# Bicycles, Bloomers and Great War Rationing Recipes

## The Life and Times of Dorothy Peel OBE

# VICKY STRAKER

PEN & SWORD
HISTORY

First published in Great Britain in 2016 by
PEN AND SWORD HISTORY
*an imprint of*
Pen and Sword Books Ltd
47 Church Street
Barnsley
South Yorkshire S70 2AS

Copyright © Vicky Straker, 2016

ISBN 978 1 47382 858 2

Printed and bound in India
by Replika Press Ltd

Typeset in Times New Roman by
CHIC GRAPHICS

Pen & Sword Books Ltd incorporates the imprints of
Pen & Sword Archaeology, Atlas, Aviation, Battleground, Discovery,
Family History, History, Maritime, Military, Naval, Politics, Railways,
Select, Social History, Transport, True Crime, Claymore Press,
Frontline Books, Leo Cooper, Praetorian Press, Remember When,
Seaforth Publishing and Wharncliffe.

*For a complete list of Pen and Sword titles please contact*
Pen and Sword Books Limited
47 Church Street, Barnsley, South Yorkshire, S70 2AS, England
E-mail: enquiries@pen-and-sword.co.uk
Website: www.pen-and-sword.co.uk

# Contents

# Foreword

A few years ago, an attractive blonde woman came into my house. 'I am Vicky', she said, 'a neighbour and a fan of yours'. And so a friendship began, based on a common interest: food. We began to exchange recipes, suggestions, cookery books and dishes. The latter was mainly a one-way 'exchange': Vicky brought me delicious bits of food to taste, which made me realise that she was a very good cook indeed.

Then, one day, I saw a pile of old books on her kitchen table. I began to browse through them and was immediately fascinated. All of the books were by a certain Mrs Peel. 'Oh', she answered, 'she is my great-great-grandmother. She wrote many books on cookery and household management.' I looked through the books with renewed interest and found most of the recipes fascinating and still feasible. I suggested to Vicky that she should write a book in which some of the recipes devised by Granny Dot – as she called her – were adapted for our time.

Vicky agreed and we soon discovered that there was far more to Mrs Peel than just her writing. She was an enlightened woman, who lived long before her time. She did not only write cookery and household management books; she wrote with great passion on other subjects too, like Women's Suffrage, homosexuality and the Great War, the work carried on by women, the rationing of food during it and the heavy burden women carried with great stoicism and dedication to keep life going on as normal as possible.

Soon I was asked to Granny Dot's lunches, Granny Dot's teas, Granny Dot's dinners, or I was given a piece of Granny Dot's cake or a few of Granny Dot's biscuits to comment on. Throughout I was very pleasantly surprised at how delicious they were. One of the things that I most like about Mrs Peel's recipes is their simplicity and the very few ingredients they contain.

Apart from recipes, Mrs Peel, in all of her books, gives advice and suggestions that are all very up to date. For instance, about fruit she writes, 'Fruit, if fresh, is better eaten raw, as in the cooking its value is destroyed. A plum or an apple eaten raw does not require any additional flavouring or sugar, but, if cooked, requires sugar at all events to make it palatable.' Comments and remarks also abound, such as these: 'It is skill, not expensive material, which is the first necessity in the kitchen', and 'People talk about plain cooking and high class cooking, but the fact remains that if you can cook you can cook.' Or, when writing about Rice Croquettes, she begins her recipe by saying, 'When bone stock is made there remains on the bones a certain amount of meat, skin and gristle which, although it has lost its flavour

6

which it has given to the stock, has still a certain value as a food. This, when mixed and added to fried chopped onion and a little Worcester sauce, well seasoned with salt, pepper and spice, is excellent and when mixed with crumbs or cooked rice can be made into croquettes or rissoles.' This is similar to how any contemporary thrifty cook will make her croquettes or polpette.

Mrs Peel gives the recipe of an Italian macaroni pie, which is her version of the many pasta pies made up and down the Italian peninsula, even making her short crust pastry with a little baking powder as many Italian cooks do. Her pudding recipes win me over completely, with her many different kinds of steamed puddings, one of the lost glories of the British cuisine.

There is an appealing 'Britishness' about Mrs Peel's recipes. Of course, there's no balsamic vinegar, molasses syrup, tahini or even much olive oil. However, her dishes, judging by the many I tasted, are incredibly good and representative of how good the food was in an Edwardian household and the importance that was given to it.

I very much enjoyed the combination of history and cookery writing, and I realised how the food of a certain era can be an important source to experience the actual life of that era more vividly.

In this informative and invaluable book, Vicky, Dorothy's great-great-granddaughter, has been able to summarise the most salient traits of Mrs Peel's productive pen.

Anna Del Conte

# Preface

I remember my mother mentioning that she had put my paternal great-great-grandmother's cookery book on a shelf in the attic room. Expecting to find a compilation of handwritten jottings, I discovered *The Daily Mail Cookery Book* (1920), a well-thumbed hardback by Mrs C.S. Peel, my great-great-grandmother. Collapsing into a rocking chair to read this book, I entered a world that would occupy my life for the foreseeable future.

Downstairs, I tapped 'Dorothy Constance Evelyn Bayliff Peel' into a search engine on the computer. It did not take me long to realise that in the early twentieth century it was common for female authors to publish using their married name, and so I keyed in 'Mrs Charles Steers Peel'. Several comments popped up, and my ancestral adventure began.

Dorothy's career started after she won a competition for a dress article for *Woman* newspaper. She gained work writing domestic articles for them and in 1898, when married with limited earnings, published her first book, *The New Home: treating of the arrangement, decoration and furnishing of a house of medium size to be maintained by moderate income*.

Domestic and culinary writing allowed Dorothy to work from home while her daughters were small. In 1903 she became Editor and Managing Director of *Hearth and Home*, *Woman,* and *Myra's Journal* until the owner died three years later. During these three years she wrote a series which included titles such as *Entrées Made Easy* (1905), *Fish and How to Cook It* (1907), *Still Room Cookery* (1905), and *Puddings and Sweets* (1905). Opening a hat shop when her children were at school led to her writing *The Hat Shop* (1914),[1] which made fun of the lighter side of running the business. A less successful second book, *Mrs Barnett, Robes* (1915), was followed by a more successful *A Mrs. Jones* (1916). When she wrote her fourth, *Tony Sant* (1920), Dorothy received a letter imploring her to stop writing novels: 'I like your cookery books, but I hate your novels.'[2] Dorothy wrote for *The Lady* and *The Queen Newspaper*, the latter position she held for seventeen years. Known as a fount of domestic knowledge, she wrote freelance articles for other publications as well as theatre criticisms, or 'notes', as she says in her autobiography, belittling her ability to critique. In March 1917 she was asked to be co-director of the Ministry of Food, advising on rationing in the First World War. Her influence was paramount, permeating into the ordinary kitchen. When her services were no longer needed, she worked for the *Daily Mail* for two years, cut short by ill health.

Dorothy Peel OBE notes. *(Imperial War Museum)*

Dorothy Peel OBE photograph. *(Imperial War Museum)*

Dorothy wrote *Marriage on Small Means, 1914*: *A Year in Public Life* (1919), detailing her work for the Ministry of Food during the First World War; *How We Lived Then 1914–1918* (1929); rationing recipe books; and a plethora of cookery and domestic books. Her interest extended to charitable work, seen in her chapter, 'The Home Life of the People', written for Mrs G.M. Young's 1934 book, *Early Victorian England*,[3] which focused on the domestic life of the poor. When her husband, Charles, became ill in the 1920s for a period of nearly two years, together they wrote a historical novel, *The Stream of Time* (1931),[4] though he did not wish his name to be attributed.

Dorothy was awarded an OBE in 1918, the very first year the award was given, for her work on rationing for the Food Economy Division for the Ministry of Food and for services in connection with the war. Her acceptance of this honour was, in her eyes, shared with housewives around the country:

Housekeeping is the world's basic profession, and the better we keep house the better people we shall be. Yet no one showers OBEs on worthy women who stay at home and bring up families, or upon those equally worthy

9

women who go into service and give not only the work of their hands but often the love of their hearts to those for whom they toil.[5]

Researching her final three novels showed Dorothy the less fortunate side to life in various organisations, among them The Children's Commonwealth in Dorset, the Infirmary in Soho, and the family centre in Peckham: 'Well, life is as it is and we can but do the little we can do to make it more endurable for those on whom it bears too hardly.'[6] She also sat on Ministry of Reconstruction Committees, which looked into the improvement of housing for the working classes and the conditions of those in domestic service. In explaining her desire to work, despite failing health, Dorothy uses a comment made by a friend of hers, that to keep busy rather than dwell on miseries can be 'translated into flowers'.

In the 1920s, Dorothy was diagnosed with diabetes and angina, which forced her to reduce her working hours. Despite this, she continued to write. 'If I had not the nine lives of the proverbial cat I should not be proposing to write any more books, for while correcting proofs of *The Stream of Time,* I fell ill with Angina, and sat propped up in a bed strewn with slip-proof, while I refreshed my failing energies with inhalations of nitrate of amyl.'[7]

Eager to read her books, I searched second-hand booksellers and eventually found most of her titles, some first editions and some later. I read each book, taking notes as I did so. Displayed on the bookshelf in my kitchen these frayed, faded tomes, published between 1903 and 1933, sometimes lacking a spine, speak to me of social and culinary history closely linked through time and progress.

Within this book are many extracts from Dorothy's works. Her writing and recipes were shaped by experiences during a time of enormous social and historical change, particularly the effects of the First World War. These are combined in different chapters, which are intended to help paint a picture of life in Victorian and Edwardian Britain. Each chapter starts with the earlier part of Dorothy's life relevant to the chapter heading, following through to the latter. In Part Two, I present some of her recipes, altered where necessary.

We may smile at her advice to housewives that champagne should be reserved for acquaintances, while wine should be served to close friends; or feel relieved that women are no longer labelled 'shameless hussies'[8] for riding bicycles, and grateful that our food choices are not limited due to wartime rationing. We may recognise the warmth that emanates through the sympathy she shows within her writing, such as for the elderly couple who worked at making nail brushes despite their fingers being cut and swollen as a result, so that they might earn a living; the plight of the Suffragettes; the hardship of food rationing; and the furtherance of social reform.

'I often regret that one cannot live backwards and in one's doing time have even as much understanding as one comes to have in one's thinking time.'[9]

# Acknowledgements

The putting together and writing of this book has been a mainly solitary project, so those I need to thank first are my husband and children for putting up with my trials and errors; my dogs for not being walked enough; and my friends for tolerating my preoccupation. Thanks particularly to Jane Southall and Rupert Brown for providing critical palates in their taste-testing. With the centenary of the First World War almost upon us when I discovered that my great-great-grandmother had done something so worthwhile, I was thrilled.

Food writer, Anna del Conte, has been my inspiration, so thanks must go to her, without whose warmth and encouragement this book may never have come to fruition. My aunt, Caroline Springfield, gave me one of Granny Dot's books in the first place, so without her, my discovery would not have been made. Finding that photography had to become one of my strengths overnight, I must thank Emma Farquhar and Sam Walton for stepping in when it was not up to muster.

Serendipity played a part with the inspirational writer, Sallyann Sheridan, being a close neighbour. Meetings as early as 5.30 a.m. took place, before my children's breakfast time, when she guided me through the preliminary stages and advised me about how to find a publisher.

Cathy Kawalek, from New York, has helped enormously in her thorough research into the life of my great-great-grandmother, which has led to the inclusion of the article from *The Queen Newspaper*, among other insights, for which I am truly grateful.

Pythouse Kitchen Garden lent me some crockery, as did Deborah Kennet, who also kept me company with the help of Granny Dot's Mint Julips on a day when I was squeezing in as much as I possibly could before the school holidays began. Minna Hepburn has provided encouragement to my social media world, as I would go back to letter-writing and telegrams if I could.

Thanks to Ben and Liz Brabyn who came to the rescue when the book cover was about to go to print and I could no longer see the wood for the trees.

I am sure there are many I have not thanked. So thank you to those I have forgotten, because I have not forgotten you; at the moment you are just not springing forth!

So I give you this book, a mishmash of the life of Granny Dot: rich, varied and slightly chaotic.

Vicky Straker
www.victoriastrakercook.co.uk

11

# PART ONE

Before the war there was a steady demand for a book by Mrs C.S. Peel, with the odd title *Ten Shillings A Head for House Books*. In these days, half-a-sovereign does not go far, so Mrs Peel is helping us with a practical and up-to-date manual called *My Own Cookery Book*, which condenses the experience gained in the lady's own kitchen during five-and-twenty years ... The monotony of the menus in British homes is bad for both body and mind; and this book shows that variety, can mean economy. We recommend it warmly.

*The Tablet*, 14 July 1923

# Introducing Dorothy

So much of life is a pigeon pie which consists almost wholly of beef, is it not?

Mrs C.S. Peel, *Life's Enchanted Cup: An Autobiography 1872–1933*

For a family taking a walk
In Arcadia Terrace no doubt
The parents indulge in intelligent talk,
And the children they gambol about.

At a quarter past six they return to their tea,
Of a kind which would not be attractive to me,
Though my appetite passes belief;

There was old leg of mutton and warm lemonade
And a large pigeon pie most skilfully made
To consist almost wholly of beef.

A respectable family taking a walk
Is a subject on which I could dwell;
It contains all the morals that ever there were
And sets an example as well.

A poem recalled by Dorothy from her childhood in the 1870s and referred to in her 1933 autobiography.[10]

I walk past the family portrait of my great-great-grandmother every day on my way to the kitchen, where I often recreate her recipes. Even my five-year-old son noticed my efforts, remarking, 'Mummy, you are the best cook in the world, but Granny Dot is better.'

Dorothy was the seventh of nine children born to Richard and Henrietta Bayliff, four of whom died in infancy. Her life began in Ganarew, Herefordshire, on 27 April 1868, before the family moved to Monmouthshire and, within a few years, to Clifton in Bristol, so that her older brothers could be educated locally. As she recalled, 'There was no money to send the boys to Eton, Harrow or Winchester. At Clifton they could be day boys and get quite as good an education.'[11]

Dorothy came from a privileged background, though her parents did not have the wealth of many of their contemporaries. They instilled in her a strong sense of charity and compassion.[12]

The Victorians were philanthropic, with many wealthy people like Octavia Hill and Angela Burdett Coutts setting up charities. Despite not being in these realms of wealth, Dorothy's parents ran a soup kitchen while living in Clifton: 'My father and mother, ill-off as they were, said that no one who asked for food should be turned away ... to save the servants we children were proud to act as servers.'[13]

Suffering from asthma as a child, Dorothy spent long periods of convalescence with her wealthier aunts in Doward House, Herefordshire. They provided poor local families with jars containing food, and black arm bands that were worn for mourning, a more regular occurrence before vaccinations and accessible healthcare became commonplace. More lavish social occasions were enjoyed by her aunts than Dorothy was used to, which she could not help but contrast with the comparative frugality of her parents.

Family photograph. (Mrs C.S. Peel, *Life's Enchanted Cup: An Autobiography 1872–1933*)

| Aunt Charlotte | Aunt Marianne and Edwin Scobell | Aunt Susanna holding Carli | Markey and Percy Hart Dyke | Parents Richard and Henrietta Lane Bayliff and Jenny, the nursery dog |

A FAMILY GROUP IN THE LATE SIXTIES
The ladies are in mourning for their mother, Mrs Robert Peel

Rather than send her away to school, Dorothy's father educated her. He was able to do so because he was in the army, Adjutant of the Monmouthshire Volunteers, which enabled him to move to different areas of the country. Her parents became more financially strained when her father was ill so that 'being on the threshold of a successful career', he was forced to leave the army, which cut his income drastically. Dorothy commented, 'No wonder my father looked anxious and my mother sighed.'

While being taught to read and write by her mother, Dorothy did not enjoy being tutored by her father: 'I hated my lessons because he laughed at my mistakes and sometimes repeated them in public. This teasing I could not take good-humouredly; it was the beginning of such tiresomeness on my part as [sic] eventually caused me to be sent to a day school.'[14]

A description of playing the piano with a fellow school pupil illustrates the embarrassment she felt during performances:

> I learned to play 'The Turkish Patrol,' 'The last Rose of Summer,' and a duet called 'Bluebells,' which I performed at the school concert in the company of a fat girl singularly like an amiable pig in a maroon velveteen frock, who thumped solidly in the bass while I, clad in a starched white muslin inherited from Carli and still tightly pigtailed, ambled uneasily about in the treble. Any guest who had a sense of humour and no ear for music must have enjoyed that concert.[15]

Schooling did not become compulsory until 1880 when Dorothy was 12. An Act of Parliament was passed which stipulated that children must be educated between the ages of five and ten, either at school or at home. By the age of 10, in order to help provide for their family, as long as children had reached a certain educational level, they could leave school and be sent to work. Girls with wealthy parents often had governesses while their brothers were sent to boarding school. Those who did go to school were educated under a strict Church of England doctrine which safeguarded their innocence and sense of decorum. While the boys were educated intellectually, the girls were educated socially, the expectation being that young ladies would marry someone able to support them financially, their duty seen as providing a comfortable home life, with the help of servants, for their families.

The grandmother of a friend of mine, Mamie Charlton, met Dorothy in Northumberland when Cecilia, Dorothy's eldest daughter, had moved there through marriage. Her memory is of a tall lady wearing 'London clothes' who was great fun, not a surprising description considering the character which her books exude:

One hot summer night I woke, terrified ... Down the stairs, a slip, a bump, a wild rush past the passage where the bear caves were, through the lighted ante-room ... On the terrace sat my father, my mother and a strange lady and gentleman, playing whist. Imagine that, playing whist, out in the garden in the middle of the night! Suddenly there came to me the knowledge that Mummie and Paito were not just our parents who belonged to us, but people who lived a life of their own with which we children had no connection. Mummie picked me up, I sat on her knee, Paito brought the couvre-pied and wrapped it round me ... the air was so still that the candles burned without a flicker, and the baize on the card table and the red of the hearts and diamonds were brilliant in their light. There was a lovely smell, for but a yard or two away bloomed the lily trees.

Then there was a noise of horses, a shining of lights. A pair-horse brougham[16] was at the door. 'Good-bye, good-bye.' Then bed, a drink of nice cold water, Mummie's door open, the light shining through.[17]

Dorothy spent time with her paternal grandparents, of whom she was very fond. In her autobiography, it is clear that her grandfather, a respected man of the cloth, lived his life to the full. Many of his decisions may now be frowned upon, but at the time, seemed to be accepted with a smile:

Grandpapa was tall and as heavily built as his phaeton,[18] with a red face and beautifully curly white hair, whiskers, chin beard and shaved upper lip. He wore a top hat and white tie; only young clergymen wore clerical collars then. He had inherited a comfortable little income and, just as he went up to Oxford, someone had left him a couple of thousand pounds. So he had lived richly and horsily, winning a bet that he would drive a four-in-hand keeping the wheels of one side of the coach on a track of half-pennies. By the time that he took Orders the loose thousands had been pleasantly squandered. He further impoverished himself by building a vicarage which cost far more than he had expected it to cost and consistently living beyond his means.

Grandpapa was a muscular Christian and had a way with him, and if on a Saturday night the hullaballoo at the 'Labour in Vain' grew too violent he would be asked to look round, and thought little of taking two young men by their scruffs and putting them into the ditch conveniently placed on the other side of the road.[19]

When Dorothy was a child in the 1870s and 1880s, all was far from equal: 'In the little church, in those days, the men sat on one side, the women on the other, the children on benches under the belfry.'[20]

16

Watched over with a beady eye, it was ensured that nothing offended Dorothy's innocent mind. She writes of an occasion when staying with her aunt: 'newspapers were still forbidden, and the novels were tried out by Aunt Markey, and if in one, otherwise innocuous, she found something not fitting for our budding minds, she clipped the pages together and bade us not undo them.'[21] Strict application of acceptable codes of conduct in her upbringing imparted a reverence in Dorothy for her elders:

There was an upright piano with a front of faded red fluted silk and a stool which twirled up and down. Once I twirled it with such a will that the top twirled off. I had killed the piano stool. What would they do to me? A green sensation took possession of the pit of my stomach. That rat-in-the-trap feeling of being helpless in the hands of grown-up people who can do just as they please is a horrible one. Aunt Mary, who was always kind though generally uninterested, screwed the top on again. The feeling of relief made me feel faint and limp and always after that if I 'touched' – 'No, don't touch that, Dorothy' – I touched with care.[22]

Such veneration and desire to look at what was forbidden led to self-reflection. In her autobiography, Dorothy tells us that as a child her creed was to be kind to animals and poor people because not to be so was 'unthinkable', not to be rude to servants, 'though I sometimes was', and that it was wrong to be greedy though 'how greedy I could be. Pease pudding, a loathsome yellow mess. Now be a good girl ... Dot, do as you are told or ... consternation ... disgust ... But in me satisfaction that in the end I had punished them for their obstinate disregard of my wishes.'[23]

Later, with an adult view of herself as a child: 'Sometimes intuition and imagination may serve as well or better than knowledge, but for the most part knowledge brings power, the power to use oneself rightly. But here was I, a tall pink-and-white-faced girl, ignorant, innocent, tiresome, gauche, happy, unhappy, and always hungry for new experiences.'[24]

Concluding that many may have seen her as 'an odd young woman', with her expressing opinions where they may not have been wanted, she lived by the mischievous ethos that 'Although it was wrong to lie, it seemed to me that I was by no means the only person who did it. On the whole I concluded that I would be good, provided that to be so was neither too dull nor too difficult.'[25]

As was expected of her, Dorothy hoped to fall in love with someone who could support her financially: 'I always hoped that I might marry a Duke but, naturally, I never did. There are so few Dukes and so many girls who want to marry them.'[26] Prior to their marriage, Dorothy and her second cousin, Charles Steers Peel, were together under the happy yet reluctant eyes of family. It transpires that the reasons were not only financial, but that Charles was four years her junior, a fact which

17

Dorothy seems to have concealed in her autobiography, the date of which starts in 1872 instead of her birth year of 1868. Their marriage was consequently disapproved of and in her autobiography, Dorothy sympathises with her family's concern from her altered viewpoint as the mother of two daughters, without divulging the reason for her parents' disapproval.

Charles trained as an electrical engineer which, by the mid-1890s, would have brought in an annual salary of in the region of £110. In the last decades of the nineteenth century the founder of the Salvation Army and Methodist preacher, William Booth, estimated that a working family needed an income of £50 a year just to get by and between £57 and £78 per annum to be 'comfortable'.[27] Nevertheless, for the standard of living Dorothy's parents hoped for their daughter, Charles's income was considered insufficient.

To alleviate their concerns, once she was married Dorothy knew she needed to find work to supplement their income: 'Naturally it was strange to think of their daughters earning money, but undoubtedly the money was very useful and even nice girls were now beginning to go about by themselves and to be independent.'[28]

Legally, a wife belonged to her husband and he was expected to provide for her financially both with what she may have brought into the marriage and with his own money. Records of women who worked are not clear because often none were kept where the work was considered to fall within the domains of the home, such as being a seamstress or helping with the family business. Coming from a middle/upper-class background, there is no doubt, however, that Dorothy's working was unusual. It may be assumed that because her work was concentrating on domestic and culinary matters, she met with less objections than she may have done otherwise.

Dorothy and Charles married in St Paul's, Knightsbridge, in 1894. In the early years of marriage, they started with an allowance from her father-in-law which ceased on his death. They struggled a little, relying on what they earned themselves alongside 'a small share' of her mother's income:

In those days there was work for those who would do it and, as we found, little difficulty in earning sufficient for our needs. Nevertheless, the sudden cessation of what we had regarded as our safety income was, naturally, a shock – but one which taught us some understanding of the anxiety suffered by those for whom the dividing line between enough and nothing is a month's or a week's notice.[29]

A man is expected to know his job and to do it. A woman must first prove that she knows her job, and then do it unless her opinion clashes with that of a man, when it is taken for granted that the man must know best and the woman should give way.[30]

# CHAPTER 1

# Visiting, Parties and Royal Encounters

Paito's father and mother were still living in their pleasant vicarage at Albury in Hertfordshire. Although but thirty miles from London, it might have been three hundred. Only one working man in the village had been to London.
Mrs C.S. Peel, *Life's Enchanted Cup: An Autobiography 1872–1933*

Dorothy's social life in the 1880s involved a great deal of 'visiting'. Compared with the speed with which we travel today, to journey by carriage was slow and necessarily involved a longer stay due to hours spent in transit with the need for coachmen to rest and horses to be watered. Dorothy writes of many visits, including staying with friends in the mid–1880s. She describes a lengthy dressing process, being laced up by a helper who may miss a button hole and have to start all over again. Straight bits of hair may escape after using curling tongs which she would 'frizzle' off, while buttons on kid gloves may come off at the last moment.

The first time she went to stay at a very smart house, Brynkinalt, on the Shropshire-Welsh border, she and her sister, Carli, were the only guests without their own maids to help them. Having had her shoes and boots taken to be cleaned, they were not returned, which led to her frantically rush down the back stairs where she found a footman who helped her find them.

What agitation lest the housemaid should not appear in time to do me up and I should be late for the stately dinner, served on those silver gilt plates which never were hot and on which knives and forks squeaked shrilly.

Before I left, kind, grand, severe Lady Trevor, who was my hostess, tipped me Five Pounds – riches. I did not know if I ought to accept such a magnificent present; then suddenly her severity melted, she became just a friendly soul, kissed me, told me that I was a dear child, that my red sailor hat was rather flighty looking, that young girls could not be too careful, and that when she was a young girl with a small allowance her godmother had always tipped her. This was an amusing visit.[31]

19

Often Dorothy found the most generous people were those who had the least and, in contrast, those who had the most looked after their pennies to a disappointing extent:

> I must own, however, that in some of the mansions of the rich in which I was a guest the conversation was not gay. The respectable rich are apt to be dull, and often the richer people are, the more do they love economy. On one occasion my sister and I dined with some important folk in company with two other ladies – a squire's wife and a parson's wife – with their menfolk. How we small fry would have loved to hear of the doings of the great world, to know what that terrible Mr. Gladstone said to the Queen, and if Mrs. Langtry really was as lovely as people said. But instead the after-dinner interval before the arrival of the men was spent in a dreary description of our hostess's efforts to discover the cheapest shop at which to buy little boys' sailor suits.
>
> Imagine too, my disappointment when I was invited to spend the day with old friends of my father's who, as the phrase goes, rolled in money. They took me to the Academy. Then, although it was raining and my best frock and hat were becoming more and more speckled, they waited for an omnibus and in it we returned to eat mutton in a vast, drear house in Grosvenor Place. They asked me, who of necessity seldom travelled in any other vehicle, if it was not quite amusing to go in an omnibus, which people of their kind seldom did. They also said that they did not go to the theatre often because it was so expensive.[32]

At this time, Dorothy, aged 17, had moved to Twickenham with her family. She describes it as the countryside with large gardens and houses, 'and quite a rural little patch between it and Richmond'. Why her family moved here, she did not know.

In old family albums, photographs of Dorothy show her turned away from the camera, or hiding under a hat; even in a family portrait with her husband and elder daughter, my great-grandmother, she is sitting at an angle so that only her cheek is visible. The unfortunate consequence is that, to my knowledge, there are no photographs of Dorothy as a young woman, images which would be perfect in complimenting her description of 'visiting' with Charles:

> The first time we went to stay, after our marriage, at a big country house for a ball, I wore my tiara, three small diamond stars surmounting a diamond bandeau. The tiara was the pride of my life. We young folk went to the ball in the omnibus and took hours getting there and back, for the roads were covered with snow which balled in the horses' hoofs. The two chief ladies drove in the brougham.[33]

Portrait of Dorothy, Charles and Cecilia Peel. *(Author's portrait. Photography by Sam Luke Walton, Hole and Corner Magazine)*

Hunt balls in the 1890s were much the same as hunt balls are now, but dinner parties were different. They began earlier – at seven-thirty or a quarter to eight – everyone was paired off strictly according to rank, and they walked in procession. The menus were longer. There might be two soups, two fishes and two entrees, though this two-and-two business was beginning to be old-fashioned. Then came the joint, game, two or even four sweets, and a savoury and, in some old-fashioned houses, cheese and celery and old ale as well.

Modish folk dined a little later and were content with one soup and one fish, but at large parties they were generally provided with two entrees. Bridge as an after-dinner amusement came in a little later, but it took a considerable time to penetrate into squiredom. In the houses of the rich, Baccarat might be played. In such houses one met with elaborate and luxurious bathrooms, lace-trimmed sheets and pillow cases – fashions looked upon with aversion by folk such as our relations. There would be tea in the great hall, the women wearing tea gowns, the men still in their tweeds.[34]

'The season' to which Dorothy refers in the following extract is the time during which débutantes were presented at Court, from about May until July each year. This involved entertaining in the hope that daughters would meet a suitable spouse:

Dinner parties during the season were large and formal, but the two-and-two procession of dishes was now démodé; soup, fish, two entrees (one white, one brown), joint, asparagus or a mousse of foie gras, a sweet, a savoury and dessert, at which ices were served, sherry, hock, champagne, port, and liqueurs with the ice were now considered sufficient.

After dinner the men stayed downstairs for a considerable time while the ladies chatted; and when the men re-appeared, chatted a little more or played Bridge, which was then becoming popular.[35]

The 1890s had come to be referred to by some as the 'naughty nineties' which, from Dorothy's experience, was more for its illiteration than actual value. Fancy dress balls were held at Covent Garden, after which – Dorothy describes – passageways were littered with drunk people at the end of the evening. Girls were able to go to music halls with a chaperon, unless married, in which case they may take a box or stall. The Empire Music Hall was popular, with a reputation for being quite daring. Its existence was protested against by some for being unsuitable for young ladies, until it was then deemed a 'Truly a respectable Court' by Queen Victoria. When escorted by Charles and one of her brothers, Dorothy saw it as no more than a meeting place for young men and women.[36]

Politics did not interest Dorothy until during and after the war when work for the Ministry of Food and for the improvement of life for poorer people in the 1920s absorbed her. Prior to this time, describing a dinner party she went to at the house of a supporter of Gladstone, the Liberal Prime Minister, instead of commenting on the political conversation, her focus was on the delicious dinner she was given of 'chicken done in some delightful way and ice in the shape of peaches'.[37]

Dorothy and Charles gave parties quite regularly. A description of one evening paints a picture of this part of life for them and its propriety in the early 1900s:

Our tall, elegant butler, Clements proved a friend in need. We were expecting friends to dine and were dressing when the maid informed me that Sir

Somebody and Lady Something had arrived. This puzzled me for we knew no such people. Also it was now but twenty minutes to eight and our own party was timed for eight. We descended hastily to find an ancient lady in a cap and shawl and a still more ancient gentleman whose head drooped low on this breast as if from the weight of his flowing white beard. They said how d'you do and did not seem in the least surprised to see us. I began to wonder if I was mad. Did I know them? Had I asked them to dine? And what was going to happen now, for by no conjuring could our dining-table accommodate more than eight persons. It seemed terrible to say, 'We don't know you and you must go away' to such a pair of pets. Then Clements appeared and bent over the old lady. 'If you please m'lady, I think there has been a mistake. Mrs ___ from next door is expecting you to dinner at quarter-to-eight.'

Just as obediently as they had accepted their unknown host and hostess did they allow themselves to be coated and shawled and delivered next door.[38]

Death duties, which were introduced in 1894, broke up many family estates. Increased taxes forming part of the People's Budget 1909/10 impacted upon the middle and upper classes. These and the influences of war made their financial situation less stable, which in turn led to more spontaneous and less formal dinner parties: 'After the War, the unstable economic position which makes it impossible to know what the income may be from month to month, causes a restlessness which shows itself in the informal "throwing" of parties, rather than the carefully planned giving of elaborate parties such as were a feature of my young day.'[39] And so the way was paved for the more informal parties of today, less elaborate and sometimes spontaneous gatherings.

## Drawing Rooms and Courts

'In the life of a Victorian debutante, there were probably few experiences more exciting than her presentation to the Queen at Court.'
Dawn Aiello of *Victorian Lace, Presentation at Court*, Thehistorybox.com

Either a young lady would 'come out' at a debutante ball, or following her presentation at Court, after which she was able to enter into 'Society'. A letter would be written to the Lord Chamberlain suggesting suitable candidates for presentation. Strict rules were involved in being presented. Both who you were and what you wore was of utmost importance. Either your family had to be aristocratic or your father must be in a particular profession, such as working as a barrister or a member of the clergy. A line was drawn between professions so that being the daughter of a solicitor or a general practitioner meant that your presentation at Court would not be accepted.

Wearing the correct dress, feathers and jewellery involved hours of preparation. Lessons on deportment would enable a debutante to glide effortlessly across the floor to the queen where she would kiss her hand and perform a deep curtsy which would have taken weeks to master. When leaving the Court, the debutante would have to exit walking backwards as to turn one's back on royalty was not acceptable. The following extract from Dorothy's autobiography gives us a flavour of what the event was like:[40]

It was in the May or June of the year after my marriage that I was presented. Drawing-Rooms then took place in the afternoon and refreshments were not provided. The business of dressing began quite early in the morning. There were not then the number of hair-dressers' shops that there are now. Very great ladies might have their own hair-dressers whom they took with them when visiting their friends, but generally speaking the lady's maid did her lady's hair. If a lady did not keep a maid, she did it herself, employing a hair-dresser only on special occasions. On Drawing-Room days fashionable hair-dressers might begin their rounds as early as eight o'clock in the morning.

We wore full evening dress made strictly according to regulations, Court trains, and feathers, and carried the large shower bouquets which had lately become fashionable. The court train was long, lined, padded, and trimmed, and therefore more sumptuous looking than the shorter trains which are worn to-day.

We started for the Palace long before the luncheon hour, and our carriage took up its place in the Mall. Members of the great families still used their State carriages, driven by a white-wigged coachman who sat alone on the hammer cloth, while a couple of footmen in State liveries, their hair powdered, stood at the back. Persons of lesser degree also prided themselves on the smartness of their horses and carriages and the liveries of their coachmen and footmen, who wore posies of flowers in honour of the occasion.

Such a fine show attracted crowds of sightseers, whose comments were occasionally difficult to bear with equanimity.

Arrived at the Palace, those who knew the ropes generally left their wraps in the carriage to avoid the delay caused by reclaiming them from the cloakroom. At the foot of the Grand Staircase we met a friend and her mother. Sally was one of those girls to whom things always happen at the wrong moment; when half-way up the staircase her flannel petticoat fell off. It was a modish garment, gored into a shaped band and embroidered. Without a moment's hesitation she stepped free of it, gathered it into a bundle, and threw it at one of the Beefeaters who lined the staircase on either side. Never shall

I forget the face of that man, as, mouth open, eyes staring with horrified astonishment, he clasped that petticoat to his breast.

If I remember rightly seats were not provided, and as everyone was anxious to reach the Throne Room before the departure of Queen Victoria, who when tired would leave the Princess of Wales to represent her, there were some unseemly scrambles.

At the entrance to the Throne Room each lady handed her card to the Gentleman appointed to receive it, while two other Gentlemen took her train from her arm, upon which it had been folded, and arranged it. Our names were announced and we entered the Throne Room.

I am glad I was not too nervous to take in the scene; the half circle of Royalties and their ladies and gentlemen brilliantly dressed, brilliantly jewelled, and in the centre a little red-faced sad-looking old lady in a widow's cap, and old lady-like, black evening dress, high in the neck and with sleeves reaching below the elbow, across her breast the Garter ribbon.

Her Majesty was not a beautiful old lady. She had a rudder-like nose and her blue eyes protruded. Yet such is the power of personality, a personality formed by the living of an upright life, that I doubt if anyone who ever saw her could forget Queen Victoria. After passing the Queen, upon whom one must not turn one's back, one progressed in a sideways fashion, pausing at intervals to make the required number of curtsies. After that there was nothing to do but to go home again.[41]

Cecilia, the elder daughter of Dorothy, was presented during the reign of King George V, at the first garden party after the war. There were also representatives of the Women's War Associations and notabilities from Allied countries. Denise, Dorothy's younger daughter, was presented to Queen Mary. In contrast to Queen Victoria who spent her life following the death of her husband, Albert, dressed in black, Queen Mary 'wore a gown and train of gold, the train of enormous length, a tall crown of pearls, the only touch of vivid colour in her dress being the blue Garter ribbon'.[42]

The next event on the programme on a Drawing-Room day was the Drawing-Room Tea at which relations and friends gathered to admire us in our finery.

After the accession of King Edward, Drawing-Rooms became Courts, and took place in the evening. A luxurious buffet-supper, accompanied by particularly good champagne, was served from tables set out with the Royal gold plate.

When I presented my younger daughter, Courts were again held in the evening. We watched the Royal procession leave the Throne Room.

After the dreariness of the War and early post-War years, the ceremonial of a Court, even though shorn of some of its former splendour, because the trains were shorter and there were few bouquets, was like a scene out of a fairy tale.[43]

## Royal Encounters

Dorothy writes of further encounters with the Royal Family worth mentioning. During the 1902 Coronation of King Edward VII when she was living in Brompton Square:

We saw the procession from a stand on Constitution Hill, and the only person who made any great mark on my mind was the lovely Queen Marie of Roumania, to whom years after, when she was Queen Mother, I had the honour of being presented. Then she had lost the slimness of youth, but her beauty was magnificent and her personality overwhelming.[44]

While at Marienbad Spa with a friend, Alys, who was almost blind:

The King [Edward VII] approached and stopped to speak to a friend. I, naturally turned away, but Alys, who had no idea that His Majesty was anywhere in the vicinity, did not. Before I could attract her attention, a fierce little man in a Homburg hat hissed in her ear, 'You are requested not to star-r-r-e at the King.' 'I have never even seen the King', protested Alys, continuing to stare directly at him, an accident which evidently much amused His Majesty.[45]

What a rushing, glittering time it was, that of King Edward's reign. The Court set an example of splendour, and American, South African, and Jewish magnates were made welcome. Social conventions became less strict and, where rank, or position gained by outstanding mental capacity backed by wealth had been passports into exclusive society, now money, unbacked by other qualifications, began to talk, though not invariably to just those people to whom it desired to talk.

There was a vast amount of entertaining of a lavish order, with red carpets and awnings, rows of men-servants and champagne suppers ... Even people of no account like ourselves were affected. We went to quantities of all kinds of parties and when we could get away took a holiday abroad or rented a house in the country, sufficiently near London for Charles to travel up and down to his office and for me to keep in touch with my newspapers.[46]

Everyone, I think, felt sorry that he should have lived so short a time to enjoy the Kingship which for so long had been denied him, but his death did not mark the end of a period, as that of his Royal Mother had done, and neither was it mourned by members of the general public as a personal loss....

King Edward's funeral was a red and gold and gorgeous pageant, but it did not touch the heart as that of the Queen had done. As the cortege passed I was struck by the way in which the visiting Royalties chatted with each other, and even laughed. His Majesty, ex-King Alfonso of Spain was the only one whose face bore any look of grief.[47]

CHAPTER 2

# Victorian Food

The food was good and plain, served on a polished mahogany table from which, at the 7 o'clock dinner, the cloth was removed before dessert, which consisted of biscuits, home-grown fruit or oranges and now and then figs, almonds and raisins or home-made damson cheese.
Mrs C.S. Peel, *Life's Enchanted Cup: An Autobiography 1872–1933*

Dorothy writes of her childhood in the 1870s and 1880s, which appears enviable in its wholesome and local simplicity:

At Easter, if we children were on a visit, Grandmamma asked other children to tea; but not on Sunday, for there was no Sunday party-giving in such circles in those days. We hunted for Easter Eggs which the hens laid, the cook boiled, and Grandmamma painted red, green or blue and decorated with little landscapes, bunches of flowers, or animals.

The cook who boiled the party eggs presided over a large stone-floored kitchen in which was a large coal range. Before it lay a black and red rag carpet, and red Turkey twill curtains gave a cosy effect. The bread was homemade and on baking days a widowed ex-cook came to help with the baking and the housework. She was a brisk woman with sparkling eyes, who never took off her black bonnet, merely untying the strings, and she wore pattens on which she click-clacked from kitchen to washhouse, where was the brick wood-heated oven. On baking days I was allowed to visit the kitchen and make plaits of dough, which were baked and served for nursery tea.[48]

Our food was plain, our house simply furnished, and I recollect that Mummie declared that never did she have some homely dish such as liver and bacon but my father brought someone home to lunch. That was some half century before the introduction of the liver treatment for pernicious anaemia and the insulin treatment for diabetes, treatments which have sent the price of liver and sweetbreads soaring. It was in the very early days of imported meat and great was the fuss when my father suggested its use. Butchers with

28

polite scorn said they did not keep it and there appeared in *Punch* a picture of a lady who, having bought imported meat elsewhere, apologises to her butcher for the smallness of her meat bill owing to presents of game. 'Yes, M', it's plentiful in July' returns the butcher.[49]

Aunt Charlotte did the housekeeping and kept 'a good table' consisting of excellent joints (the day of imported meat had scarcely dawned), large hams and tongues, Stilton cheese, trifle, meringues, delicious calves foot jelly and raised pork pies and curry made from jealously-guarded recipes.

The store room was an earthly Paradise with cupboards full of jams and pickles, boxes of macaroni and preserved fruits, bags full of rice and tapioca, blue-papered cones of sugar, chests of tea, canisters of coffee, sardines, anchovies, soap, candles, string, brown paper, kitchen paper, stationary for the writing-tables, pens, pencils, boxes containing India-rubber bands, and a large pair of scales.

My Aunts dug their cheese with a scoop made of silver with a long ivory handle. It was my ambition to dig the cheese ... I approached my Aunt Marianne and told her that I would have my dinner with her and dig the cheese. She looked at me from under her sideways-tilted hat, through her eye-glasses which sat crookedly upon her handsome nose, and replied mildly, 'Well, if you must, you must.' And so it was.[50]

Eating only what is on your plate and not asking for more is alien to most of us now, but Dorothy recollects that in 1884, aged 16, she felt that: 'Only girls who were on particularly intimate terms with one another would admit that they could be so gross as ever to desire a second helping.'[51] Dorothy's early encounters with food involve mishaps and embarrassments:

That winter I went to a party at Courtfield, the home of a houseful of handsome young men of the Catholic faith. I fell in love with two of them ... But what really mattered ... was that I disgraced myself at tea. My partner in sin was a chocolate éclair, a dainty new to me, which when bitten basely spat out custard. The custard dribbled all down my party frock, even on to my new blue ribbed silk sash with fringed ends ... I felt utterly ashamed and convinced that everyone was looking at me, and scorning me as a little girl who could not even eat her tea tidily.

Food often played me dreadful tricks, for at my first dinner party I cut off the top of an ice pudding and it went whizzing on to the floor and turned me from a pink and white girl in a white frock into a sort of shameful Mont Blanc of a person who would go through life labelled as the girl who did not know how to help herself to ice pudding.[52]

On one occasion when departing on a speaking tour, Dorothy's husband, Charles, bid her farewell on a train and gave her a 'dinner basket for the journey. The piece de resistance – a chicken leg – was extremely elegant and slim. While dining somewhat unsatisfyingly off this dainty a small and fossilised roll and a disheartened tomato', her travelling companion 'fussed and fretted' at the delay to the train. To cheer him up, Dorothy offered to share hers, which he accepted:

> Judge then of my amaze when as we drew into the station that base young man flung open the door, snatched up the small case which appeared to be all the luggage he possessed, hurled himself out of the carriage, and as the French say, 'running with all his leg,' made a bee-line for the Liverpool train! Running is not one of my accomplishments, especially when encumbered by a heavy dressing-case, and I arrived panting on the platform to behold the Liverpool train dwindling in the distance. Surely I may be forgiven when I vow that never again will I share insufficient chicken legs with strange young sailor-men.
>
> It was late and dark, bitterly cold and raining fast as I made my way to the nearest hotel. There I found the night-porter drinking tea and eating bread and butter in the office. I asked him if he could procure some tea for me. He regretted that everything was locked up. Moved to pity by my cold and wearied appearance he offered to get another cup if I would not mind sharing his meal, and once again I realised that all men are not evil at heart. So we sat in the office and discussed Trade Unionism over our tea and bread and butter... That night porter was a charming and interesting old person and I much enjoyed my nocturnal tea party.[53]

Dorothy's autobiography also describes an enviable scene in the early part of the twentieth century in Switzerland, where each winter she spent a month or two, taking her children and a friend, to be joined later by her husband:

> How lovely it was to start out, she with her sketching, I with my writing things, our luncheon packets fastened on our luges, to sit and paint and write and eat in the brilliant sunshine amongst the fast-frozen snow on which the pine trees threw shadows of deepest blue, to pause on the way home and drink coffee and eat croissants and cherry jam at the village cafe.[54]

# CHAPTER 3

# Servants

In the case of a lady the housemaid should return about fifteen minutes before dinner time to see if her help is required. She should then ask at what time the guest wishes to be called, if she takes early tea, and if the bath is to be hot or cold, in the bedroom or in the bathroom.

Mrs C.S. Peel, *How to Keep House*

In 1901 1.5 million people were employed in domestic service, the vast majority of whom lived in accommodation provided by the employer, usually within the same house so that they could attend to the wishes of their employer throughout the day. In Victorian times, having a servant was the want of not only the wealthy upper classes and aristocracy, but of the burgeoning middle classes. The upper middle classes tended to have at least two servants, often a cook, a charwoman (by the late 1920s to be referred to as a 'Daily') and possibly a nanny or butler. The lower middle classes, if they were able to afford it, would have a 'maid of all work', often a lonely and dissatisfying job which was never complete. This less attractive occupation, together with women's increased desire for independence, was reflected in their roles, shown in the 1911 Census, where the number of people in service decreased to 1.27 million, despite a rising population.[55]

When Dorothy was a child in the 1870s, female servants were referred to as servants, as opposed to maids, which became common parlance after the war. Her parents, who were not very well off, employed servants who assisted with the running of a soup kitchen from their home in Bristol:

Our staff then consisted of a tall, stout, cheerful Devonshire woman; a thin, sad elderly house-parlourmaid, a nurse, and a boot boy – the cook called him a 'limb'… The cook, Mrs Snow, was a dear soul ... and made Cornish pasties and Saffron buns and would have made clotted cream had we been able to afford it. 'Keeping down the house books' was one of the bugaboos of Mummie's life. Every week did she produce them for my father's inspection, a procedure trying to both.[56]

31

Dorothy's aunts lived in a more lavish style with a number of servants plus a footman who wore 'a blue coat with plated buttons and a yellow and blue striped waistcoat'.[57] She describes staying with her paternal grandparents and the everyday duties of the servants in their home:

> Although the house was a fair size, lighted by paraffin lamps, and everyone had a daily hot bath carried to their room, there were but two servants, aided twice a week and on special occasions by the widowed Emma, and the daily task of boot and knife cleaning, water pumping and coal carrying by a man of all work. Neither Grandmamma nor aunt ever did any domestic work, but everything seemed to get done satisfactorily.[58]

By many, servants were not viewed with respect. This is illustrated by the patronising attitude of a *Punch* cartoonist implying that a maid does not understand the implications of warfare, 'Oh, no, ma'am, I've left off worrying now. He can't walk out with anyone else while he's there.' If this view was commonplace among employers it is not surprising that the number of people in domestic service diminished as more employment opportunities arose:

> Young men who will walk out and take off their hats to 'young ladies' in shops and in offices will not consort with domestic servants. Well-to-do servants desirous of taking a holiday in a boarding-house must conceal the fact that they are in service ... The names 'slavery,' 'skivvie,' and 'Mary Jane' are employed, and in music-halls and in comic papers servants only too often are depicted as ugly, ungainly persons with caps on one side and smuts on their noses.[59]

During her childhood, the staff employed by Dorothy's parents earned less than they were to earn in the 1900s, yet worked harder. 'Our cook earned £20 a year, the house parlourmaid £18, the nurse £22, while the gardener's daughter was content to sew all day for 2/- and some food. When there was a party a woman from the village came for 1/6 day and food, to help in the kitchen and pantry.'[60]

When visiting very large country houses in the 1890s, Dorothy realised how much work went on behind the scenes:

> one might find one bathroom in a country house, and sometimes electric light, but for the most part candles and paraffin lamps, baths in the bedrooms and great crackling fires, which, in the houses where comfort was studied, were lit at 7 o'clock in the morning and kept up until bedtime, and in houses where comfort was not studied were just beginning to burn when one came upstairs

to dress for dinner. What with making up fires and carrying cans of hot water before breakfast, luncheon, tea, dinner and bed–time, housemaids worked hard for their living.[61]

In 1897, when visiting Paris for the first time, she stayed with her cousin who had 'taken a sumptuous flat in the Avenue d'Iena'. There were four staff – an elderly couple, a footman and a maid. Dorothy comments on how efficient the staff were in comparison with those in England. This helped sow the seed for *How to Keep House*, in which she gives details on the effective running of a house, aimed for the guidance of its mistress.

A close friendship was formed between many servants and their employees. When Paul, the 'gentleman friend' of Dorothy's nanny, returned after a length of time away as a soldier, she found them in a passionate embrace which she knew was 'very rude'. Both Dorothy and Nanny pretended this had not occurred, but in time her nanny had to leave due to being pregnant. Dorothy writes that after the war people's attitudes changed towards unmarried mothers, before which they were viewed with harshness and were called names. Yet her mother, 'though she might speak severely, did what she could for Nursie, for she was a woman with a pitying heart.'

Prior to the early 1900s, Brompton Square in Knightsbridge, London, had been frequented by prostitutes, and before that had been a rural neighbourhood where theft and murder had taken place. Considered a newly respectable area, Dorothy lived there with her family, employing servants:

> a Norland nurse, a parlourmaid, a housemaid, and a cook. Later we kept a manservant who had been head footman of three, and asked £70 a year. The cook, a very fair cook too, earned £28. If my memory serves me rightly, the Norland nurse's salary was £40. Norland nurses, who were women of the educated classes trained at the Norland Institute, wore a special uniform and were a novelty. Later, while our second child was in the nursery meal stage, we had a between maid.[62]

Domestic staff who worked for Dorothy are spoken of affectionately, particularly Alice (whose recipe for *Poulet Marengo* appears in Part Two). When Alice left to be married, Dorothy found it difficult to replace her which led to her working alongside her cook, experimenting on how to efficiently run a kitchen. Using this experience, she wrote articles for *Hearth and Home* under the title of 'Ten Shillings A Head for House Books'. Complaints were received from readers, one calling her a 'mischief maker'[63] who felt they were unable to look after their home and feed their family on that sum, and others thanking her for the consequent efficiency of their expenditure. This again broadened her reputation so that letters replied to through work for the *Daily Mail* Food Bureau, *Hearth and Home, The Queen* and *The Lady* amounted to many thousands.

It was not plain sailing for all of her staff, and one cook seems to have experienced mental health problems, 'We returned to find Ellen mad; a sly, smiling kind of madness. She had made a pie with a lovely crust and still smiling carried it into the dining-room. Its inside consisted of hay. Even though the cook is mad, one eats, but that pie we could not consume.'[64] We are not told what happened to Ellen; I would hope that the empathy shown in other parts of her writing led to Dorothy helping her resolve her problems.

In 1906 Dorothy published *How to Keep House,* advising young ladies on what they were to expect of their staff:

> Throughout my married life I have had to keep house with regard to cost and yet, like most women, I have desired to provide good, wholesome, plentiful and attractive food. This I have tried to do with the help sometimes of a cook-general, sometimes of a single-handed cook with or without help from a charwoman. But always cost and labour have been considered in some measure and thus it comes about that the book which I now offer to the public is exactly what its title implies.[65]

The duties expected of each member of staff were very particular:

> There are several varieties of cooks, not only, as the unlearned man might suppose, the good cook and the bad cook: there is the cook-housekeeper, the professed cook, the cook, the plain cook, and the cook-general ... on the house-parlourmaid's afternoon out (the cook) must answer the door and take in drawing-room tea.[66]

Within Dorothy's advice, the needs of the servants and the 'mistress' are focussed on equally, the onus being on the 'mistress' to look after the interests of her servants. Dorothy shows understanding for both:

> The success of all housekeeping depends upon the spirit in which the head of the household approaches the subject. If she looks upon it as an evil and is too bored to take an interest in it she must expect failure. If the mistress despises her household duties the maids will probably follow her lead. On the other hand, a really intelligent woman who wishes to have domestic comfort in return for what she spends will make herself thoroughly familiar with every detail of management and so be able to steer her family ship safely through all kinds of troubled waters.[67]

In addition to the salary earned by the servant, tips were given by visitors to the household. These were considered so high that they may hinder friends from visiting:

> The custom of tipping servants in private houses is one which most people deplore; but until the owners of large households combine to put a stop to it, the guest can do nothing.
>
> Meanwhile, people who are badly off are frequently deterred from availing themselves of invitations the acceptance of which would give pleasure to host and guest alike, simply because the visit would entail a heavier expenditure than the guest could afford. Considering that high wages are paid to servants in large households, that many of them are only employed in order that it should be possible to entertain, and that they are engaged with that end in view, it seems unnecessary that they should be paid two sets of wages, one by the host, one by the guest.
>
> As things are, the upper servants often receive as much in gratuities as in wages, therefore the master who attempted to put down the tipping system would be rewarded probably by finding himself servantless.[68]
>
> It is evident, therefore, that the young girl and the impecunious young man and the young couple of modest income cannot indulge in too extensive a course of visiting.[69]

An extreme view is expressed of the lavish nature of those in wealthy houses in the late Victorian and Edwardian period. While the extravagance refered to was of course not the case for all houses, it as an example of what contributed to the demise of many estates. This was added to by taxes such as the land tax introduced as part of the Government's People's Budget 1909/10, championed by David Lloyd George and Winston Churchill. Comparing and contrasting the efficiency of her cousin's servants in France, Dorothy concluded that 'everything was as well done as it would have been in an English house where double the number of servants were employed.'[70]

> In the rich years of the late Victorian and Edwardian periods, the extravagance in many large houses was appalling ... In allowing such a state of affairs the careless rich created social plague spots ... When Mr. Lloyd George's policy began to impoverish the great land-owners they were forced to enquire into the upkeep costs of their households ... In many cases, to shut up the house at all events temporarily was the only thing to do.[71]

Taxes meant reduced incomes which impacted upon the ability of householders to employ servants. So began the necessity for the housewife with servants to play a more active role in the upkeep of her home:

> At the moment I know a woman whose husband fills a high position who, to meet a shrunken income, has become her family's cook. Another, the wife of a man whose family forty years ago lived in a palace, has done likewise and yet another, brought up in affluence, cooks and does all the housework, with the help of a young nurse, and none of them makes any to-do about it.[72]

Among the servants may be a lady's maid who would assist with the everyday care of her employer. In *The Hat Shop* Dorothy gently mocks her wealthier customers: '"Oh, I've left my purse," she cried breathlessly, "and please tell Madame Delaine to keep that nightgown for me. I'll pay for it myself, and I'll get my maid to come for it."'

Servants played a significant role for many people until the war, when Dorothy says, 'the servant shortage had become acute: Dismiss them indeed! We were thankful if anyone would condescend to apply for our situations.' She desired the kind of innovation which was to come about later in the century in domestic matters: 'by making use of mechanical appliances and by building and furnishing houses in a somewhat different way, we could eliminate from one-third to half of the hard and dirty domestic work which now must be performed in them.'[73]

Time-consuming labour-intensive methods of cleaning, such as using tea leaves to clean a carpet and washing clothes using a mangle, have been replaced by the use of modern domestic appliances. The greater freedom we now enjoy due to the hard work of our ancestors has impacted our lives, easing the burden of domestic work, and increasing autonomy for all. I end with a comment from Dorothy, thankful that we are no longer restricted by such margins: 'The personal charm of the hostess counts for something even among people who are so dependent on luxury as the English upper classes.'[74]

CHAPTER 4

# Admirers, Marriage and Intrigue

As a little girl I had often fallen in love. Now, being fifteen and looking older, I found that 'males', as our housemaid called them, fell in love with me. I felt deliriously pleased about this because, having been richly teased by my brothers, I felt doubtful of my charms, and being of my time, I knew I must try to get married. Not to be married was to announce oneself a failure ... I knew also that one must not appear to wish to be married though really one was secretly longing to be so.

Mrs C.S. Peel, *Life's Enchanted Cup: An Autobiography 1872–1933*

The interest shown in Dorothy by young men conjures up the most wonderful innocence, a privilege of youth:

A rather horrid young man, then home on leave from his regiment and acting in some theatricals, to which I was allowed to go because Paito and Carli were performing, brought me sandwiches and lemonade at the party which took place in the green room, and on meeting me again at the tennis club asked me to go for a walk with him on the Downs. Palpitating with excitement, feeling steeped in vice, I went. He tried to kiss me. Deeply offended I walked home alone. Yet I admit that I longed to meet him again... However, my morals were strict and I took no further notice of him.

I did not like any of my admirers, but I did like having admirers. It was comforting, it made me feel that should my brothers again call me suet pudding I could bear the insult calmly.

It was very difficult to be a nice young girl and yet not too nice. To be too nice led to dullness and young men, though in theory they approved of dull girls, in practice left them to be wall flowers. Indeed, unless you were a beauty or an heiress it was very anxious work being a young girl in the days of my youth.[75]

37

The ridicule of her brothers caused Dorothy to doubt her charms. They told her that she was fat and danced like a 'coal heaver hopping in a public house' and that when she sang she had a 'voice like a cheese mite'. When attentions were paid, she accepted them reluctantly. At a party with her aunts, she was asked to dance by a Mr Smith whom she describes as looking like an ape with his gloves having split, so large were his hands, and that 'he did something with his feet, but dance he did not.' Mr Smith fell in love with Dorothy, 'poor man, I suppose he had to fall in love with someone.' Despite being told by her aunts that her behaviour that night had been 'marked', perhaps the result of indulging in too many meringues, Mr Smith was allowed to visit Dorothy until she was relieved that they put a stop to further meetings.[76]

When I was 17 and had an admirer who was interested in mesmerism and lent me a book on the subject, he, proper youth, went to the trouble of sewing up certain pages. Naturally, I neatly unpicked them and returned the book re-sewn, being careful to sew the original buttonholes. The information contained in these censored pages was to the effect that mesmerism if practised on the expectant mother might possibly affect the unborn child. In those days nice girls did not recognise babies until they were born. That troublesome process over, it was quite proper to gush over them.[77]

Until upper-class and aristocratic girls were married, their social life depended on being chaperoned. Dorothy writes of an occasion prior to her marriage when she was taken to a dinner for a well-known dancer in a Richmond Hotel where she says that her 'country bumpkin' eyes were opened easily.[78]

'Coming out' balls took place when young ladies of the aristocratic and upper classes were eighteen years old. They would be formally introduced to Society and would meet potentially suitable husbands from the same background:

I still looked forward to coming out at a ball in all the glory of a tight white satin bodice, and tulle waterfall skirt ... I came out at a Military Ball at Shorncliffe Camp. This time it was all a ball should be, more indeed than I had dared to hope a ball could be. Emmie, (a friend) who had just been presented, wore her Court dress of white tulle with a white satin bodice and trails of white Gelder roses, and I, because we were feeling very poor just then, wore an almost new ball dress of my sister's which she had not needed to take abroad. It was a pretty dress of filmy lace flounces with regulation boned bodice. An admirer sent me a "spray" of gardenias wired with their stalks wrapped in silver paper. We went to the ball in a fly.[79] All Folkestone went to balls in flies, which generally smelt of straw. We each danced every

38

dance but never more than three dances with the same partner ... There were other balls that winter, and at these our conduct degenerated; we danced many more than three dances with some partners.[80]

## Competition Winner

'Poor we were not, but in comparison with other people of our world, badly off we were. Yet no one seemed to think that anything could be done about it if you were a girl, as you were so you remained unless you made a good marriage.'

Mrs C.S. Peel, *Life's Enchanted Cup: An Autobiography 1872–1933*

Division was made between classes. There were the aristocracy who were independently rich and titled; the upper class who were independently rich; the middle class who had professions; and the working class who worked in areas such as domestic, factory, railway and coal mining. There was also what was termed the 'underclass', which included prostitutes and people of ill repute.

Dorothy's decision to work was unusual within her social background, though the seed had been sown by her cousin, Mrs Talbot Coke, who wrote on house decoration for *The Queen Newspaper,* while Dorothy's sister, Carli, illustrated them:

If one person could write why not another? I had a liking for my pen. As a small girl at Wyesham I had written in printed characters in a copybook a novel called 'Three Figures of Mourning,' a fine title, but before its time, for the vogue of Russian dreariness had not then set in. At the age of sixteen I had written a sickeningly sentimental novel called 'Poor Teddy,' which was a falling off in the way of titles.

Now, on the way to stay with friends, I had bought at a railway bookstall a clever little paper called *Woman*, which later on was edited by Mr Arnold Bennett. A prize was offered for a Dress Article. I opened my travelling-bag, found pen, ink, and paper (there were no fountain pens then), wrote an article, and won the prize. A week or so later I received a letter asking if I would care to call on the Editor with a view to writing further articles. From that time, except that I still lived at home and was boarded and lodged, I became financially independent. My parents were surprised, and so was I. It seemed that they had two clever daughters instead of one.[81]

I now wrote for *The Queen*, which was then edited by dear old Miss Lowe who wore a mushroom hat tied under her chin and looked like Queen Victoria. *The Queen* had a great prestige. Advertisers humbly asked for space in the

39

paper. Once I, going to a certain shop to write a notice of its wares, was kept waiting and not too politely received. I told Miss Lowe what had happened. She struck the bell on her desk. 'Ask Mr. Dash (the Advertising Manager) if he will be good enough to speak to me.' 'Will you kindly tell Messrs. So and So that we are unable to accept their advertisement. I require that representatives of *The Queen* shall be treated with consideration.'[82]

*Hearth and Home* employed Dorothy as Editor when the position became vacant. As well as this, she continued to write domestic articles and to freelance. Her short stories and reviews on books were published by various magazines and papers, thus broadening her reputation.

I wrote for both *Hearth and Home* and *Woman*, which now was edited by Mr. Arnold Bennett ... He was a plain young man, a raw young man and afflicted by a violent stammer, but one who already knew what he meant to do. Under his direction *Woman* was a brilliant little paper.

I entered his room one day with an article. He took it, read a few sentences; then looked up at me. He leant back in this chair and his limbs stiffened, as happened when his stammer overcame him. 'W...w...w...why do you not l...l ...l...learn to write?' he enquired. Probably by then I was earning considerably more than Mr. Bennett, but I had the sense to know that I could not write, and that he could. I replied humbly that I would gladly learn. How did he think that I should begin? 'I will teach you,' said he. Kind man, he little knew what a task he had set himself. Presently, 'Did you not learn grammar?' 'I think I know the difference between a verb, an adjective and an adverb.' He sighed... no, it was a hiss rather than a sigh. He hissed with exasperation. 'You must learn and I certainly shall not try to teach you. I know a Miss So and So who might be able to give you lessons.' Miss So and So did give me lessons. She taught grammar to Board School Children, but she never taught me. I seemed to be incapable of learning grammar. A combination of words sounded right or sounded wrong, and thanks to my father's refusal to let me read trash, my ear was accustomed to the sounds of words well used.

Arnold made me write articles; he made me strike out superfluous words; he made me put away what I had written, produce it again and then decide if I had written what I meant to write or if I had merely imagined that I had written what I meant to write. He asked me why I wrote 'can' when I should have written 'may'. I did not know. I am not sure that I know now. He spoke of the balance of sentences, the weakness caused by over emphasis. He read the articles which I brought to him, recast sentences, put out a word here, a word there, substituted the right word for the wrong, until from muddles of words they became ordered presentments of fact or opinion. He suggested to me that words did not mean what one thought that they sounded as if they might mean, they meant just what they meant; that, and nothing more. He said that women were idle and would not take the trouble to learn their jobs, that authorship is a trade as well as an art, and that authors who wrote what no one wanted to read and muddled contracts and excused their foolishness on the plea of artistic temperament deserved to go hungry and generally did.[83]

I made what was for a young woman journalist in those days a comfortable little income, and as my young man had now become an electrical engineer we thought that four years was long enough to have been engaged and announced our intention of marrying.[84]

## Marriage

'I have yet to be convinced that life can be of any use to anyone if it is not ruled by love, for it is the mental effort born of love that makes life beautiful.'
Mrs C.S. Peel, *Life's Enchanted Cup: An Autobiography 1872–1933*

When I bought my wedding outfit, the underclothes of girls such as I were made of white cambric, trimmed with lace and threaded with baby ribbon. We wore woven combinations, and flannel petticoats which were embroidered and scalloped with white filoselle silk, and stiffly-boned stays. Waists were small. Although I was all but 5 feet 8 inches in height my waist measured 22 inches. My going-away dress was made of a brown material called Zibeline, my hat of brown felt was trimmed with sable tails and gardenias ...

My wedding dress was of white satin, the skirt bell-shaped with a stiff frill, tacked on the inner side of the hem to make it set properly. The Court train was of brocade. I wore orange blossoms and my mother's Brussels lace veil. Our relations continued to disapprove of our approaching marriage but they did it so nicely. My mother was devoted to Charles, his father and mother were kindness itself to me. So many young women seem to find it necessary to quarrel with their mothers-in-law. I loved mine and she was always the dearest friend to me.[85]

My soon-to-be-husband, having finished the task of electrifying the town of Antwerp, was now at Dewsbury. He applied for leave, which was granted. The wedding day was fixed. An old friend of Clifton days Mrs. Bengough, lent us her house in Wilton Place and we arranged to be married at St. Paul's, Knightsbridge.[86]

There was an influenza pandemic, also known as 'Russian Flu' or 'Adriatic Flu' first recorded in St Petersburg, Russia, in 1889. It caused particular concern because in London the mortality rate was five times higher than the average in Great Britain.[87]

> Then I fell ill. I had influenza very badly. The wedding must be put off. It should not be put off. I rose from my Twickenham bed and with my family came to London. Our friend and doctor, the late Dr. Leeson, arrived the next day and by means of a strong pick-me-up administered while my veil and wreath were being arranged enabled me to walk up the aisle and down again.[88]
>
> I am told I was married by several clergymen at St. Paul's Knightsbridge. I may have been, but all I remember is that I came out of a mist to find brother Dick, who gave me away, knocking an elbow into my ribs, and whispering,
>
> 'Stick it out, old girl, stick it out,' and then went back into the mist again.
>
> We went away in the wrong carriage, the coachman making no protest, and that evening my small bridesmaid succumbed to an attack of measles.
>
> Waking about four o'clock next morning and feeling desperately influenza-ish, I was fed by my devoted bridegroom, lovely in pink and white striped pyjamas, upon Brand's jelly. My careful mother had included the jelly in my outfit, but had forgotten to add a spoon. Being a resourceful lad, Charles was not deterred by that, but used my shoe-horn instead.[89]

Dorothy's honeymoon was cut short by Charles's work so that when he was asked by the firm he worked for to go to Tenerife to electrify a villa, they extended their curtailed honeymoon.[90]

> When I was a child the average 'nice' married woman knew nothing about birth control. Although my father and mother were badly off and had no desire for a large family, they had nine children. When I married, young people were practising birth control by methods which could not be depended upon and which were only whispered about. Today people discuss birth control with the same freedom as they discuss the latest novel or an earthquake in Japan and it is practised in all strata of society, except, perhaps, in the one in which it is most needed, that is, amongst the poorest and most degraded of the community.[91]
>
> Having children has its delights, but they are nothing to the delights of friendship with grown-up children, to whom you have ceased to be a policeman; while a lover is not to be compared with a husband who, after thirty-eight years of married life, is one's best friend.[92]

Daughter Cecilia Straker, Dorothy Peel, son-in-law Harry Straker, sister Carli Peake, brother-in-law Harold Peake, husband Charles Peel, brother Dick Bayliff seated. *(Family album)*

**Intrigue**

'Falling in love is part of one's education, but for the most part a restless, teasing experience.'[93]

Insight into this reference is given in her autobiography where Dorothy writes of while staying with cousins in 1898, and visiting gambling rooms in Monte Carlo.

One evening the rooms were so crowded that I could not get near enough to play at my chosen table. A tall, fair, powerfully built Englishman standing near me took advantage of someone moving from the table to make way for me to approach it. I played for some time and won; once or twice the unknown helped me to rake my winnings in. When I moved from the table I thanked him. To my surprise he followed me:

'Be careful where you go with that amount of money on you,' he advised.

43

'Thanks, I am joining my cousins, I shall be all right,' I replied a little stiffly.

He looked at me for a moment. 'Monte Carlo isn't London. One does things in Monte Carlo that one doesn't do elsewhere. Can't we meet again?'

I wondered if we could. There was something very attractive about that Englishman. Of course he might be a crook but I did not think he was.

After I agreed to that meeting I went to look for my host. He seemed pleased, but walked as though his boots were tight. They were, he had won, changed it all into notes, and packed them away in his boots.

"Who is that tall fair man over there?" I asked.

'So-and-So-quite a nice chap – why do you want to know? Does he love you?'

'I think so,' I laughed.

'Bless you. It's good to be loved,' said he.

We did meet again; we spent a day up in the hills, lunching at a little inn under a pergola of vines at a table spread with a blue and white check cloth, upon it a long baton of bread, a basket full of oranges, set off with a spray of fresh orange blossom and toothpicks in a wine glass. As we sat there eating an omelette, followed by veal cutlets and drinking a pinkish fragrant wine made in the hills above Mentone, a bank of white cloud formed, blotting out the world beneath.

That was a good day. I enjoy the memory of that day. After I married there were no more love affairs for me, but I have watched the course of many. Ninety-nine times out of a hundred they create more trouble than they are worth. And yet ...'[94]

CHAPTER 5

# Bicycles and Bloomers

People tended to stay for longer before the days of cars and buses. When staying with friends in the country during the summer, they might stay from 10 days to a few weeks.

Mrs C.S. Peel, *How to Keep House*

Until the introduction of the motorcar in 1911, people travelled by Phaeton, Victoria, Barouche, Brougham, Hansom and Fly carriages. These may be hired using a Jehu, the equivalent of a taxi driver. A coachman to look after the carriage and horses was required, as well as an extra pair of hands, so that the coachmen could drive in shifts.

Dorothy's paternal grandparents fetched their guests using their cumbersome four-wheeled Phaeton, which could seat two in the front with a hood and one in an uncovered seat at the back. At times they hired a Fly with straw on the floor: 'Our darling little Aunt Charlotte, our mother's eldest sister appeared in the brougham drawn by a large roan horse with a Roman profile, called Hector, who was driven by a crotchety, grey-faced, grey-whiskered coachman, wearing a cockaded hat and a sand-coloured livery coat with plated, crested buttons.'[95] As well as a Brougham, her aunts owned a wagonnette and a high cart, which was used by their groom when he collected items such as fish and newspapers.

Dorothy writes that in 1888 before motorised transport, other than the use of carriages, the train was used for travel further afield: 'We were independent by the help of the train, for except for a few abandoned females in bloomers, ladies did not yet ride bicycles, and omnibuses did not rush about the roads of Twickenham and its surrounding suburbs.'[96]

Dorothy recalls her brothers being at Clifton College 'perched on bicycles with huge front and minute back wheels', which must be the Penny Farthing, though they were called bicycles until the introduction of the modern safety bicycle.[97]

Initially, it was considered indecent for a woman to ride a bicycle. Dorothy recollects that when she was a young girl 'two women in bloomers came bicycling through Albury village and stopped to inspect the church. A crowd collected and several boys threw stones at them, encouraged by their mothers who thought it a right and proper way to treat such shameless hussies.'[98]

45

"Do you know I once actually saw the Kaiser riding through the streets of London as bold as brass. If I'd known then what I know now I'd have told a policeman." (*Punch Magazine – Brock, 1917*)

It was not until 1896 when the safety bicycle was introduced, that they became more widely accepted: 'smart women mounted the new safety bicycle, and in especially cut skirts with deep inverted pleat at the back, a shirt, high collar, and sailor hat would convey their bicycles to Battersea Park and there mount them.' The bicycle saw the beginning of less restricted travel for women, 'and so began the downfall of the chaperon, completed by the motor car and the War'.[99]

Before motorised transport, Victorian morals were strictly applied to women and their modes of travel:

> Young ladies in Society seldom walked alone except in retired situations, and never in Bond Street, Piccadilly or St James's Street. For a girl to drive alone in a hansom was still rather fast, and never did a lady travel on the top of an omnibus ... Grand ladies did not travel in omnibuses at all. They had broughams, Victorias or barouches, and the Park in the late afternoon was a parade of beautifully dressed women, fine horses and perfectly appointed carriages.[100]

In the early 1900s the motorcar enabled the wealthy to travel with ease, going away for weekends rather than longer periods of time necessitated by use of the horse and carriage. With shorter visits came lighter luggage in the form of suitcases and a hat box instead of heavier trunks. In the early days of the motorcar, before roads were tarmaced, to be covered in dust at the end of a journey was par for the course. Driving was initially reserved for men, until women had to learn to drive in taking their place when they went to war. This, in turn, led to women's increased post-war freedom. The arrival of the motorcar, however, was not met with immediate acceptance.

> A modern minded squire who bought one of the first motor cars and appeared at a [Hunt] meet in it caused a veritable stampede and was almost cut off by the County. Gentlemen of static minds refused to allow cars to be brought to their front doors; the motoring visitor must leave his disgusting vehicle in the road. Earlier, horses had been terrified by the bicycle, which in my early girlhood was ridden by men only.[101]

Whether Dorothy owned a car in her early years of marriage is unclear, though I assume that they did not own one until they had saved for it in later years. When she did travel by car, however, she recounts that it was considered a treat:

> In our early married days to go out in a motor car was an excitement. We women wore motoring caps or bonnets, and wrapped our heads in gauze veils, took our knitting or a book, some biscuits and chocolate, knowing that we might sit for hours by the roadside while our men-folk tinkered with the insides of these wilful machines. We returned covered with dust, for roads had not then a tarred surface. The clouds of dust caused in dry weather by a flock of sheep, a wagon, or even a carriage, is a sight which we seldom see now. Then, if driving in open carriages, ladies wore dust cloaks generally made of biscuit-coloured tussore.[102]

In 1933, by which time the car had become more commonplace, Dorothy tells us of how it was not uncommon for a family to have a car, often starting up a business to fund it:

> The cheap motor car has also had a great effect on social life. Faced with the choice of a solid house, a nursery and children to put in it, or the possession of a car, the car wins the day, and in order to afford it, the house becomes a bed and breakfast dwelling, which may be run with little trouble or expense.[103]

Travel by train became more widely accepted following its use by Queen Victoria in the mid-1800s. Travel by bicycle, and then car increased mobility and thus broadened working life choice as well as opportunity for travel. In *How We Lived Then 1914–1918*, Dorothy writes of changes in transport and as a result, the environment, enabling the growth of industry, recreational and social lives, alongside the unburdening of social restrictions with which improved transport was linked:

> We look back during the first fourteen years of the century to a world less hurried and noisy than it has now become, owing to the increased use of motor-vehicles and of aeroplanes; to cities less congested with traffic; to roads and streets unadorned by direction lines and arrows; to a country not yet traversed by arterial motor ways; to a London which knew not the rotary traffic system nor the severe, factory-like buildings which to-day look so startling to eyes accustomed to a cosier style of architecture.[104]

CHAPTER 6

# The Treatment of Animals

Few people protest against the tight bearing reins which tormented the horses, because they made these unfortunate animals look so 'smart'. To be smart and to look smart was then and for many years after the ambition of all those with social aspirations.

Mrs C.S. Peel, *Life's Enchanted Cup: An Autobiography 1872–1933*

Dorothy's autobiography is littered with references to animals. Among them is the treatment of pigs, her first experience of which was when a sow died, leaving nine piglets behind. She and her older sister, Carli, brought them up by hand, moving them to a 'cucumber frame in the wash-house' until they were old enough to feed themselves and move back to the sty. Their grandparents employed Jawker, a man who helped out. He chose to return the piglets to the sty before they were ready, which resulted in all but one dying, for which she could not forgive him.[105]

In the early years of her marriage in the mid-1890s, living in the minster town of Dewsbury in West Yorkshire, she discovered to her horror that she was living opposite a butcher's shop:

Pigs began to scream. Poor things, of course they screamed; they did not want to die, and to die so cruelly. With the unseeing eyes which men have, my Charles had not noticed that opposite our lodgings was a pork butcher's shop. He was out all day, he did not hear those agonies. I flung on my outdoor clothes and walked the streets, to return, to listen ... and when all was still to go home again.

That evening I talked to Charles about pigs. He said pigs had to be killed like that, but I knew that they had not. Not because I had studied the gory subject, but because women, being intuitive beings, sometimes do know what they have no reason to know. And now I know that I was right; but still, in spite of humane killers, some people will go on murdering pigs brutally.[106]

49

Returning to London from her honeymoon in Folkestone, cut short by Charles being called back to work, she wrote: 'There was fog. Then it began to drizzle. The roadway was like ice. Our horse fell. Charles and a policeman and the driver put it on its legs again and we proceeded at a walking pace. Every few yards an omnibus horse was down. How I hated to see the struggle of the poor brutes.'[107]

Dorothy's care of animals extended to her opinion on hunting and shooting. Despite being brought up with such sport, in later life she condemned the killing of animals for sport:

> cruelty necessitated by sport ... is not only allowable but even praiseworthy ... Although I, too, had been brought up in this tradition, I was beginning to dislike it. I felt that the killing and, worse, the maiming of animals and the trapping of all the little beasts known as vermin should not be regarded as sport, that is amusement. When it is necessary to kill, then kill quickly, but not for fun.[108]
>
> I have sometimes ventured to suggest ... that in sports which involve cruelty, it is not only the animal which suffers. Those who find amusement in giving pain are sinning against their own natures. But history teaches that there is in humanity a passionate dislike of change except in dress and that changes of thought, as a rule, come slowly.[109]

During weekends, before exercise in the form of golf or other ways of keeping fit became popular, people would spend time in country clubs. The Princess of Wales shared Dorothy's view on animal welfare, refusing her patronage of the Hurlingham Club until one of the entertainments, the shooting of trapped pigeons, was stopped.

It appears from the fur she is wearing in her OBE photograph, that Dorothy did not object to wearing it until the 1920s when the wearing of animal fur for decoration was popular, perhaps causing her to consider its use:

> We put a vast amount of trimming on our hats then, and they were perched on the top of our heads. I had a sealskin jacket and a sumptuous sable tie sent to me from British Columbia by my brother Hugh. Although I was disgusted by cruelty, I do not think it ever occurred to me to wonder how those poor little sables had been caught. To-day I would not wear the fur of a trapped animal even were it given to me.[110]

Dorothy gives recipes where every part of the animal is used so that if thrift is demonstrated in its use, a little goes a long way. While this was practised during and after the First World War due to limited supplies, Dorothy's words may be applied to the higher cost of buying free-range or organic meat today:

50

To judge by letters which have appeared in the daily press and from private conversations it would seem that many people think that to abstain from meat on one of two days a week and to limit their total consumption to 2½lb. per head per week is a restriction which may seriously affect their health. To be quite frank, it may affect their greed, but it certainly will not adversely affect their health; indeed, there seems good reason to think that less meat-eating would improve the health of the well-to-do.[111]

Finding humour in straightened times, Dorothy tell us of a yellow labrador in *A Year in Public Life,* who gained from the culinary labours of a public kitchen during the war:

The enterprising and social yellow dog which attends all functions ... decided to attend the opening of the Westminster Bridge Kitchen, and I discovered him, having dodged through a compact mass of legs and squeezed himself behind the counter, sitting licking a pink mould with the greatest appreciation. And I now confess that in spite of the fact that I was, as people used to call me, a lady Food Controller, I did not interfere. He liked that pudding so much and he didn't look as if puddings often came his way. Presently one of the servers came and shoo'd him off, but I noticed that she did not remove the pudding. I meant to have done so but just at that moment the Queen took her departure and I had to attend to other matters. I often wondered who ate that pudding, because the yellow dog had licked it very neatly and it still looked quite shapely and shining![112]

CHAPTER 7

# Charity and Compassion

How many of the worthy people who go and 'talk to the poor' could attempt to house, feed, and cloth a family of six or seven on 25s. to 30s. a week (quite an ordinary pre-War wage); work surrounded by a tribe of little children; be kept awake at night by a teething baby, and remain cheerful and uncomplaining? Many a time I have been asked to go and talk to working mothers. If I have ventured to do it I have returned feeling that I have learned from them far more than they have ever learned from me.

Mrs C.S. Peel, *Life's Enchanted Cup: An Autobiography 1872–1933*

Poverty was widespread in Victorian England, necessitating enormous need for philanthropy. Dorothy writes of the contribution her aunts made, issuing 'stores ... bi-weekly to the servants', and keeping a slate on which to note orders of food. Spare vases were put aside for those who needed them for flowers, and a '"bag of black" which provided mourning armbands or a pair of bonnet strings or a child's sleeve ties for village families too poverty-stricken to purchase funeral garments. Here too were rolls of old linen, cotton wool and bottles containing household remedies for the sick poor.'

I was interested ... to see on a tray on the sideboard a collection of jam pots. These were brought to my aunt, who placed in them helpings of roast mutton and vegetables. Paper covers bearing the names of the recipients were twisted over them, and later old men or women or small girls or boys, called for these dinners and took them away.[113]

A Parish Nurse was then unknown and neighbours helped each other in times of sickness. Hall, Vicarage and the larger farmers distributed gifts to the respectable poor, and the unrespectable and the Dissenters went without.[114]

Following the introduction of the State Pension in 1909 and unemployment benefit in 1911, which was labelled 'the last defence against extreme poverty' by *The Times,*

52

improvements were seen in the standard of living for working-class people. Until this time, there was a greater onus on charity, for those with to help those without. In the late 1880s, when Dorothy was a child, her family perceived it as their duty to provide what they could for the poor.

A local vicar would decide who was in the greatest need of charity so that the aunts never actually visited sick or poor themselves. The 'suitable cases' came to the back door and were interviewed by Aunt Charlotte in the servants' hall before being given their donation. Dorothy's mother visited those to whom she donated by horse and carriage, the sight of which, she says, excited them.

This was a world away from the welfare state and education in which we now live. A hairdresser, who used to visit Dorothy in her home, collapsed while with her and died soon after. Having been neglected by family who were unable to support her, she had a job which barely paid for her lodging. Unable to feed herself properly

> Her one extravagance was the purchase of newspapers which offered money prizes for competitions, and the necessary stamps and envelopes. She told the woman (landlady) that some day she knew she would win a prize – perhaps a thousand pounds. A thousand pounds! A penny for a paper, a penny for a stamp, twopence for a few envelopes ... and that night to bed – hungry. But tomorrow, perhaps, a thousand pounds.[115]

Dorothy became interested in the plight of prostitutes while researching one of the four novels she wrote. A woman who was employed to work among them told her that finding work for the prostitutes was difficult, and unless they were taken off the street by a man who had taken a liking to them, 'the life gets its claws into them, and after a time they are useless for regular work.'[116] 'I ... remain convinced that physical union, unless it is combined with mental union, is worthless and that paid prostitution is hideous and as degrading to the purchaser as to the purchased.'[117]

Dorothy spoke with Mrs Pember-Reeves, with whom she worked at the Ministry of Food, in some women's prisons. Their audience consisted of young women and girls. 'What were they? For the most part prostitutes and petty thieves. They filed into the clean bare room in silence clad in ugly caps and shapeless dresses.' Dorothy doubted whether they should be in prison for the offence of prostitution, for which the majority were being punished, questioning why it is that men are not punished for 'like offence'. She goes on to question why prostitution is not legalised, suggesting that with men finding pre-marriage celibacy difficult, prostitutes may be viewed as, 'women who minister to their needs (who) are good citizens'. Rather than labelling these houses as 'Maison Toleree', Dorothy suggests calling them 'Maisons Recommandees', labelling prostitutes as 'martyrs in a just cause': 'if prostitution is anti-social, if it is a degradation so great that women prostitutes are classed as outcasts, then let us cease to cultivate an intolerable hypocrisy which permits the punishment of one sex for the sins of both.'[118]

Details of the abuse of young children whom Dorothy saw in The Children's Commonwealth, a home in Dorset, are upsetting and a sorry part of life, of which, I hope, we are increasingly aware and able to prevent:

> A very young lady who had attached herself to the gardening party, was the Colony's pet, then aged two-and-a-half. She was the incestuous child of a little girl of thirteen, who after the baby's birth screamed so terribly at the mere sight of her that she had to be taken away. Another girl, pretty, fair, graceful, who was helping with the work of the guest house, had at the age of fourteen been purchased by four sailors. She seemed happy there, but was very silent. God alone knows what were the memories of that child.[119]

When a bill that established the Society for the Prevention of Cruelty to Animals was presented to The House of Commons in 1924, Dorothy writes of her being told that it had been met with 'catcalls and derision'. At the same time, the House was 'vastly entertained by the idea' of a Society for the Prevention of Cruelty to Children. Parents and carers of children were deemed to be entirely responsible, and their care was not the business of others. Not until the neighbour of a child who was being abused contacted the police telling them that an animal next door was being cruelly treated, was the NSPCC founded in 1884. Dorothy felt passionate about the rights of girls and women. Even though it could be proved that a child aged thirteen entering a disorderly house was innocent, she was considered legally to have consented to her undoing. In 1871 the first proposal to change the age of consent from thirteen to sixteen was put forward. It took fourteen years for it to be raised, finally in 1885. 'Do you think that had there been women in Parliament then, it would have taken fourteen years to raise the age of consent?'[120]

Dorothy's compassion extended to many aspects of life and she had an understanding, beyond many, of how ordinary people lived and struggled. At a demonstration kitchen, the aim of which was to show its audience how to make do with food rations, Dorothy writes of a woman with four children in tow, and four at home. She admired the woman's dedication and 'the way in which this mother jogged and patted her babies into quiescence' while listening and taking notes which 'would have filled a conjurer with admiration ... the way in which many working-class women keep house and bring up their children on minute and fluctuating weekly incomes resembles a very clever conjuring trick, of which I for one have never learned the secret.'[121]

In the 1890s, the imprisonment of Oscar Wilde was the 'cause celebre of the day'. Dorothy enjoyed his plays and wrote of 'the charm of his conversation and of his smile'. He was convicted and imprisoned in 1895 for two years of hard labour for his homosexual relationship with Lord Alfred Douglas, the son of the Marquess of Queensbury. 'The trial, the subsequent life and death of this highly-gifted victim of mental processes which are still obscure were tragic indeed.' Dorothy's response to the 'jeering chants' of people outside the court following the trails was to write, 'Let us pray to whatever gods there be that we may be pitiful of all distress.'[122]

When seeing a play in Covent Garden, called 'White Cargo', the subject of the play was a 'brilliantly clever doctor' whose turning to the bottle was killing him. In the hope that someone may have sent him a letter, he looks hopefully at the postman, and on realising that he has none, turns back to the bottle. Dorothy felt let down by the cruel reaction of the audience who 'laughed' at the demise of this man.[123]

To end this chapter on a lighter note, Dorothy's empathy extended further than perhaps that of many of us so that when the nurse who looked after her first baby, Cecilia, 'extended her attentions to my husband, the fact that he could not see his way to accept her advances seemed to have caused no ill feeling, and we all parted the best of friends'.[174]

CHAPTER 8

# Fashion

She came in and fell in love with that new muff and stole – you remember, the one in velvet and fur with the tiny flowers....

Toque and veil removed, the trying-on process began. The customer sat in front of a large glass, tightly encased in corsets of the wrong shape, while Mademoiselle set elegant pieces of millinery upon her much crimped wig or part-hairpiece.

Mrs C.S. Peel, *The Hat Shop*

The onset of war, the subsequent introduction of women wearing trousers through their work for the war effort, the riding of bicycles, the arrival of the motorcar, as well as women getting the vote, are just examples of changes which took place in the first quarter of the twentieth century. Consequent adjustments in lifestyle led to enormous alterations in fashion during Dorothy's lifetime.

Victorian formality dictated what Dorothy wore during her childhood, with skirts involving several layers and hair neatly put into place. Such form is also seen in her description of tennis fashion: 'There was no tennis court at the Vicarage, but I remember that at one house to which I was allowed to go, Mr Archer Houblon, a local magnate, played tennis in a top hat.'[125] The practicalities of wearing trousers in sport took a while to emerge. 'Women skiers then wore skirts half-way between knee and ankle and knickerbockers beneath. The result when they took a toss was a trifle comic; undoubtedly the modern trousered outfit is more workmanlike. But it needed the War to accustom us to women in trousers.' Comparable impracticalities did not improve in the near future, with skirts with bustles, stiff white linen collars, ties and 'mannish straw hats' being worn by women for at least the next twenty years.

Dorothy's description of her aunt sounds like that of the perfectly dressed Victorian lady:

Aunt Charlotte was tiny and fair, with smoothly parted hair, a bonnet, exquisite little kid boots, which she bought from a celebrated London bootmaker, and in winter a sealskin coat, in summer a silk jacket trimmed with lace and jet. And always she carried a sweet-smelling green Russian leather bag containing, amongst other things, a boxful of pink and white caraway comfit [recipe in Part 2]. And always she wore a rakish-looking eye glass firmly fixed in one of her pretty blue eyes.[126]

Dorothy's own sense of dress was dictated by what was accepted as well as the confines of her mother's choice: 'Mummie, who had the same kind of taste in dress as in houses, dressed us in hideous clothes and plaited our hair in tight pigtails which were tied together with brown ribbon, looped back and again tied at the nape of the neck, just as Carli's had been when she was confirmed. We looked clean, tidy, ladylike and very plain.'[127]

When staying with her 'Grandmamma' in the vicarage, Dorothy attended tea parties. These were formal occasions and in her memoir she describes the clothes she wore for them:

> I remember that at one of these parties    Margaret and I wore dresses which Aunt Charlotte had bought for us at Jolly's. They were very grand, made of white Bolton sheeting, the underskirts box-pleated, the over-skirts turned up fish-wife fashion and much bunched at the back. The edge of the fish-wife draping was faced with red, and the dresses had red belts, red buttons, and red collars inside which was some scratchy goffered lisse frilling. 'Tuckers' were worn inside the high collars of all our frocks. These noticeable toilettes were completed by Tuscan straw hats turned up at the back with bows and streamers of red ribbon, white gloves and black silk stocking and laced-up boots. I was fat and Margaret was thin and, with our hair tightly drawn back and pigtailed, we must have looked a striking pair.[128]

Dorothy's Aunt Marianne married later in life, to a 'kind ginger-whiskered sporting little man'. She describes how she remembers his dress as 'cord breeches and gaiters, a black and white check tweed coat, and a square-shaped hard felt hat'.[129]

Admitting to an intense dislike of her maternal 'Grandmamma', portrayed as spikey with 'a long, thin, pointed nose', Dorothy goes on to describe her clothes thus: 'full skirts, paramatta boots with patent leather toe-caps, a cap with lappets and a lace chemisette and undersleeves'.[130] On baking days and when there was need for additional help with housework, Grandmamma employed a widowed woman 'with sparkly dark eyes, who never took off her bonnet, merely untying the strings, and she wore pattens on which she click-clacked from kitchen to washhouse.'

In the 1880s, then Dorothy was a teenager, 'nice young girls' did not powder their noses, 'if they shone, they shone'.[131] Bustles were in fashion. By this time,

Dorothy had developed an interest in her appearance, which her mother deemed as unhealthy. She tied her bustle so tight that it 'stuck out aggressively and waggled' when she walked. This was before the days of cushioned bustles, in which case metal steels, which ran into the material, may stick out when the bustle strings were tied too tight. Pain was endured in order to look the part – these were the days of high-boned collars, which rubbed on necks, and stays that were stiff. So awkward were these strictures that the Rational Dress Society was founded in 1881 in order to curb such extremes of fashion which might lead to ill health.[132] Hats were secured with long hat pins through hair, gloves were tight, and boots were buttoned.

In 1901, the restriction on mixed bathing was lifted. During Victorian times, showing even an ankle was frowned upon, and servants had to help women from the sea without being seen by men. From 1910, views on swimming attire became more relaxed. Until then, however, there were restrictions in place during daylight hours, and it was not allowed on Sundays, Christmas or Easter. Dorothy questioned such restrictions:

> There was no mixed bathing in our nursery. If one is to believe that 'virtue' is a virtue, then perhaps Puritans and the Fathers of the Holy Catholic Church are right in their insistence on the necessity for the teaching of modesty as we understood it. Nowadays some think that nakedness and modesty are not akin. Are they right? Thank heaven one cannot know everything or even be expected to pretend that one does, and so I ask the question but leave it to be answered by someone else.[133]

Dorothy tells us that swimming attire changed from full dresses for ladies at the beginning of her life to one-piece swimming costumes towards the latter part. When she was visiting Switzerland in 1910, French women arrived wearing sleeveless dresses 'cut low under the arm' which caused a 'shocked sensation'; never before had being sleeveless been accepted.

> The vagaries of fashion cause one to ask, is there such a thing as decency in dress, or only custom? In my youth, had a woman worn the kind of evening dress or bathing dress which she wears to-day she would have created a riot. We bathed in a loose trousered garment with a tunic reaching nearly to the knees, and even when so clothed hurried into the sea and, our bathe finished, hurried out again and into a dank smelling, sandy floored bathing machine.[134]

When going out in central London, it was considered acceptable in Dorothy's early years to wear a dinner jacket. By the 1920s, this had lapsed to tweed coats, frowned upon by some:

Fashionable men wore frock coats and striped trousers, a pearl pin in their cravats, shining top hats and patent leather boots. There was no lounging about Piccadilly or Bond Street or St James's Street in tweeds, and no one would have thought of going to a restaurant or the stalls of a theatre in day clothes or even dinner jackets. Smart young men had private hansoms or hired a hansom by the day with a Jehu in a buff-coloured box-cloth coat with large pearl buttons, a button hole, and a very curly, very shiny top hat.[135]

**Home Interiors**

The Victorian love of embellishment was reflected in their homes as well as in their clothes. In her autobiography, Dorothy vividly describes her bedroom. In the late 1890s when she moved with her husband from Dewsbury to London, she paid £80 a year for a flat in Greycoat Gardens, Westminster, which is in the region of £8,300 today. With two sitting rooms, two bedrooms, a bath-dressing room, and a good kitchen with electric light, she 'was proud as a dog with two tails' of her new home: 'My bedroom was quite in the mode, with pink striped paper powdered with talc so that one strip was plain and one shiny, curtains of ivory Holland and under-curtains of ivory-spotted net, ivory-enamelled furniture with Carton Pierre enrichments, and a pink carpet.'[136]

**The Hat Shop**

After the closure of three women's papers for which Dorothy worked, she took a break. Now a lady of leisure, she found that 'too much amusement did not amuse' her, and so in about 1908 she decided to start a hat shop, in partnership with a friend who had recently been widowed.[137] The polished dress sense of the French was seen by Dorothy during her visits to France in the interests of millenary, as well as to stay with cousins:

> In ... 1897, I paid my first visit to Paris ... To see well-dressed French and American women was a valuable education to me ... French women, then as now, dressed quietly for the street. Their neatness was exquisite and every detail of the toilette was carefully thought out; English women on the other hand were apt to overdress and to be untidy. They did not think out the ensemble and often spoilt the effect of a good dress and hat by an ill-chosen handbag or the wrong stockings and gloves.[138]

Despite the admiration commonly held for French fashions, Dorothy found that her clients were reluctant to try on hats which were genuinely French because they were regarded in reality as needing adapting 'to fit the English face and taste'. At the same time, to know that a hat was in the best Paris shapes was of the utmost importance to customers.

Influenced by the church, the wearing of hats had been considered essential since the Middle Ages. This English culture continued until just after the Second World War when from 1940, material had been rationed. To wear hats every day was seen as a frivolous use of material. Combined with the impracticality of wearing hats, this led to their gradual demise. Until then, millinery was big business, also providing irresistible temptation to shoplifters.

There are stories within *The Hat Shop*, involving the surreptitious means by which even the wealthiest ladies tried to obtain beautiful hats or items of clothing without payment. On one occasion:

> a beautiful and well-known young woman ordered an expensive blouse which I had bought in Paris. Three days later it was returned rather crumpled. In the box was a note from our customer to a Mrs. So-and-So in Walham Green asking her to copy the blouse as quickly as possible and to return the model to us. Pinned to the lining of the blouse was a note addressed to us in which our client explained that she hoped we would not mind her returning it, but after trying it on she had found that it did not suit her.[139]

Dorothy tactfully refrained from naming these individuals. She does however, mention the names of celebrities whose custom she enjoyed; Dame Ellen Terry, the leading Shakespearean actress being one, 'who sat in the shop fascinating us while Mademoiselle altered a model until it conformed to Miss Terry's idea of what a hat should be'.[140]

While meeting glamorous customers, Dorothy also spared time to ensure her assistants were well treated. They were allowed a ten minute tea break at 11 a.m. followed by a lunch break at midday, during which they cleared the workroom and could cook their lunch in the kitchen on two gas rings which had been provided for them: 'Our workers were generally very gay; they would sing at their work, and chatter like a cage full of birds. The word of the head milliner was law, and any conversation not approved by her was brought to an abrupt end.'[141]

In *The Hat Shop*, Dorothy uses one of the characters to illustrate ways around owning several hats: 'She has worn that black hat all the summer and there's been a different coloured feather in it every day. I believe she has a feather for every day in the week and puts them all on together for Sunday.'

A milliner often provided specialists in hair treatment, face massage, manicure and chiropody. While Dorothy had little knowledge of millinery when starting out in the business, she felt she 'knew a good hat when (she) saw one'. Within *The Hat Shop* perhaps the character of the proprietor, Madame Delaine, may be compared with Dorothy, going into the millenary business with great common sense despite 'her profound ignorance of the trade upon which she had embarked'.

In spite of owning a hat shop, Dorothy makes fun of the hat of a young woman who is reading her unfinished autobiography, 'Put that hat on a St Bernard dog, a cow, a leopard, and it would cease to be a dignified animal and become a figure of fun. Why should it not have the same effect on a woman? It does. I laugh at her; I love her; I wonder if her clothes express her, because if so.'[142]

**Change**

The Suffrage Movement saw conflicting interests in fashion. Dorothy gives example of men who saw long skirts as feminine clothing; with women desiring to be equal to men, some began to despise glimpses of femininity, such as the edge of petticoats under the skirt of anyone involved in the Suffrage Movement.

The war began with newspapers continuing their fashion pages, much as they had always done, with images of the latest fashions to which their readers could aspire. Yet, as the war went on, it became less fashionable to wear the most up-to-date clothing, and instead, the latest thing was to dress down, in accordance with the hardship of those at war. Dorothy gives us an example of this in her autobiography:

> The *Queen Newspaper* took the lead in publishing articles on the responsibilities of women. In a fine anonymous article it was pointed out that 'the tables that are to-day laden with luxurious food belong to enemies of the commonwealth,' and women were asked to save, and to dress plainly, and reminded that before the end of the American Civil war women who had been rich were clothed in dresses contrived out of cotton bags.[143]

Concentrating on fashion seemed superfluous in light of the devastation taking place on the Western Front. The *Daily Mail* changed the title of its fashion page to 'What Women Can Do?' This led to voluntary groups being set up, and women began finding their place wherever their skills may best be applied.

Fashions altered during the war, making way for more practical clothing necessitated by women stepping in to take the place of men at war. Change started with the shortening of dresses to knee length with the 'chemise dress': 'one notes that skirts are becoming a trifle shorter, that khaki is a popular shade, that a veil with a tiny velvet aeroplane upon it is described as being extremely chic.'[144]

Bloomers were worn by some for cycling but aside from that, trousers were not a part of women's dress until the First World War. Before then, no matter how impractical the dress, it was worn with as much dignity as possible.

By 1917 the 'silk stocking craze' was ubiquitous. Working for the war effort meant that many women, for the first time, had their own money, enabling them to buy stockings, which perhaps symbolised their new found independence.[145]

59

A Bill-Poster Girl. Note the Queen's Mary's Army Auxilliary Corps Posters. *(WAAC)* (Mrs C.S. Peel, *How We Lived Then 1914-1918*)

The Government established the Women's Land Army in 1915 to alleviate the strain on the workforce. The impracticality of wearing a dress while doing practical work was not immediately recognised: 'At that time skirts were long and women when they did field work drabbled about in muddied petticoats which cramped their movements and added to the fatigue of their tasks. It did not seem to occur to the wiseacres who objected to their dress that it was possible, as was done later, to suit the clothes to the occupation.'[146]

Stern messages were sent:

You are doing a man's work and so you are dressed rather like a man; but remember that because you wear a smock and trousers you should take care to behave like an English girl who expects chivalry and respect from everyone she meets.[147]

Dorothy writes of the reaction towards the wearing of trousers involving some disapproval from those less willing to accept this necessary change:

In 1917 this change made it possible for two land girls on leave, wearing their uniform, to enter a smart London restaurant, order as good a dinner as food scarcity permitted and sit unconcernedly smoking their cigarettes until it was served. This attitude of mind was not, however, universal, and an old, decrepit male who acted as doorkeeper in a certain Ministry incurred sharp reproof because he was found sniggering and making rude comments behind the back of a land girl who visited the Ministry on some business.[148]

Wearing trousers was not welcomed by some women, particularly those who were older:

Some of the older women considered trousers indecent, others objected to wearing them because 'the fellers would laugh.' One elderly woman ... refused to wear the trousered and overalled uniform ... An exception was made in her favour.' When the King visited she, 'cast away her skirt and put on trousers. 'Why,' said my sister, 'you've got your trouser on, Mrs__.''Yes,' said Mrs. ___, 'I'm a loyal women I am, and I put 'em on to please the King, and I'll take 'em off again to-morrow.'[149]

The importance of dressing correctly was taken over by admiration for women: 'Now one sees land girls in their breeches and smocks walking about in Piccadilly, and the only glances bestowed upon them are those of admiration for their neat appearance.'

First week

Second week

Third week

Fourth week

*Punch (Punch Magazine, W. Bird, 1918)*

As the war continued, dress shops sold little but black and white day clothes because so many women were in mourning. At the same time, the craze for nightclubs was increasing, the overall instinct being to make the most of life: 'Men used to come to dine and dance at night, and go out the next morning and be killed.'[150]

Dorothy's eldest daughter, Cecilia, was a teenager during the war, she writes of her dancing with more abandon than prior to it. Shops selling 'dance frocks' thrived[151] and in 1917, despite rationing restrictions and increasingly exorbitant food prices, women were spending more on dresses than ever before. The women spending the money were those who had gone to work during the war, never before having earned their own wage.

Tailors who had experienced a rush in the supply of uniforms at the beginning of the war were in debt where they had formed the habit of giving long credit, and the man whose suit had been made had lost his life at war.[152]

Instead of containing pictures of the latest pretty fashions, magazines and newspapers featured 'descriptions of chest protector waistcoats lined with odd bits of flannel, operation shirts, body belts, many-tailed bandages, Japanese heelless socks, pneumonia jackets, Warleigh leggings and gas masks.'[153]

The life-changing episode of war brought about modernisation of fashions due to work practicalities and financial austerity with men at war not bringing in salaries. Increased involvement of women in wartime roles, and the Suffrage Movement also influenced their appearance with everyday dress becoming less ornamental and more functional. These changes were historic in their long-term evolution.

CHAPTER 9

# The Suffrage Movement

I have only once been there [the House of Lords] myself, and then it was to listen to the speeches of various old gentlemen who continually referred to women as 'irresponsible persons'.

Mrs C.S. Peel, *Life's Enchanted Cup: An Autobiography 1872–1933*

In early 1914 the daily newspapers contained disparaging titles such as 'Can Women understand Politics?', 'Is it feminine to Vote?' and 'What will Women do with the Vote?'[154] The plight of the Suffragettes, their demand that women should have the vote, and with it the ability to work in professions alongside men, was met with abounding disregard. This is illustrated in Dorothy's novel, *The Hat Shop,* where she gives an example of how the Suffragettes were viewed by many: 'But it all comes of young women not being content to stay in their proper place. But we won't say any more about that. Juliet, my dear, don't fuss about so – it would fidget me if I ever allowed myself to be fidgeted.'

During Dorothy's childhood in the 1870s, she tells us that women were viewed by the majority as 'less capable of being educated than boys', which meant that 'the faintest tinge of 'Blueness' was considered to make them so unattractive that it might prevent them from receiving any invitations to become wives and mothers.' A woman's wish to be educated was ridiculed because her brain was viewed as being incapable of learning: 'Only Heaven knew what would happen if women went to College – or rather probably more would be known about the matter in Hell.'[155]

In her autobiography, Dorothy tells readers about her own experience of gender inequality, while growing up in late Victorian society:

For the greater part of their grown-up lives, the men I knew preferred to be with other men. Even at parties they liked to collect in groups and especially was this noticeable in the country. In my youth men stayed almost all the evening after dinner in the dining-room. Now since nothing is as it used to be, a fact which worries many people greatly and does not worry me at all, men do mix more with women, and even find it possible to talk with them on any subject. I look back on men who flirted, who chatted, who paid compliments, but on few who conversed with women on terms of equality.[156]

Divorce was frowned upon in the Victorian era, therefore, Queen Victoria did not allow divorced women to appear at Court. It was suggested by Lord Salisbury that this rule should also be applied to men 'guilty of matrimonial misconduct'. The general consensus remained, however, that 'men were men' and being so, were unable to help their transgressions.[157]

The fight for women doctors was brutal. Dorothy tells us that at the thought of women becoming a part of what had always been a male profession, any chivalry and propriety expected in men left them:

> The men students wished to prevent the five women students from entering the building. When the ladies appeared, the gentlemen sang, shouted, jostled, threw mud and slammed the courtyard doors in their faces. The ladies remained calm; a janitor managed to open a little door and they entered and went to their classroom, which was in possession of more young gentlemen. The professor turned them out. A moment or two later a sheep was pushed into the room. 'Let it stay,' said the angry professor, 'it has more sense than those who sent it here.' The male students afterwards said they understood that inferior animals were not to be excluded from the classes – hence the ladies and the sheep.[158]

From the onset of war, hospital units were managed almost entirely by women doctors. Despite this, their efforts were not recognised by the Red Cross until early 1916, when a Government Committee was formed specifically for allowing the replacement of women to fulfil the roles of men who had gone into the military. By 1917 it was thought that this amounted to six million women, some earning as much as £2 or £3 per week (£206–£309 today).[159]

Dorothy wrote that she was not a feminist, but 'one of those sane people who think that as "male and female created He them", the best brains of both sexes are needed to conduct the world's affairs.' Dorothy took an interest in the Suffrage Movement, though not as much as she would have liked, with writing work taking up her time.

> It was in the middle of the nineties that I decided to invite my friends to a Suffrage Debate and asked the Suffrage and the Anti-Suffrage Societies to provide two speakers. Having a liking for hearing both sides of any question, I looked forward to an interesting afternoon. The Suffrage speaker made a brilliant speech, but the Anti-Suffrage representative crumpled. One of the

few suggestions which she put forward in support of her cause was that as the Virgin Mary had not had a vote it was unnecessary for any other woman to have one.

It was daring of me to stage this debate, for Women's Suffrage was one of those subjects which excited passionate feeling. Many men, and women, too, thought that if women were enabled to use political power directly rather than indirectly by exploiting their sex or using the power of money or social position, the British Empire would crumble to ruin.[160]

Dorothy's work brought a certain amount of insight into the male view of 'womanly domesticity' that if women are to focus on matters outside of the household, its successful running may be neglected.

During the First World War, the various Suffragette organisations put their resources at the disposal of the Government, so that political activities may be set aside and their energies devoted to the war effort. This offer by Suffragettes was initially disregarded by the Government who, in time, were pressured to accept it through the absence of working men who had gone to war. Dorothy tells us that women taking over 'has since become the settled policy of the Government, and is known by the somewhat curious name of "dilution of labour"'.

While working for the Ministry of Food in 1917, despite the opinion of men that food 'was a woman's question', the appointment of a Food Commissioner or even Assistant was not designated to a woman. Dorothy goes on to say that during the war, the country would not have successfully continued to run without the valuable work of women. This was thanks, in part, to the Suffragettes:

On Saturday, July 17th, 1915, a pouring wet day ... [Suffragettes] paraded London to force upon the attention of the public their demand to be employed in order to free men for the army. "We demand the right to serve," was inscribed upon their banners. Both public and politicians had now changed their tone, and these thousands of rain-soaked women were described as a "touching site." "Their spirit is splendid," said the Press, which was not what it had said about processions organized by suffragettes in former years. Mr. Lloyd George declared, "This procession will educate public opinion." Possibly it did, or more probably it was stern necessity which educated it, for it was becoming more and more tiresome to wait a long time for everything from a railway ticket to a cup of tea in a tea-shop.[161]

In 1914, due to the outbreak of war, 24 per cent of women were working in roles traditionally filled by men; by 1918 this number had risen to 37 per cent. The number of women in domestic service decreased as a result of their recognised ability to

The contribution of women. (*The War Illustrated*)

69

work outside of it. Example of this is seen by their increased involvement in the post office in *How We Lived Then 1914–1918*, 'This year we have lost 1800 men clerks and substituted 1300 women, and the figures were finished only one hour late.'[162]

Work for the civil service provided both independence and increased wages so that their number rose from employing 33,000 women in 1911, to 102,000 by 1921. In 1918 Millicent Fawcett, a pioneering Suffragette, summarised the effect the war had on the plight of women, 'The war revolutionised the industrial position of women – it found them serfs and left them free.'[163]

With so many clergy serving overseas at war, it took until the summer of 1916 for women to be able to speak in Anglican churches. And even then, they were allowed only to address women and girls: 'That a woman might have something of value to say to men regarding the spiritual life was unthinkable.'[164]

Reflecting on when women were finally given the vote in 1918, Dorothy comments:

The general public felt that [women] had been so useful during the War that they might be given a vote, much in the same fashion as a biscuit is given to a little dog when it has done its tricks nicely. So in 1918 women over thirty became citizens, and my Lords sat down and sighed that the Country was going to the Dogs. (In 1928 the vote was granted to women of twenty-one on equal terms with men.)[165]

CHAPTER 10

# The First World War and Rationing

The world must prepare for the greatest catastrophe that has ever befallen the Continent of Europe. The consequences, both direct and indirect, will be incalculable.

Sir Edward Grey, *The New York Times*, 22 July 1914

**War Declared**

At the end of July 1914 the papers announced, 'Fall of prices on Stock Exchange: Financial Condition Grave'. This had been prophesied at the end of June when it was announced that all of Europe were arming. The British Fleet was at sea and was now in a position of extreme gravity. On the last day of July of that year, the nation was told that Europe was drifting into a disaster and the archbishops of Canterbury and York appealed for the prayers of the nation.[166]

In her autobiography, Dorothy writes of the run-up to war:

Charles came home from London saying that there had been remarkable scenes in the City, that the Stock Exchange was to be closed until further notice, and that after the Bank Holiday, gold was to be called in and paper money issued.[167]

On Bank Holiday war was the only topic of conversation. In three months the whole affair would be over. A retired colonel who came to tea assured me that everything was arranged, and that the organisation was perfect. Yet in spite of that assurance, a week or two later wounded men were loaded into filthy cattle trucks; the dead, the dying and the wounded were crowded together in ships and in the Casino at Boulogne, hastily converted into a hospital, the stretchers were packed close on the floors, the veranda, and the garden paths, and the cries of men, to whom no attention could be given, were heard throughout the night.[168]

On Sunday, Germany attacked France and violated Belgium, our Army was mobilised, and the Reserves called out. Great Britain declared war against Germany as from 11 p.m. on August 4th.[169]

71

**Women and the War Effort**

'Considering the suffering and discomfort due to these causes, to the shortage of fuel, overwork, personal unhappiness and general mental strain, the people as a whole remained wonderfully calm. They grumbled, but their grumbling was chiefly an emotional outlet. Directly they understood the position, though they might still grumble, there remained the determination to 'stick it,' to do their 'bit' and to win the war.'

Mrs C.S. Peel, *Life's Enchanted Cup: An Autobiography 1872–1933*

Women on the Home Front and men past fighting age of forty-one were called upon by the War Office to fill the positions of the working men who had gone to war. Additional jobs were created and needed to be filled for its efficient running. This was done using propaganda posters made by various organisations including the YMCA, YWCA and the Salvation Army.

Those who were financially independent were encouraged to volunteer:

Practically every woman who could spare time to work outside her own home was working. Everywhere there were workrooms, in which hospital necessaries were made and canteens, not only for soldiers, but for war workers.[170]

The Voluntary Aid Detachment (VADs) had been established in 1909 by The Red Cross and Order of St John. Its main aim was to provide female volunteers to nurse in the field and in hospitals in the event of war. By 1914 there were in the region of 74,000 volunteers.

Dorothy does not write about her family very much, but there is mention of her elder daughter, Cecilia, working in the kitchen in an officer's hospital in Cadogan Square. VADs who were working far from home slept four per room in the attic of the hospital.[171]

Meanwhile, Dorothy's husband, Charles, carried out munition work for the Admiralty. Being forty-two and above military age, he was a Special Constable and: 'had a rough time amongst the looters in a poor part of Chelsea, where in the end the Specials had to be augmented by a squad of that body, drawn from another part of London.'[172]

The Women's Royal Naval Service (WRNS) and the Women's Auxiliary Army Corps (WAAC) were established in 1917. The former fulfilled widely varying roles from cooks to decoders of naval messages. The latter was linked to the Women's Legion, which helped substitute women in place of men in army roles behind the lines, including cooks and waitresses, and also in convalescent hospitals and rest

VADs. *(Family album)*

VADs. *(Family album)*

VAD letter. *(Family album)*

TERRITORIAL FORCE ASSOCIATION
OF THE COUNTY OF LONDON
VOLUNTARY AID ORGANISATION

County Director's Office,
24, Eaton Square. S.W.1.

To Commandants of Women's Voluntary Aid Detachments.

I am anxious that the Women's Voluntary Aid
Detachments of the County should know of the splendid
impression made by the V.A.D. Contingent in the recent
procession to Buckingham Palace, on the occasion of the
presentation of an address to Their Majesties.

As the Senior branch of   Women's Service in the
Country, the representatives of the Voluntary Aid
Detachments rightly took the foremost place in the
procession and from every side have been sent to me
expressions of gratification, not merely at the fact,
but also at the appearance of the Contingent.

In my opinion, far too little recognition has been
given to the work of members of V.A.D's in Hospitals
and other spheres, and it is my endeavour to secure a
better recognition of that work.  The fact that their
service is quietly rendered in the wards of Hospitals
rather than before the public eye, far from detracting
from its importance, adds to it the further value that
it is work for the sake of the work itself, and for
those to whose welfare it is vital; and needs no
stimulus of popular applause.

The Voluntary Aid Detachments have for nearly four
years contributed a splendid unselfish service without
which the Hospitals could not have carried on: whether
recognition of the work comes early, late or not at all,
the memory of that work will not fade from the memory
of those who have reaped the benefit of it and its
result will always stand as a lasting monument of its
value.

County Director.

camps. Recruits, aged twenty and upwards, were able to work overseas in France and there was also a Motor Transport Section where women worked with motorcars.

By the end of the war, there were almost 40,000 women working for the WAAC. Despite Queen Mary assuming the position of Commandant-in-Chief of the corps in April 1918, it dissolved in May 1920. The final women's military organisation, founded in 1918, was the Women's Royal Air Force (WRAF), which employed 8,400 women as clerks, storeswomen, sailmakers, fitters, riggers, mechanical transport drivers and cooks.

In Dorothy's wartime memoir, *How We Lived Then 1914–1918,* she includes an extract from the diary of a VAD volunteering in a London hospital. This paints a picture of the suffering and consequent value of such volunteers:

The terrible suffering of some of those I nursed added to my exhaustion. I think that the uncomplaining bravery of the men made it all the more heart-

Russian hospital, South Audley Street. *(Family album)*

breaking. Probably had I been trained I could have endured it better, for after a time if one is to do one's work one is forced to become less sensitive. I look back on that time with such a loathing of war that remembrance becomes almost physical pain.[173]

The Director General of the Army medical service, Sir Alfred Keogh, helped establish auxiliary hospitals within private homes and buildings in order to ease the strain on the military hospitals. Over 5,000 homes were offered so that in April 1915, the War Office issued an announcement that they did not need any further offers. Funding came from a variety of sources, among them, voluntary donations, contributions from the War Office and private funding. Within a family photograph album, which belonged to Cecilia, are some poems written by officers in the Russian hospital based in 8, South Audley Street, London. It was funded by a Russian Diplomat, Monsieur Mouravieff-Apostol, who had given up his career to manage his wife's vast estates in the Ukraine. She acted as commandant of the hospital.[174]

The Rubaiyat o the Brothers Bing
Awake! Nurse Harvey with a cup of tea
Doth coax us gently from obscurity;
And Lo! The little Welsh girl passes by
And there is no more sleep for you or me.

Here, with a broken arm or leg, or brow
Or collar-bone, or severed nerve – with thou
O rarest spice, with wondrous healing charms
And hospital were paradise enow!

With dinner you may milk or water drink.
(of cider there's a secret hoard I think)
But when night-sister, smiling, comes to thee
With darker draught, take that, and do not shrink!

They say the young and reckless oft frequent
'The Flea and Flatiron' on liquor bent;
But those who wisdom
And field rank attain
Contrive, (with sister's aid)
To have it sent.
Some against time with
Jig-saws madly race

76

With matron's help the work
Proceeds apace -
Bunny, enrapt, forgets her half-days off;
(Caruso almost puts a piece in place!)

Lucifer Bing, by Captain H. R. Mallett
There is a sluice although it hath no key,
There is a door, through which one cannot see.
Would you believe me were I to suggest
'twas never entered save by V.A.D.?

When V.A.D. with Lightning tread doth pass
Among the tables laden high with glass
And on her joyous way encounters on
oh shades of ronuk! Some (damned) spot, alas!

Ah soon! Too soon, shall we be desolate
The 'Russian's' being closed by cruel fate
And we must all unaided go our ways
Sans Bunny, sans Caruso, and sans Kate.

Despite successfully undertaking the working roles of their husbands, fathers and brothers, contributing to the war effort through working in munitions factories and volunteering, seen as independent, women were paid lower wages than men, often half the 'family wage' of their husbands.[175] While this money may have helped alleviate the increasing cost of food and the gap left by the absence of a family income, it was not enough to stop many falling upon hard times. This was something that Dorothy's work made her acutely aware of: 'There was much talk of food, for prices continued to rise, and women whose husbands had been called up were in many cases obliged at once to cut down their expenses, and to find ways of living more cheaply.'[176]

In addition to the financial hardship many endured, women working in roles traditionally fulfilled by men also had to face some male objection to their work. If women were able to fill these roles at a cheaper wage, trade unionists asked what was to stop their employers from continuing to employ women at a lower rate when the men returned from war?

In *How We Lived Then 1914–1918*, we are told of the intolerable conditions of the munitions factories in which women had to work. There were no arrangements for workers to be fed, and as many as six girls would sleep in one room at night and six others during the day, with no time for the cleaning or airing of beds. Dorothy tells

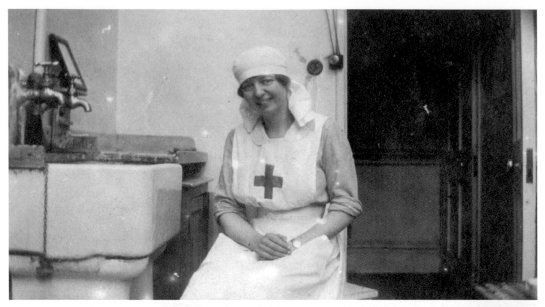

Bunny. *(Family album)*

Caruso. *(Family album)*

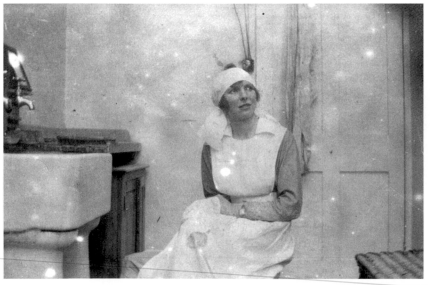

Lightning. *(Family album)*

These three VADs feature in the poems on the previous page.

Replacing the work of her husband at war, as a sweep. (Mrs C.S. Peel, *How We Lived Then 1914-1918*)

us that the Prime Minister, Mr Lloyd George, undertook to take drastic measures to improve the working environment so that hostels were built and canteens started as well as providing the means for girls to heat their own food if they bought it. A favourite method of marking their potato was to stick a hatpin in it.

> One point which struck me was that the better-class girls, who all their lives had been well fed, were not as hardy as the lower-class girls, who brought both to work and play an extraordinary amount of energy. It was not an uncommon thing for these girls to work all day and to dance practically all night, while the ladies went home exhausted after their day's work.[177]

INDIGNANT WAR-WORKER: "And she actually asked me if I didn't think I might be doing something! Me? And I haven't missed a charity matinée for the last three months" *(Punch Magazine – Baumer, 1918)*

Advising on food economy, Dorothy had to speak in a variety of venues:

> I had to do some outdoor speaking and also spoke in between the turns at music halls and cinemas, which was not easy, as what one had to say had to be condensed into a few words.[178]
>
> By the winter of 1914, London had gone back some twenty years as regards lighting, and by the end of the War it was almost as dark in the

London streets as it had been in the Middle Ages. When, in the later years of the War, it was my duty to go into parts of London hitherto unknown to me, in order to speak at meetings, I did not enjoy groping about in the dark.[179]

By that time [1917] the war had changed our lives completely. All formal entertaining had come to an end. Practically every woman who could spare time to work outside her own home was working.[180]

**Suspicion**

As the war progressed, the attitude of the British people became increasingly suspicious towards foreigners. German nannies were regarded with care with tales of weapons found in their trunks being bandied about.[181] Many people with a German sounding name changed it, for example, Bernstein became Curzon, Steineke became Stanley, and in 1917, Mountbatten became Windsor. Shops ran by Germans were ransacked, though Dorothy tells us of a bakery run by a German woman whose business was protected by her customers, due to the kindness she had shown them over the years in allowing payment dates to be extended.[182]

Dorothy was living in Chelsea, London, during the war and, by order, everyone had to have blinds which were drawn at night during black-outs, so that the enemy could not see where houses were. If you forgot to draw your blind, the police would telephone and you would be fined if the offence was repeated. Groups of lighting were dimmed so that the view of the City from Hampstead Heath was diminished to just a mild glow.[183]

**Air Raids**

'[O]n looking north-east over the houses I saw a cloud of aeroplanes. Then the guns began.'

Mrs C.S. Peel, *How We Lived Then 1914–1918*

The first air raid took place on Christmas Eve, 1914, in London. As soon as the familiar sounds of air raid sirens were heard, people found refuge in dug-outs, tube stations and the basements of large buildings. In areas such as Dover, where bombing raids were more frequent, these refuges sometimes had electric light, seating and beds, given the length of time they needed to be occupied.

At one time air raids happened on thirteen consecutive nights. Where homes were destroyed by bombs, shelter was sought in a variety of places. Overleaf is a picture of an upturned tree being used by a family in the countryside, where there was no alternative:

The *Daily Mail* offered insurance for those who felt the aftermath of air raids. Dogs and pet birds were found crushed, while it was not uncommon for a cat to

81

Air Raid warning. (Mrs C.S. Peel, *How We Lived Then 1914-1918*)

Family seeks refuge after their home has been bombed. (*The War Illustrated*)

escape unharmed.[184] Less damage was done in some areas such as Ramsgate than expected, as Dorothy noted:

On one occasion though 10,000 sheets of glass were smashed and 660 houses damaged, the total casualties in that town were only twenty-four killed and fifty-one injured. It was during that raid that a man and a woman were buried in the ruins of the "Bull and George Inn" and the barmaid had a wonderful escape, for she had just left her bed when a bomb passed through the centre of it.[185]

Babies and little children being taken to an air raid shelter. (*The War Illustrated*)

Among the horrific consequences of air raids, a girl died when a bomb exploded at her feet while at the garden gate she waited for her parents to arrive. Another bomb hit twelve children as they walked to Sunday school. One lady recounted to Dorothy that a woman walking behind her with a basket met her demise a few seconds later due to a bomb landing on her. Afterwards, this lady wrote that walking through Grimston Gardens was 'like walking through a thin coating of ice on a winter's day, which crackled and broke under one's feet'.[186]

In the absence of an air shelter, it was advised that the safest place to protect your family was in the basement, which generally housed the kitchen. Family and servants would often gather on the kitchen stairs, where they would continue with the book which had been set aside to be read aloud in such events, or to knit or sew.[187]

83

Panic ensued in attempts to seek shelter in underground stations; 'I shall never forget the sight at Holborn Station. The girl who was working the lift kept her head but was quite powerless to control the mob, and Miss Bellis and I stood by her and helped as much as we could.'[188] Once sheltered in the deep basement of Harrods, impromptu concerts took place, one performer being a young employee who was admirably tuneful with a toothcomb. In the underground, air shelters and basements, families often would settle down to a picnic for the duration.

Dorothy writes of the confused response to cheering when the 'large silver cigar' of a Zeppelin travelled through the sky before bursting into flames: 'I began to cry, 'Hooray! Hooray! too. But suddenly I stopped. We were cheering while men who were after all very bravely doing what they thought it their duty to do were being burned to death.'[189] In her autobiography, she adds:

> Following a meeting, I jogged off to the hall alone in an ancient fly driven by an ancient man. The roads were slippery and I feared for the horse. Presently there came a droning sound; the driver stopped, clambered from the box and opened the door of the fly, 'If you've no objection ma'am, I'll come inside, I like to feel a bit between me and them planes,' said he.[190]

Dorothy writes of tempers which flared during raids. The following describes the wife of a constable who was on her way to work during the raid which left the most lasting impression on Londoners – the daylight raid of 13 June 1917:

> There appeared to be about thirty large black planes travelling slowly, and a larger number of smaller planes flying faster. Some of them seemed to drop out of the clouds and began firing at the larger planes, which continued in formation, led by one well ahead of the main body ... I ran into Hyde Park House and made for the stairs leading to the basement. By this time the noise was deafening. The basement was packed with women clerks, some of them crying hysterically. One seized my arm, 'Oh, I am going to be killed, I am going to be killed,' she moaned, pinching me so violently that, what with pain and excitement, I so far forgot my manners as to reply, 'If you pinch me like that I hope you will.' She stood staring at me with her mouth open, the picture of idiocy. A girl nearby who had also been crying, remarked quietly, 'You are not very sympathetic.' 'I am sorry,' I apologised, 'but she pinched very hard.'[191]

Dorothy's daughter, Cecilia, narrowly missed a bomb explosion when she became impatient of waiting for an air raid and 'walked along the Embankment towards Charing Cross, and had just got into a taxi when a bomb exploded, wrecking a tram

MRS. GREEN TO MRS. JONES (who is gazing at an aeroplane ) "My word! I shouldn't care for one of them flying things to settle on me." *(Punch Magazine – Belcher, 1917)*

car and killing and injuring several people'. She had two further lucky escapes; one was when she decided not to travel home from Ireland on the *Leinster*, only for it to be torpedoed; and another when a bomb fell in Piccadilly when she was at the theatre with friends. When travelling home by tube, they decided to walk instead. Had she exited a matter of minutes earlier, she would have been part of the wreckage caused by the bomb.[192] Lucky escapes for some and not, of course, for others, came when it was thought that the enemy was aiming for the houses of Lord Northcliffe, owner of the *Daily Mail,* and of Mr Horatio Bottomley, Liberal MP and proprietor of the *Financial Times*, who had said, 'Germany must be wiped off the map of Europe.'[193]

Air raids became a part of life so that some, when partying, would take shelter, and when it was over, continue with their revelry. People got on with life as best as they could, shown in an experience related by Dorothy:

[I was] in a room full of men, a mass of khaki broken here and there by blue naval uniforms. We were eating our soup when suddenly the lights went out

85

– an air-raid warning, but no one appeared to be in the least alarmed, and in spite of the fact that we had but a glass roof between us and possible bombs, the waiters produced candles and dinner went on just as before.[194]

In total, 1,413 civilians[195] were killed in the United Kingdom as a result of air raids and 3,407 injured. After fifty-nine aeroplane raids in 1917, one taking place on five consecutive days, 619 deaths and 1,650 injuries, the strain took its toll, some talking of 'air raid aches'.[196]

Taking refuge in Admiralty House, Hyde Park Corner, during a raid, Dorothy found that she had a rare free afternoon. She went to her club to have 'luncheon' and to play bridge. Feeling faint, she called 'no trumps', only to come round again and see the hand on which she had called and almost faint again. On the way home in the 'omnibus', it skidded violently. Dorothy writes that she found herself saying aloud, 'Well, I can't bear *this*, it's *too* much,' and then began to cry.[197]

**Passing the Time**

In trains and omnibuses and parks, in restaurants and canteens, people knitted. It was soothing to the nerves to knit, and comforting to think that our knitting might save some man something of hardship for everyone was haunted by the knowledge of what suffering had been, and must be, endured in order to win the War.

Mrs C.S. Peel, *Life's Enchanted Cup: An Autobiography 1872–1933*

Wartime life led to an increase in people frequenting night clubs and to the loosening of previously strict rules and curfews for many. While Dorothy may not have allowed Cecilia to go to certain nightclubs, she says there was plenty of dancing in private houses.

Mothers insisted on their daughters being accompanied by other girls who they knew well. Were they to be accompanied by a man on the way home, they should be with a friend. 'Most of the dances were small, champagne was not provided, refreshments were simple, and a pianist took the place of the pre-War band.'

Cecilia and I worked for some time at the Liverpool Street and Canon Street canteens. She, in addition to suffering from foot trouble, had been obliged to undergo an operation for appendicitis, but was not recovered and began to work in the Air Ministry, where by the time she was twenty ... was in control of eighteen clerks. Like most of her contemporaries, she worked by day and danced by night.[198]

The war saw a shift in dancing style, with jazz becoming the rage. The motto, 'Eat,

86

drink and be merry, for to-morrow we die', led to marriages taking place within days of people meeting.[199]

In addition to the lapse in strict social form, people tended to visit fortune tellers, palmists and crystal gazers: 'The mental strain and desire to forget led to an increase in drinking, drugging, gambling, dancing, and an utter breakdown of what people of my generation considered to be sexual morality.'[200] With so many dying during the war and fear of a reduced population, illegitimate children were called 'war babies ... because of the fear that without the illegitimate child, the population might be too seriously depleted'.[201]

THE CAPTAIN: "Your brother is doing splendidly in the Battalion. Before long he'll be our best man." THE SISTER: "Oh, Reginald! Really, this is so very sudden." *(Punch Magazine – Pegram, 1916)*

**Food Restriction**

Time after time men and women have said to me of food: "I don't see why I should not have it if I can afford to pay for it." That there might come a day when money would not buy bread seemed to be beyond their comprehension.

Mrs C.S. Peel, *A Year in Public Life*

The gravity of food restriction and the need for the people of Britain to play an active role in ensuring that the nation was well fed, took some time to penetrate. Some of the older generation who had seen warfare, were able to understand, as related by Dorothy when an aged man who had fought in the Crimea said:

There was a man as 'ad some'ow got a bit of tobaccer, and an officer who 'ad none come along. 'Say, me man,' he says: 'I'll give you a sovereign for a bit of tobaccer.' But the man 'e says: Well, sir, a sovereign ain't no more use to me 'ere than it is to you, and I'd rather keep the tobaccer.' That'll show 'em as money ain't everything always.'[202]

Before the war, Britain imported up to 70 per cent of its food, most notably from Canada and America. When compared with pre-war prices, by the end of the war the price of food had increased by 170 per cent and by 1920 was at its highest, having increased by over 200 per cent. Germany started the war with sixteen submarines, which torpedoed 750,000 tonnes of Allied shipping. By 1916 with unrestricted submarine warfare and additional submarines, Germany torpedoed hundreds of thousands of tonnes of shipping carrying imports. Numbers increased until the authorities feared that Britain would be unable to feed its population. Food reserves were down to supplies for just six weeks of food.

As early as August 7th, 1914, a Cabinet Committee on Food Supplies began to function, and some maximum prices were fixed. These prices seemed high to us then; they were nothing to the prices which were to come ... But if the prices of ordinary necessities rose, that of the luxury foods fell. It became an economy to feed on luxuries for there was a collapse in luxury trades and in the wine trade.[203]

Entertaining in a lavish manner was considered 'vulgar' and to dress in clothes which were not 'the quietest' was deemed inappropriate: 'Clever skits appeared in *Punch* of aristocrats clad in rags and tatters, whilst the new rich flaunted their new finery.'[204]

Procuring linen was almost impossible so that at the end of the war when an acquaintance of Dorothy's was staying in a hotel in Berlin, in the absence of sheets, he found curtains were used as bedding.

People were panic-buying[205] so much so that a well-known provision firm said that eight days of normal business were done in one. This led to angst among those who could not afford to and had the adverse effect of increasing prices, which fuelled the black market so that those with money were able to buy extra food, while others went without. Hoarding took place and when discovered, the goods were requisitioned and a fine imposed. The use of every part of food available became an absolute necessity. The Defence of the Realm Act (DORA) had been introduced in 1914, to ensure that food never ran out, and over two and a half million acres of land was procured for farming.[206]

Hens born after 1 January 1916 were entitled to 2oz of feed per day:

> One pictures those youthful hen birds hatched since January 1st applying for certificates on behalf of their owners to the local Food Control Committee. Knowing the excitable habits of hens, it was doubtless even more difficult to persuade them to fill up their forms correctly than it sometimes proved in the case of their owners! Heaven knows what happened when a White Minorca filled up by mistake the form of a Yellow Wyandotte or vice versa. If this Poultry Food Order was issued uncorrected it must have done something to lighten the gloom of life in war-time.[207]

At the beginning of the war, daily newspapers continued for a while in the same way they always had. They tended to include articles on 'Housekeeping in War time' and 'Economy Columns'. 'The papers were depressing reading for the housewife. The price of bread rose by a halfpenny a four-pound loaf, and it was said that we had only a month's supply of meat if our overseas supplies were stopped.'[208]

By 1917, however, the position was grave and something had to be done to ensure the continued supply of food for the nation:

> home reserves were dangerously low. There was food and [*sic*] to spare in other countries, but to bring it to our shores necessitated the use of ships, and the supply of shipping was becoming shorter. Further, of the available shipping a considerable proportion was needed for the carriage of munitions. It was, therefore, necessary to increase production and reduce consumption. To do the latter, waste caused not only by throwing away food fit for human consumption, but waste occasioned by bad or improper cooking must be reduced to a minimum.[209]

The following note, which appeared in *The Times* newspaper in Paris in 1918, illustrated the increased cost of absolute essentials during the previous four years:

> To feed four people in a working-man's home, for bread, meat, bacon, butter, eggs, milk, cheese, potatoes, dried vegetables, sugar, salad oil, paraffin, and methylated spirit, the average cost per annum, according to prices in the third quarter of 1914, represented 1003f. In 1915 and 1916, at the same season it had risen to 1235f. And 1420f. Respectively, while in 1917 it was 1845f. By the end of June this year it had increased to 2331f. This latter sum represents the enormous increase of 132 per cent over the prices before the War. No wonder it is hard to make both ends meet and that there is a cry for increased salaries.[210]

Dorothy writes of a man who, despite his severe wartime injury, was calm in his dissatisfaction of what was he was eating: "'Fish Rissoles should be made of fish," was the message. I sent a note in return: "Sir, perhaps you have not observed that we are at war and there is a food shortage." The poor man had had a leg off and was wounded in the head, so if anyone knew what war was he did. I found this out afterwards, but in the answer to my note all he said was: "Dear me, is that so?"'[211]

Within her books on rationing, published in 1915, 1917 and 1918, Dorothy writes that 'To shun waste, to get out of our foodstuffs the full measure of nourishment – these are essential principles in war-time cookery; and I should like to see the words, "Make do" on the walls of every kitchen in the land.' She aimed for her uplifting words to encourage housewives to move forward with a positive frame of mind, 'Here the good housewife (whose goodwill and good temper have been a national asset in these times of shadow and anxiety) is shown the way by which to make the best of war-time foodstuffs.'

'Let us remember at all our hearths the bravery of the men who through perils of the seas bring food to our shores. Remembering that, we shall practise economy in a thankful spirit.'[212]

## Queuing

So great were the discomfort and ill-feeling caused by the food queues, and the suspicion that the rich were obtaining more than their fair share of eatables, that the demand for compulsory rations became more and more insistent.

Mrs C.S. Peel, *How We Lived Then 1914–1918*

Queuing helped force local authorities to adopt rationing schemes:

The queue scandal was of far more importance than the hoarding scandal. I have vivid memories of bitterly cold wet days during that winter, of dismal dirty streets and those shabby depressing-looking shops common to the mean streets in the poor districts of all great towns. In rain and sleet, in bitter winds, in snow, women and children waited, women with shawls over their heads, carrying baskets and babies ... women who shifted their living burdens from one arm to another to ease their aching – women with their hair arranged in row after row of metal curlers – women in capes and men's caps – little down at heel children clutching baskets, fish baskets made of string or American cloth. Often in spite of cold and weariness there was a flow of wit and humour, and sometimes a late comer would try and sneak in at the head of the line and then would come trouble promptly allayed by the large policeman who kept law and order in these strange gatherings.

Food queue scenes. (Mrs C.S. Peel, *How We Lived Then 1914-1918*)

The queues were a very real hardship, and it was little wonder that the poor resented them bitterly, knowing as they did that the rich escaped this experience.'

Despite the hours of queuing, which housewives were having to endure in order to feed their families, Dorothy gives an example of the patience of some:

'Why wait hours to get meat?' I asked a woman once, 'when you could get fish without waiting?'

'My 'usbin 'e wouldn't eat fish for 'is dinner,' was the reply made in a tone which would not have surprised me had I suggested a diet of rattlesnake. On another occasion when I asked the same question a lady looked at me with kindly tolerance. 'An' get a black eye for me pains,' she cheerfully observed.[213]

# TWO NOTABLE WOMEN
# OF THE HOUR.

## By MAUD STEPNEY RAWSON.

Mrs C. S. PEEL. [Olga Baswitz.

Mrs PEMBER REEVES. [Swaine

her work and personality that she has become known, and no one was more surprised than herself when the Government approached her and asked her to deal with this burning question of national household economy. Like Mrs Pember Reeves, she is a moving and powerful speaker, and for the last year and a half has given innumerable addresses on the subject of the National War Loan.

Not only does she deal with the present problems of domestic life, but looks far ahead to those days after the war, when homes that are broken up shall be re-established, and when new houses shall arise more fitted to the needs, and, alas! reduced incomes of many of us. "I cannot too often emphasise the fact," she says, "that women are wasting their health, energy, and charm in a quantity of unnecessary household toil from which they might be

NO APPOINTMENT of the heads of a Government section during this war has given more complete satisfaction than that of Mrs Pember Reeves and Mrs C. S. Peel to the co-directorate of women's service in the Ministry of Food, and, oddly enough, nothing could be more marked than the personal contrast between these ladies as you see them standing in one of the suite of beautiful salons at Grosvenor House to-day. These rooms have witnessed many brilliant gatherings—balls, concerts, bazaars, conversations. The frescoed ceilings alone remain witness of those days of gala before the war. These famous walls, with their pictures and curios, are now protected by a covering of grey, and in place of the furniture and hangings you see but a few office tables and chairs. Grey the background and grey-green the quiet garden on which this salon gives, but there is nothing grey, either in the outlook of the atmosphere of these two representatives of a department of National Service so intimately affecting their sex.

Here, is Mrs Pember Reeves—small, slight, with inexhaustible intensity of purpose and fullness of experience underlying her great charm of manner. She has been working in the Ministry for some time before her appointment to this directorate. In her public character she scarcely needs introduction to our readers. As the wife of the Minister of Labour and Education in New Zealand, who subsequently held the posts of Agent-General and High Commissioner for that Colony, she has taken an active part in great movements both overseas and in the Mother Country. Both as writer and speaker she has long been famous to many audiences, and especially to all her compatriots who care for the status of the poor and the conditions of bread-winners of all classes. For eight years she worked amongst the latter, the result of her sympathetic co-operation being published in her well-known book, "Round About a Pound a Week." With an immense grip of detail gathered during those years she has developed remarkable powers of organisation. She is instinct with energy, infallibly responsive, always gracious.

Here, on the other hand, is Mrs Peel—tall, finely moulded, calm, and equally inspired. The public enthusiasm which greeted her appointment is highly gratifying to the staff and readers of this paper, to which, as expert on matters domestic and artistic, her talents have long been attached. She comes on her father's side of a military family, and her husband is a distant cousin of the late Speaker. At the age of eighteen she entered the world of journalism, had instant success, and was placed on the staff of several newspapers, eventually becoming not only editor in chief of three women's weeklies, but managing director of the company which published them. As the author of three published novels (a fourth is only delayed owing to her new post), she shows herself as one who has not only observed life truly, but writes of it from her heart. Her keen interest in working girls and women, especially those engaged in the millinery and dressmaking trades, comes out vividly in her first two books, The Eat Shop and Mrs Baraat—Robes, while a third novel, A Mrs Jones, exhibited her psychological gifts and sympathy with human nature. She has also worked as book reviewer, theatrical critic, has travelled widely, and her charming house, until the war, was always a centre of interesting people. Never a self-advertiser, it is entirely through

delivered if the average English house were to be carefully organised and provided with labour-saving devices in regard to light, heat, and water arrangements, and—where possible—a lift for carrying heavy objects."

For many years she has longed also to see domestic service put on a different footing. "If in all other departments of life which concern our physical and moral welfare we demand expert assistance and advice—dentist, doctor, nurse, clothier, and so on—why should we be content to employ people less skilled for the feeding of our households, the nurture of children, and the comfort of our homes? Two things are needed—a more liberal attitude on the part of the mistress, a more intelligent attitude on the part of the maid. Better conditions for the worker, fixed hours for labour, a minimum wage, will, I feel, overcome the dislike to domestic service. As far as possible needlessly heavy or dirty work can be minimised by the labour-saving devices alluded to. Above all, we must have better-class women in domestic service, and I would have them come forth fully trained from a domestic school and provided with uniform. To supply those homes which cannot include a resident servant I would have a separate organisation for outside domestic workers, also certificated and uniformed, who would come in by the day or for a fixed number of hours according to requirement. This high standard of what must be a properly recognised profession demands inevitably equal efficiency in the mistress of the home."

As mothers—for both have charming and gifted daughters—as gentlewomen who have made their homes their first care while their hearts have been open always to the needs and the suffering of the working world, Mrs Pember Reeves and Mrs C. S. Peel stand as unique figures before the public at this moment. They are here not to compel but to appeal. They have placed all their powers of mind and heart at the service of their country. Only true hearts can touch hearts. Only large brains can carry truth home to many of those outside official circles who only faintly realise the need of England.

This section of the Food Department dazzles the enquirer with no complexity. Here is no official fuss, no great staff, clerical or other, no arrogance of authority, no whirl of activity that the eye can see. But though no newspaper paragraphs give daily reports of the progress of their work, organisation is going on at lightning speed. The machinery is being set in motion all over England of this great campaign to protect the poor of all classes by appealing to the richer ones to put down extravagance that all may have a sufficiency. This point needs explanation. The great appeal that will issue in the written and spoken word is one that covers all classes. The wage-earners, while they receive every encouragement towards thrift, must and will be helped by the willing sacrifice and co-operation of their richer compatriots. Bread is a greater necessity to the wage-earner than to those who can afford a greater variety in diet and the little extras which supplement bread. But the rich are not to be fleeced, nor are a shortage of nourishment and resulting panic entailed in any sense. It is simply, as Mrs Peel says, that "England is put upon her honour." By that act England enrols us all in her Imperial Army-at-Home. With the sweetness and penetration of a silver trumpet call her appeal goes forth to-day to carry to the homes of

the Empire the song of her heroism, the poignancy of her need, the joy of service in her honour. Who shall dare to turn a deaf ear to her messengers led by such women as the two here delineated?

### SHORT MEASURE.

IT WAS A DAY OF THAW, following a night of frost and sprinkled snow. The morning was heavy with mist, and as I rode along there was a musical running of water in the ditches, the million drip, drip of sodden trees, and rime-encrusted grass turning to liquid diamonds under the touch of the sun. The road was ridged and broken by the continual passing of lorries and waggons on this great coastward highway, and mud spurted from the wheels of the bicycle in a wake as neat as swathes of hay.

Out of the mists loomed, human and comfortable, the roofs of a little hamlet, set, like so many of these Wealden villages, T-shaped to its church, which stood, grey and solid, aloof in the flagged churchyard :

A land of hops and poppy-mingled corn,
Little about it stirring, save a brook.
A sleepy land, where under the same wheel
The same old rut would deepen year by year;
Where almost all the village had one name.

Little, indeed, stirring this grey forenoon, save some woman about her morning's business, and an old roadman taking his "elevenses" of bread and cheese beside the half-cleared ditch. The same wheel, indeed, in faded blue and red, ruts the familiar lane from the farm, but under far different guidance this year. The farm-help, proud wielder of his elder brother's waggoner's whip, scarcely reaches to the wise team he swings more by familiar usage than by force of arm. As for the names, the flag-draped roll of honour in the church porch blazons them in the service of their King; not in any great variety, indeed, but good ancient names of the Weald, in threes and fours and fives. One recognises the same names in many generations on the encrusted gravestones, with the skull and crossbones roughly chiselled above. "A sleepy land," and yet the call of the wild sang later in their ears than in most Englishmen's, for they were the last to yield to conquest, and they wrung their own terms from Duke William, these Men of Kent in their forest dense. In later centuries these same woodland ways provided ample scope for evading the excise officers when nights were favourable and "poor, honest men" beached their cargoes among the wild sand dunes of the Marsh.

The brasses and marbles in the church show them dead in many lands—in India, in the days of John Company, in Gibraltar, Jamaica, Egypt, and South Africa, under the old colours for the most part, and in many a famous fight by land and sea. The hamlet is probably remoter in proportion now than it has ever been; but at the first thrill of the drum the old spirit flamed afresh, so that when the Derby scheme came into operation scarcely a new name was added to the long roll of honour which had gone before. And they have paid their share of the toll. The scroll in the porch is flecked with red; and in the church, below a rusty sword and scabbard, sheathed for ever long ago, two laurel wreaths tied with purple, drooping ribbons, caught up with the badge of a great regiment, enclose the parchment which is inscribed already with not a few names. Young lives all, like the young regiments they have helped to create. But

It is not growing like a tree
In bulk, doth make men better be;
Or standing like an oak three hundred year,
To fall a log at last, dry, bald, and sere.
In small proportions we just beauties see,
And in short measure life may perfect be.

GUENN F. NEWNHAM.

*The Queen Magazine Article. (Department of Special Collections and FIT Archives)*

92

**Ministry of Food**

He that wastes today will be hungry tomorrow.
Mrs C.S. Peel, *The Victory Cookery Book*

By 1917 Dorothy was well known for her domestic and culinary writing. Her cookery books had become popular and the advice given in her articles and to the men at war who wrote to her, well received. One example is a man who wrote asking for recipes: 'They have made me cook of the Officers' Mess,' he explained, 'God help them.'

With her domestic and culinary reputation preceding her, Dorothy had spoken on behalf of the United Workers and later, the National War Savings Association.[214] Mr Prothero, President of the Board of Agriculture, asked her to make an appointment to discuss her work. Before that meeting was arranged, she was 'summoned' to the Ministry of Food to see Sir Henry Rew, the Agricultural Statistician. Sir Henry asked Dorothy to accept a responsible position in the Ministry of Food in Grosvenor House, Park Lane, with Mrs Magdalen Pember-Reeves, starting in February 1917. Their task was to help ensure the successful allocation and use of rations during the war.

Mrs Pember-Reeves was referred to as Dorothy's 'twin', due to their working in close proximity. In *A Year in Public Life*, Dorothy describes her colleague: 'Mrs. Reeves, of Scottish parentage, was born and brought up in New Zealand, educated at Christchurch, and married at the age of nineteen. It was after the birth of her two elder children that, "feeling so dreadfully ignorant", to use her own words, she returned to college.'[215]

The Pember-Reeves's came to live in London when Mr Pember-Reeves became High Commissioner for New Zealand. At this point Mrs Reeves saw the poor conditions in which so many working people lived and 'began to work for (their) betterment'. This led to her being asked to work for the Ministry of Food with Dorothy:

'Well, my dear', she remarked, looking around our ballroom, 'so here we are.'
'We are,' I agreed. 'But there doesn't seem to be very much else here, does there?'
Then, quite unknowing of the laws which control such matters in Government offices, we proceeded to explore, vent on discovering furniture for our ballroom ... finding a carpet looking like a gigantic Swiss Roll.
It was a happiness to me to work with Mrs. Reeves, for though our lives had been lived under very different conditions, our experiences have led us to form to a considerable extent the same conclusions, and we worked in sympathy and close understanding.[216]

Dorothy tells us of frustrations as well as experience gained while working within the Ministry of Food:

Mrs. Reeves and myself worked quietly on as best we might. Life at Grosvenor House was an 'Alice in Wonderlandish' performance, for having with much trouble found the croquet ball, the hoop vanished, and having found the hoop and again picked up the ball the mallet disappeared. As for myself, I began to feel like an anxious, painstaking little dog whose master throws stones into a muddy pond from which no matter how industriously the poor dog scrapes and scratches no stone can be disinterred. Becoming tired of this game of seek and not find I concluded that it would save trouble to say 'Clever man, nice stone,' as the stones splashed into the pond, and then to arrange my own work in my own fashion.[217]

The only town to which Mrs Pember-Reeves and myself journeyed together was Liverpool, which city took a leading part in the Food Economy campaign. The Lord Mayor, the Lady Mayoress, Sir Max and Lady Muspratt, asked us to lunch at the Mansion House, and kindly sent the Lord Mayor's carriage to get us and convey us back to the hotel. Imagine how proud and important we felt driving through the streets in such an equipage. But no – I do not believe Mrs. Reeves ever felt proud and important, though I frankly own that I did – whenever I could discover an opportunity of so doing.

During my time in the Ministry of Food I saw so many things made in the great factories of this country that I learned a great respect for the work of men's hands. Now I can scarcely bear to see even an empty cardboard box thrown away because with the vision of the thing comes a vision of the life of he who made it.[218]

When I wash my hands my nail-brush brings me another vision – a lively old gipsy-like woman and an older silent white-bearded man with the face of a dreamer, living in a little room under the roof, most of which was taken up by the bed. These old people put bristles into nail brushes. They sleep, eat, and work in that one room, from the walls of which the paper hangs in tatters. 'The landlord 'e's done all 'e can, dearie – but the damp's right in that corner.'[219]

The hands of these two old folk are cut and scarred with the wire with which they work, but 'Oh, we don't think nothing of that, dearie, but I mus' say I do wish as we 'ad room for another table; it's a job clearing up all them bristles when it comes dinner-time.'

I make many pictures out of what I see and hear and read – some of them beautiful pictures and some such that I would I could put them out of my mind once and for all.[220]

During the 313 working days of that miserable anxious twelve months between March, 1917, and March, 1918, I travelled about England from Plymouth to Newcastle, addressed 176 meetings – more than one every other day – spent a week in France studying mass feeding, attended numerous conferences, wrote thousands of letters, interviewed hundreds of people, 'fed' the Press, and prepared leaflets for the use of the speakers and recipes for the use of war foods which were issued in millions, prepared new speeches to suit the ever changing conditions created by a World War, and not infrequently drafted replies to questions asked in the House.[221]

With the food supply at an all time low, it was necessary to ask audiences whether they would prefer to lose the war, allowing ships to leave America free from warfare so that we may be well fed, or to continue as they had done to that point and risk increased hunger. 'There was but one answer to that question,' Dorothy wrote.[222]

By 1917, food shortages were so severe that it became a summary offence to throw rice at a wedding and the sale of luxury chocolates was stopped. The feed of animals was restricted so that horses, cows and even London pigeons were rationed. Corn could not be fed to 'cobs, hunters, carriage horses and hacks'. Bread could not be thrown to pigeons. One man who was arrested for feeding bread crusts to pigs pleaded in his defence that they would have otherwise been wasted as navvies would not eat crusts. To feed or adopt a stray dog was an offence. Any strays had to be handed over to the police.[223]

Bakers were ordered to bake only Government regulation bread, which consisted of a mixture of barley, rice, maize, beans, oatmeal, with the addition of potato (see recipe for Maize Potato Bread in Part 2). Dorothy describes the disappearance of the local 'muffin man' who used to carry a tray of muffins, or crumpets on a baize-covered tray upon his head, ringing a bell to alert people of his presence. Her hungry mind then comes into play when she admits to questioning the use of a crumpet or muffin without the butter or 'marge' with which to spread it![224]

The head of the Ministry of Food was Food Commissioner Lord Devonport who, in December 1916, divided the country into sixteen areas for the purposes of rationing. There were 2,500 Food Control Committees to help with the administering of the rations. A careful system was put into place ensuring the fair and equal distribution from and for wholesalers, retailers and consumers.

Although France and Britain received imported food from America, the Prime Minister, Lloyd George, implemented food rationing, though not enforced, as soon as he agreed that it was absolutely essential, and America had become involved following the bombing of the passenger ship, the *Lusitania* which killed 1,198 civilians. The Royal Family took on voluntary food rationing, in the hope that their example may be followed. It was necessary, however, for the Government to introduce compulsory rationing in January 1918.

In Britain the aim was that, for most people, their standard of living would not alter greatly during the period of rationing, due largely to the centralised distribution of food supplies and the work done by the Ministry of Food in ensuring that people received enough nutrition. In *How We Lived Then 1914–1918,* we are told that among the poorest in some cases their nutrition improved: 'Though low wages explained to a great extent the under-nourishment, lack of knowledge of what to buy and how to cook it was, as it still is, responsible for some of the malnutrition both of the rich and of the poor.'[225]

While working for the Ministry of Food, Dorothy was sent by the Permanent Secretary to study French methods of mass feedings. The success of these mass feeding regimes necessitated Dorothy's visit with a view to obtaining useful information to help with Britain's food restriction.

Despite grain production in France falling by 30 per cent in 1916, and some farms being abandoned, this state of shortage was offset by imports and companies being encouraged to put canteens into place for their workers. Not only were these a success, but larger companies provided crèches and infirmaries, which eased the burden on women who had gone to work while their husbands were at war, later implemented in Britain.

In addition to this, an 'Allocation Millitaire' of one franc and fifty centimes for the wives and fifty centimes for the children of men at war was paid by the state in order to help alleviate the strain of reduced wages in the absence of the fathers: 'In providing everyone with the necessities of life it has been the main cause of domestic peace and calm.'[226]

While Britain and her allies were supporting each other during the food shortages, Germany was not faring so well. There was a prolonged blockade of imports by the Allies from 1914 to 1919. This was further worsened by the 'turnip winter' of 1916, which followed heavy rains and potato blight so that turnips were being used in everything from soup to bread. Despite starting 3,000 public kitchens, the calorific content of the food available was not always enough to provide sufficient nutrition so that as little as just 1,300kcal per day were consumed at times, less than half the recommended daily allowance for working men.

Germany did not succeed in implementing successful rationing. Farm produce was limited since many of the men had gone to war and so, by 1917, there was very little for them to eat. Civilian mortality rates rose by a third.

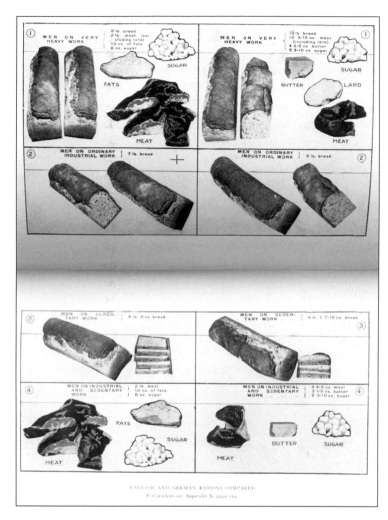

English and German Rations, compared. (*Mrs C.S. Peel, How We Lived Then 1914–1918*)

## Public Kitchens

The Public Kitchen is an institution (which should bear no relationship whatsoever to the charity soup kitchen), in which food is prepared with scrupulous cleanliness, cooked with scientific knowledge, and sold at such prices as the customers can afford to pay, cannot fail to prove of inestimable benefit.

Mrs C.S. Peel, *A Year in Public Life*

During their time with the Ministry of Food, Public kitchens, later to be called National Kitchens, were started by Dorothy and Mrs Pember-Reeves. 'Women of the Labour Party were interested in these kitchens, which they thought might ease

Dorothy Peel with Queen Mary and Princess Mary opening the 'Food Kitchen' in Westminster Bridge Road, London. *(PA Photos Limited)*

the life of the working-class women and ensure for them and their families better food.'[227]

Buildings which housed inessentials, such as public swimming baths, were requisitioned. The idea was to save food, fuel, labour and to provide nourishment for all. This had become a concern to the nation since German submarine warfare had torpedoed merchant ships carrying sugar so that fruit, for example, could not be preserved for the winter months. As well as providing necessary nutrition, if a large number of people took advantage of the public kitchens, cooking at home with less regularity, not only would fuel be conserved for use in war time, but the money saved by the housewife on fuel would go towards the increasing cost of food. These kitchens were often opened by the queen or another member of the Royal Family:

> many of them (people using the kitchens) omitted to bring any kind of receptacle and rushed home again, arriving purple and panting with a jug or basin in order that they should not be too late to be served by the Queen. One old man managed to pack a surprising variety of foods into a newspaper.

While the queen was ladling out rice pudding a very old man ambled up and bought meat, vegetables, and pudding, which he proceeded to place all together on a very dirty plate and cover with a still dirtier piece of newspaper. This evidently distressed the Queen. He then shambled out, never having realised that it was Her Majesty who had served him. This fact apparently was explained to him by the crowd outside, for shortly afterwards he returned, took up his position in front of the Queen, and solemnly waved his hat three times at her.[228]

## Public Speaking

Mrs Pember-Reeves and Dorothy travelled around the country public speaking in order to advise on food economy:

Experience in War Savings work had proved to us that the first task of any speaker is to obtain the sympathy of the audience, and this is not affected by preaching and lectoring. Mrs. Reeves never made a truer statement than when she assured our speakers that to succeed they must rely on the right intention and intelligence of the public and not mistake difference of opinion for lack of goodwill, for the whole nation, whatever its political or other beliefs, is alive with intelligence and desire to do right, though differences exist in people's minds as to the best way of doing right. Such differences must be met with understanding. The watchwords of the speaker must be goodwill and sympathy.[229]

In the early days of the Food Economy Campaign before compulsory rations had come into force, Dorothy was welcomed by a 'Member' in front of an audience she had travelled some way to address on food economy. He proceeded to inform them that everything would be alright and that the

food question would be settled without any necessity for voluntary effort on the part of anyone. 'And now ladies and gentlemen,' he ended, 'I am sure that our friend Mrs Peel will be kind enough to give us a few nice recipes for rice pudding.

However, I got back a little of my own later, for when question time came the audience showed itself solid for prohibition. At this I at once became Mrs. Peel whose only subject was rice pudding, and left the Member to deal with his prohibition part as best he might, which as he owned a large interest in a local brewery put him in a difficult position.[230]

Following one of her speeches on food economy, 'a large man arose, and in a sleepy good-humoured voice remarked':

99

'But what I say is, they shouldn't send such a well-fed looking lady as you talking Food Economy!'

For a moment I felt daunted, for there is no getting away from it I do look well fed. (A newspaper reporter once described my twin and I as 'Mrs. Reeves all nerves; Mrs. Peel all curves!')[231]

At Deal I faced a hostile audience. Fortunately the moment I set eyes upon them I saw that there was no need to ask for food economy here. Most of the faces which looked up at me were those of hard-worked and underfed folk. I changed my tactics; I asked them to eat as well as they could, to keep themselves healthy to help their country. Would they help the cause of food economy by influencing others who had more to spend, and so form a right public opinion?

After the meeting an old man came up to me and shook my hand. 'That was right what you said. Folk liked that and they'll do their best, they will. And,' his old eyes twinkled, 'I don't mind telling you some of 'em 'ad a bit o' muck ready in their pockets for you, so 'twas luck you said what you did say'.[232]

Scientists at the Ministry advised Dorothy on food, such as its nutritional content. As a result, Dorothy writes to soak chickpeas and then steam them in order to ensure as little fuel is used as possible so that full nutritional content may be reaped. Fat could be added to pulses and use made of them where meat was scarce. This was in part because of the productive efficiency of using grazing pasture for cereal and pulse production, due to imports being torpedoed by German submarines. While meat taken from stock bones would have lost some nutritional value, to eat it would ensure that none at all went to waste. The same applies to fish bones and advice on steaming, adding the liquid left in the saucer to dishes, so as to ensure no nutrition was lost. One person who particularly helped in his guidance was Sir Henry Thompson, who met his demise when the *Leinster* was torpedoed in October 1918.

It would be a strange thing indeed if we civilians could endure discomfort without grumbling in return for the sacrifices which are made for us by our fighting men. The words of Mr. Lloyd George come back to me: 'Be the comrades of your soldiers … if we do all we can, we shall never be able to requite our men for their agony; if we do less than all, we shall dishonour their sacrifices.'[233]

Dorothy's reputation spread further than I had anticipated. Written on one of the

Food Economy leaflets in America is a poem by Berghold, whom Dorothy refers to as 'the well-known writer on Bridge':

> In my paper I read that we none of us need
> To cook more than one dish for a dinner
> Butter-beans, for a start, will bring balm to that part
> Of women, or man, which is inner.
>
> Two ounces of rice should amply suffice
> For the 'starch of the average diet';
> While tomatoes (1 lb.) will effective be found
> Abdominal craving to quiet.
>
> To mix them aright, soak the beans overnight;
> And steam them two hours until tender;
> Then their crudeness allay with tomato puree,
> And set down, to keep warm, in the fender.
>
> Compounded with art, some stock will impart
> A rich flavour of meat to the meal;
> Serve the total, all hot, in an earthenware pot,
> (I am quoting from Dorothy Peel).

As well as her position at the Ministry of Food and continuing with her work for *Queen Newspaper,* Dorothy did some speaking for the National War Savings Association. Not content to stop there, additional spare time was spent working in a canteen, where in her autobiography, she tells us that she found that she and her fellow volunteers picked up the same habits about which they had in the past, complained to their servants:

> It was amusing to find ... Many of the ladies wasted the gas, and were shockingly extravagant in the way they cut the rinds off the bacon and spread the butter, or, as it was generally known, the 'marge.' Sometimes the washing-up was none too thorough, and invariably every shift complained that the outgoing shift had not left things properly.[234]

Further verses were written following Dorothy's public speaking, on her reputation as a provider of rationing recipes. In advising that potatoes, when available, should be eaten, jackets and all, she was 'cheered' by the following poem:

MRS PEEL RECOMMENDS US TO EAT PEEL

In ancient days the cannibal
When hungry ate his trusty pal
Or p'raps a stead off his best gal.

Thos' times have changed in many ways
It's sad to say in present days
This nasty habit with us stays.

This counsel by a worthy dame,
Whose name is not unknown to fame,
Has lately set the Press aflame.

When feeling that she wants a meal
She can't heredity conceal,
She eats potatoes and some Peel.

Dorothy ridicules herself when it comes to potatoes, telling us about a Yorkshireman in her audience who said 'Government send the Peel – happen we rather they'd send the potatoes!'[235]

**Looking the Part**
When giving talks at schools on food economy, Dorothy writes of one critic's view that 'Ladies who come talking food economy shouldn't wear patent shoes.' Not understanding the connection, Dorothy's irritation of that 'pernickety brat' combined with another critic writing that ladies who talk of food economy should not be 'dressed up to the nines', led her to 'rip off the white collar and cuffs of (her) blouse, remove the trimming from (her) hat, put it on the wrong way round, and buy an ugly pair of shoes, so that (her) appearance was sufficiently dowdy', even though the ugly pair cost more than the patent shoes.[236] Sir Arthur Yapp, in addressing meetings for the Ministry of Food in the great industrial centres found,

> his audiences both pleasant and reasonable, though they did scold him for his extravagance in wearing white starched collars! Now and then silly accusations were made against him, such as that while preaching economy he had obtained two sides of bacon for his private consumption ...
> Much about the same time Lord Rhondda (Food Controller) was accused of hoarding tea, the tea in question being required for the hospital which he maintained at his own house in Wales.[237]

**Allotments**

Many a sorrow was buried in these war gardens and many a man and woman learned the joy of tilling the earth.

Mrs C.S. Peel, *How We Lived Then 1914–1918*

So great was destruction during the war that to be involved in something which would reap rewards was met with great enthusiasm. Creating gardens in which to grow vegetables was taken on in response to the Government's 'Produce, produce, produce'. Allotments were scattered wherever there was space, even in Fleet Street, where one of the first allotments was developed.[238]

**Fuel Economy and Revised Cooking Methods**

Eat slowly: you will need less food. Keep warm: you will need less food. How we were to keep warm when fuel was strictly rationed and we were chilly as the result of an insufficiently fat diet was not explained.'

Mrs C.S. Peel, *How We Lived Then 1914–1918*

In order to sustain the efficient running of war, fuel resources had to be reserved and allocated. An example is given on the event of the Lord Mayor's banquet, where petrol was rationed, and so each guest was allocated some in order to drive to it.[239]

Fuel consumption was kept to a minimum and the money saved spent on the rising cost of food while fuel saved contributed to the war effort. Taxis were shared by as many as possible, with, Dorothy says, some passengers using the roof![240] How much coal a household was given was dependent upon how many rooms they had in the house. Increased amounts were allowed for babies and invalids. To waste the cinders left in the fire was a punishable offence. Women were known to collect refuse on the streets or washed up on the shore so as to contribute to what could be burned to produce heat.[241] Cooks, some of whom had brick wood-heated ovens which were fuel efficient during war, had to be resourceful with the heat they used:

> Now that it is so necessary to economise fuel as well as food, our methods of cooking must be revised. Various little known methods are suggested in this book, because they are economical of fuel and of labour as well as of food; and although good results were obtained in former days from other styles of cookery, now we can only practise those which are economical.[242]

Cooking multiple dishes within one pot, such as a haybox which retains heat for slow cooking, is advised:

> A haybox or fireless cooker should be used. Food can also be cooked in covered tins or jars placed in a pot and surrounded with boiling water. Several tins may be placed in one vessel, and thus a whole dinner can be cooked on one gas ring or electric plate. When cooking by gas the cook must exercise her intelligence and not use the oven for one dish. If the oven is needed, arrange to cook all other dishes in it. A little thought will show that there are numerous methods of saving coal, wood, gas, electricity and oil.
>
> Casserole cooking is to be highly recommended, if for one reason only, which is, that with the food being served in the dish in which it was cooked, washing-up is saved. For the same reason advantage should be taken of the many attractive fireproof dishes now on the market.[243]
>
> It became a fashionable occupation to tear up newspapers and make them into fire-lighters, or crumple them into balls, which helped inferior coal to burn better. Haybox cookery came into fashion, and cooks learned to steam cakes – and oh! how nasty war cakes often were – because they could not be permitted the fuel necessary to heat the oven.[244]

So low were fuel resources that a friend of Dorothy's with no coal in the house and an ill mother to keep warm, took a cab around London, stopping to ask anyone and everyone for a few lumps of coal, to take home in a laundry basket.[245] In Germany:

> The ladies I visited ... told me of the long, cold winters when hardly any fuel or artificial light was procurable. Families sat in the dark trying to keep cold, restless, underfed children happy until it was bedtime. As one of my hostesses

truly said, 'One could not put the little ones to bed at five o'clock on a winter's afternoon and expect them to sleep until daylight at eight or eight-thirty next morning.'

My hostesses had no knowledge of the way in which we had lived during the War, and they learned with surprise that fuel and light had been rationed, that we had been obliged to eat war bread, that at one time and in some places, our meat ration had been reduced to half a pound per head per week, and that the consumption of sugar, butter, tea and flour had been reduced.

Our conversations always ended, however, with the reflection that the suffering of the English had never, in any way, been commensurate with that of themselves, which was true.[246]

Fuel which had been gainfully exported from Britain before the War was not exported for its duration. Instead it went towards the War effort. During this time, the countries who had imported our fuel had found other sources. This combined with defeated Germany giving fuel away after the war, in small reparation for the damage caused, meant that Britain's coal mines were not able to revert back to their pre-war lucrative state. In their attempt to get profits back up to pre-war levels, mine owners reduced the wages of their workers who in turn retaliated. King George objected to their being called revolutionaries, saying: 'Try living on their wages before you judge them.'[247]

## The Food Controller

Such was the pressure on the Food Controller that when Lord Devonport resigned in June 1917, Dorothy noted in her autobiography that to fill his position was met with a '"dilly, dilly, dilly, come and be killed" tone about the invitation.'[248] Experience in other European countries involved in the war was that to try and control the consumption of the population was often met with frustrated anger from the people:

In Germany and Austria compulsory rationing had not prevented injustice; it had resulted in the forgery of food tickets on a vast scale, and it had not secured fair division of food in town and country. It had caused irritation and resentment, and this in a country where the filling up of forms and making of returns is generally practised and understood. Furthermore any system of rationing is costly and necessitates the services of a large number of people at a time when labour is scarce.

At this time, too, the public were very angry with the traders, whom they termed 'profiteers', and the traders in their turn were angry because what they deemed fair trading was termed 'profiteering', while the Ministry of Food was faced with the problem of reconciling the views of buyer and seller; limiting prices and yet keeping up supplies – tasks to appal the bravest man.

At last came the news that Lord Rhondda had accepted the post of Food Controller. Every one realises that it was a plucky action on his part to undertake so difficult a position, for there was then no reason to suppose that he would achieve less unpopularity than had fallen to the lot of other Controllers.'

The new Minister made his first public appearance at Grosvenor House at a conference of the heads of sections ... I was the only woman present on that occasion, for Mrs. Reeves was away speaking. I am not sufficiently modern to enjoy such a position, but I did summon courage to draw Mr. Clynes' attention to the fact that no suggestion that women should serve on Food Control Committees had been made in the scheme as put before the meeting. The wording was then altered to 'at least one woman,' which if not what I could have wished was better than nothing.

I remember thinking that if only one woman was elected (which often proved to be the case) and she disliked her solitary position as much as I, I did not envy her.[249]

### The End of the First World War

Thank God that nations as individuals can forget and yet remember, forgetting that which is best forgotten, remembering that which must be remembered if humanity shall be saved from yet another Crucifixion.

Mrs C.S. Peel, *How We Lived Then, 1914–1918*

Dorothy describes the devastation of France during her visit to view their mass feeding regimes. The war was to affect people's lives as much as the landscape itself changed in appearance:

Here we were in a fruit country with great apple orchards and avenues of apple trees, and then soon there were neither apple orchards nor avenues, but everywhere trees lying dead, hacked down by the Germans before they retreated. Now the sun was breaking through the clouds and there were great patches of blue in the sky, but on earth desolation. Everywhere great trees had been felled and left to lie in cross-stitch pattern upon the roads, while roads and bridges had been destroyed to delay the advance of the French. By then, the trees had been cleared away, but their stumps rose nakedly from the weed-choked borders of the roads. There were no more villages, nothing but

THE SUNLIGHT – LOSER KAISER (as his sainted grandfather's clock strikes three): 'The British are just putting their clocks back an hour. I wish I could put ours back about three years." *(Punch Magazine – Townsend, 1916)*

heaps of stones and plaster crumbled to dust. In the fields of that beautiful agricultural country so rich before the War, now gashed by trenches and pockmarked by shells, weeds flourished and amongst them coiled the rusted remains of wire entanglements ... Just before we entered the town (of Noyon), I suddenly looked out and saw before us an enormous hole in the road. Whether the chauffeur saw it or whether by this time holes in roads were matters of little moment to him I do not know, but putting on speed he took that chasm at a leap which caused me to bound from my seat and return to it with a jerk of the neck which I felt for many a long day...

It seemed as if the world had turned to stones and dust and weeds and rusted wire. Away to the right was what had once been a railway station. An engine lay toppled over on its side, the metal rails curled fiercely yet helplessly about it as though they had once had life and had died writhing in some fierce fire.[250]

## Peace

Then, when it seemed as if the misery of the world was too great to be endured longer, there came rumours of peace. Just as in August 1914 few of us could scarcely believe that peace could come. I was at the Daily Mail when the news came through on the telephone. We opened the window wide and could hear cheering and immediately somewhere near a wheeze old gramophone began to play "God Save the King." I longed to go into the street but could not, for whatever happens, newspapers must go to press.

Mrs C.S. Peel, *Life's Enchanted Cup: An Autobiography 1872–1933*

my eyes kept filling with tears, tears for those to whom peace had come too late to save some one dearly loved ... [After work] I went through the Temple which was deserted, and up one of those little streets which led to Charing Cross, and there under an archway were two old women in jet-trimmed bonnets and capes, dancing stiffly to the strains of a barrel organ – an outmoded organ with one long wooden leg played by an ancient, bearded man who might have been Father Time himself.[251]

With news of peace, Dorothy recalled that the roar of the crowd was 'terrifying, and yet inspiring'. It seemed to her that London became a city of flags. Queen Mary came onto the balcony of Buckingham Palace where she saw people climbing into the arms of the statue of Queen Victoria, from where policemen would remove them only to find them being replaced moments later. She waved her flag vigorously, 'We loved her for doing that. It must have been a wonderful thought for them, that while all over Europe "crowns were falling like Autumn leaves" (as Mr Lloyd George put it in a recent speech), their people could welcome them so lovingly and loyally'.[252]

Dorothy expresses astonishment at where all these streamers had been hiding through the years of turmoil, only to surface so easily at peacetime. In the absence of such celebratory paraphernalia, a colonel was seen standing on top of a taxi 'beating violently a dinner gong'.

'Have we won the war?' was roared, and an answering roar came, 'Yes, we've won the War.' A song new to us was heard, 'What shall we be when we aren't what we are?'[253]

108

# To Conclude

The turmoil of war, and the misfortune of those born into circumstances from which it is almost impossible to escape, are not as acutely felt by Britons today, so our forebears must be thanked for the freedoms we now enjoy and for the improving standard of living of the average person in Britain. We can relive a very small part of what was experienced by those to whom we owe so much through Granny Dot's writing and recipes. Why not savour cheese pufflets, encounter devilled bananas and mint julip, add mace to your chicken, try mutton with veal forcemeat, and indulge in suet puddings?

My life has been enriched through the writing and recipes of Granny Dot. I owe her enormous gratitude for opening my eyes to a culinary and working world which would have remained silent for a fourth generation had I not ventured into the attic room that day.

I thought of Mrs Pember-Reeves, who once said laughingly, 'You think you can do everything.' But that was not true. I did not think I could do everything, but I did think that it was worthwhile to try to do what I was given a chance to do, to find, as someone said – but who I do not know – that those who do most make the most mistakes! Still, if one is frightened of failing one is not likely to succeed.

Mrs C.S. Peel, *Life's Enchanted Cup: An Autobiography 1872–1933*

When does old age begin? I do not know, and what does it matter? If three score years and ten is the limit of my life I have six more years to live. But now I have Angina, perhaps I shall not live to the full span of man's life here; again, perhaps I may, and longer. And what does it matter either way?

Mrs C.S. Peel, *Life's Enchanted Cup: An Autobiography 1872–1933*

# Glossary of Terms

Barouche – four wheeled horse-drawn carriage with a collapsible hood over the rear half, a seat in front for the driver, and seats facing each other for the passengers.

Bathing Machine – a walled wooden cart, sometimes with canvas walls, which may be rolled into the sea to protect modesty, usually of women. People would change their clothes in this device.

Bolton Sheeting – course, heavily twilled cotton fabric

Brougham is a closed carriage, most often with four wheels. It was an everyday vehicle used

in the latter part of the nineteenth century

Bustle – a type of framework used to expand the fullness or support the drapery of the back of a woman's dress

Caraway Comfit – see recipe on page 258

Fly – a horse-drawn public coach or delivery wagon especially one let out for hire. In Britain,

the term also referred to a light covered vehicle, such as a single-horse pleasure carriage or a hansom cab.

Hansom – horse-drawn carriage

Phaeton – a light four-wheeled open-sided carriage drawn by one or two horses.

Pattens – protective overshoes

Paramatta boots – ankle boots

Porringer – A small bowl, typically with a handle, used for soup, stew, or similar dishes.

Stays – a corset raising and shaping the breasts, tightening the midriff, and supporting the back to improve posture.

Toque – a type of hat with a narrow brim or no brim.

Toupee – hair piece of partial wig

Tuckers – lace collar

Victoria – a light four-wheeled open-sided carriage with a box seat for the coachman, drawn by one or two horses.

# PART TWO

CHAPTER 11

# Rationing and Recipes

But, alas, Englishwomen are seldom taught to cook or to realise that a cook is as valuable – more valuable, indeed – to her country than many a better-paid and more highly esteemed person.

Mrs C.S. Peel, *Learning to Cook*

The Government was forced to introduce compulsory rationing in January 1918, which extended beyond the end of the war. Meat rationing ended in December 1919, butter in May 1920 and sugar in November 1920. Not until March 1921 did the restriction on flour come to an end.

Dorothy helped aid the population in their use of the limited produce available by writing books containing rationing recipes. The *Learning to Cook* cookery book was the first of these in 1915.

Decreased imports due to submarine warfare and the rising cost of food meant that malnutrition was seen in poorer communities. With the response to the War Savings Committee imposing an Eat Less Meat Appeal in 1916, Dorothy wrote the *Eat Less Meat Book* on war rations, in 1917, and *The Victory Cookery Book,* in 1918, the former stating: 'I write it hoping that I may thereby help those people who wish to do their duty to their country, to utilise every atom of food as intelligently as possible … Only by a great and united effort can we ensure that the rising generation and the generation yet unborn shall receive their proper nourishment in the months ahead of us.' [254]

The rations of sugar, meat and fat were similar to our recommended allowance today. Their distribution meant that the calorie intake was balanced so that Britain in general was in a healthier state than before enforced rationing. This particularly applied to poorer communities where rationing imposed an apportioned and nutritious diet available to everyone. Those who could afford it were unable to buy more than their fare share which meant that there was enough to go around. Despite the rationing scheme, however, there were times when the full ration was not available and so some people were not sufficiently nourished.

With the current widespread use of domestic appliances and vehicles, our daily exercise and the amount of calories we need has decreased. This is perceived in the average recommended calorie intake in 2014 for women being 2000kcal and for men 2500kcal. This may be compared with the 3500 kcal recommended for civilian men a century before.

In 1917 Dorothy's *Eat Less Meat Book* details what recommended rations were before rationing became official in January 1918. Ration cards included coupons worth 5d each. A family or person had to register their interest with a butcher and a grocer who exchanged the coupons for rations. Schools reminded parents to include their children's rationing cards in their satchels each day. They were allocated half the weight of an adult ration.

**Comparison between Weekly Voluntary and Compulsory Rations**

| Coupon | Pre official rationing Voluntary Recommended Ration | 1918 Compulsory Ration |
|---|---|---|
| Sugar from January 1918, Not including glucose or saccharin | ¾lb/340g | 8oz/225g |
| Meat, including horsemeat | 2½lb/1.13kg | 1½lb/680g |
| Tinned food | | 2½oz/680g |
| Butter | The advice was to spread it thinly | 2oz–8oz/57g–227g Distributed according to what was available |
| Flour products not including cereals such as maize, rye, oatmeal, barley, corn-flour or rice-flour | 4lb/1.81kg for women, 3lb/1.36kg in uncooked flour 7lb/3.18kg for men in industrial or other manual work | Distributed according to what was available |

Within the meat allowance was 4oz/112g of bacon, ham or cooked meat, and 2½oz/70g of pie 'according to the estimated weight of the actual meat' per coupon. An extra 1oz/28g was allowed for meat with the bone. The weight of cooked meat rationed per coupon was reduced due to loss of fat and therefore weight, during cooking. A hare or rabbit weighing 2¼lb/1.2kg dressed for cooking counted as 1lb/453g of meat.

Suet, lard and stock bones did not form part of the rationing scheme. Dorothy notes that sparrows and woodpigeons were also not included in the ration, and potatoes could be freely used.

Flour did not become part of the official rationing scheme but was distributed and Britons were encouraged to use their bread efficiently in order to reduce waste. Flour was mixed with wheat flour, which was not a preferable option at this time, and as seen in the Maize Potato bread in Part 2, substitutes were used where not enough flour was available. Known as war bread, this was not popular and a good

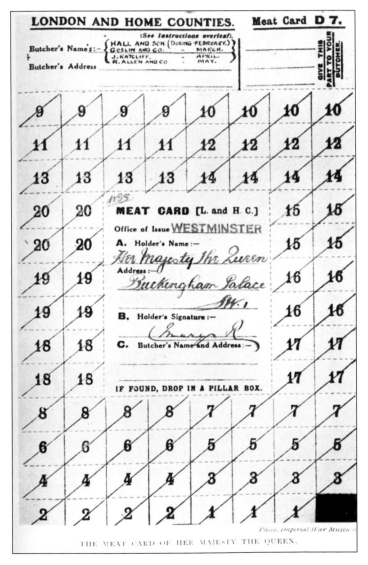

Ration card of Princess Alexandra. (Mrs C.S. Peel, *How We Lived Then 1914-1918*)

114

loaf of bread made without substitues was longed for. Despite butter becoming a luxury by Christmas 1917, not until February 1918 was it and margarine rationed. Eggs were used sparingly, often being replaced with dried eggs.

Those whose life and work involved entertaining suffered as a result of enforced rationing, as written by the wife of a clergyman:

> We have a good deal of trouble in obtaining food for the clergymen who descend upon us to help with various religious 'do's' ordained by the Bishop. These worthy men seldom think to bring their coupons. We make efforts to achieve palatable cakes with cocoa butter and make jams with glucose. The long and losing battle with 'substitutes' almost wears me out. When it came to no less than twelve parsons attending the funeral of our poor curate, who died of influenza, and expecting to be fed I nearly wept. But in the country we are rather better off than you town folk … We can in an emergency kill a duck or a chicken (though now that poultry food is so dear and 'scraps' there are none it is difficult to feed live-stock), and eggs, butter and milk are more plentiful. But oh! how cold we are with our wretched allowance of fuel. The local gas becomes worse and worse. One night the evening service had to be abandoned, as the choir began to turn green and blue and yellow and to faint, their example being followed by various members of the congregation. The boys at Mr. ___'s school were overcome at evening chapel and driven forth into the fresh and chilly out-door air to recover. Life is a nightmare of sadness and anxiety: my only pleasure that of exercising and helping to groom the remount horses at the camp near by.[255]

**Taking Advantage of the Market**

Dorothy advises to be scrupulous in taking advantage of what is on offer in order to increase the likelihood of interesting and varied food:

> Advantage must be taken of the market to vary the bills of fare with such items as peas, mushrooms, asparagus, fruit, etc., which even in these times, if there happens to be a glut or consignment that "misses the market," are sold at a low price. By buying carefully the housekeeper can often afford little luxuries. For example, one day after Christmas I found turkeys selling at 1s. 3d. the pound, the prices before Christmas having been 1s. 10d. a pound, 3 s. and 4 s. each, and 2s. 6d. the pound.
>
> Soup, roast turkey and its accompaniments, devilled biscuits, and a dessert of pine-apple for dinner, with a dish of mushroom and bacon toast for breakfast, made a pleasing change from the commonplace routine and at no extra cost.[256]

115

**Alternative Recipes**

[W]e soon discovered that there was an enormous demand for War Cookery information and recipes. People did not know how to use War flour – it made their bread and puddings heavy: they were unaccustomed to use barley and maize, and if they could not have meat and vegetables and a pudding what were they to eat? they demanded. How could they manage with so little sugar? How could they cook with so little fat?

Mrs C.S. Peel, *How We Lived Then 1914–1918*

Throughout the cookery books written by Dorothy before the war, she gave suggestions about what to add or what to substitute in her recipes. What better person, then, to advise on 'making do' in times when food was scarce than someone who had always told her readers that her recipes could and should be adapted and not read as gospel. Indeed, when Dorothy worked for the Ministry of Food, women sought advice on how to make do and they formed such long queues outside the Ministry buildings that it was necessary to make appointments at ten minute intervals.

Some of the recipes in Dorothy's *The Victory Cookery Book* were adapted during the rationing period. For example, in the absence of bread Dorothy suggests that when making bread sauce, it may be replaced by semolina or white maize meal (polenta). In making custard or mayonaise, egg colour may be used in place of eggs; where oil was not available, evaporated milk is suggested. The public had to vary their diet. At times they were told to make as wide a use of potatoes as possible; at other times, due to potato blight, they were told the opposite.

Tinned food did not feature in Dorothy's recipes outside of the rationing period. In *The Victory Cookery Book* she gives us five recipes made with just one 12oz/336g tin of salmon. Great lengths are gone to in the fifth salmon recipe, making use of the skin and bones in order to extract every ounce of flavour for a sandwich filling. Following that is a recipe for fish in batter, rather like a Toad in the Hole, but made 'with or without eggs' – not a preferable suggestion when the alternative we are used to owes much of its airiness to them. Another main ingredient, such as a rabbit, could be used to make five dishes by making use of scraps of meat from bones which could be used for soup or added to rissoles.

I have given rationing dinners to friends who, while forsaking some dishes, for example when mashed potato replaces flour, have scraped other bowls clean, and in so doing, have brought some of the past back to life.

**STAPLES**
***The Economical Use of Sugar***

Train your taste to desire less sugar. Begin by using just a quarter less than you are accustomed to use in every recipe, in a week use half as much, and soon you will be quite content with the lessened quantity.

Mrs C.S. Peel, *The Eat Less Meat Book*

Nearly 70 per cent of the sugar imported into the United Kingdom was beet sugar from Germany and Austria; therein lay a huge problem. Three ships containing sugar were sunk by German submarines in one week. Hopes of preserving the fruit by making jam and bottling it in sugar syrup were dashed. The absence of sugar was never explained, disclosure of the real reason considered inadvisable.[257]

The population of the United Kingdom during the war was approximately 45 million, many of whom added dry sugar to their hot drinks. The sugar does not all dissolve, and so Dorothy advises people to use sugar syrup instead of granules to reduce wastage. She also suggests that bicarbonate of soda should be added to stewed fruit such as rhubarb and gooseberries, thus neutralising the acid and reducing the amount of sugar needed. Glucose was cheaper and more easily obtainable than sugar. When making jam, therefore, a proportion of each is suggested. The use of honey is also recommended.

People worried that if their children did not have sugar they would die. Dorothy tells them that considering it was only introduced into the country 200 years earlier, their fears were unfounded.[258]

### *Fats*

Note – It may happen that a sauce is needed when no fat can be spared. In that case sauce may be made as follows: Take some flour and mix it to a smooth cream with enough cold liquid, which may be stock or water or milk, or milk and water, according to the sauce needed. Boil the remainder of the liquid and add the mixed flour, stirring until it boils. Then season and finish as directed.

Mrs C.S. Peel, *The Eat Less Meat Book*

During the rationing years, fat was in short supply and was obtained from wherever it could be found. It may be gleaned by skimming stock, nuts, cheese, milk, anywhere possible. Dorothy writes of a fashion in army camps for brewing tea in a caldron which had previously contained soup, the tea tending to have a fatty film over its surface as a result. So scarce was fat that she suggests this valuable commodity should be added to the fat collected by the army and navy to provide soap, or to go to other Government departments who used surplus for glycerine for ammunition. Dorothy advises not to buy new soap, which would melt too quickly, and to save on washing-up by using it as efficiently as possible.[259]

It was not uncommon for a man, in wooing his favoured lady, to bring along a parcel of butter. One such tale meets a sorry end: the butter was dropped, a puppy ate it, and then 'with utter disregard for war-time economy' threw it up on the drawing-room carpet.[260]

Beef dripping should be kept separately for cake and pastry making. To add bulk and fat content, gristle is used in dishes such as rissoles.[261] Gristle features widely in war time recipes. At the end of a recipe for 'Cobbler's Pie', which involves a potato suet paste filled with chopped potatoes and onion mixed with gristle from bones, we are advised that 'savoury herbs can be added, and just a sprinkling of vinegar or Worcester sauce will add piquancy to the boiled gristle.'[262]

I followed Dorothy's instructions on clarifying fat after roasting some beef bones for stock or roasting a joint (lamb fat does not taste good so avoid at all cost!). I put it in a clean bowl and added boiling water, then left it to cool and removed the cake of fat from the surface which I used to make some pastry for pasties and tarts. Not only is doing so thrifty, but produces a lighter texture.

Whatever the era, however, there are always shortcuts – I bought suet from our butcher in order to make a suet pudding from Dorothy's recipes, only to later read: 'when you can buy Atora beef suet ready flaked, why buy butcher's suet, which must be freed from skin, etc., and finely chopped.'[263]

### *Flour*

The abstention from all unnecessary consumption of grain will furnish the surest and most effectual means of defeating the devices of Our enemies.

King George, *The 'Eat Less Bread' Campaign*, 1917

The journalist, Mr Kennedy Jones, who was appointed Director General of Food Economy, alerted the British public to their habit of wasting, on average, one in every twelve month's supply of bread. It was so scarce that potato, when available, was often used in its place. Dorothy notes: 'A very rich woman, wearing hidden underneath her dress a beautiful pearl necklace, was amongst the refugees. On several occasions she offered pearls from this necklace and on one occasion the whole necklace in exchange for bread – to find that bread was of more value than pearls.'[264]

The price of flour increased in the run-up to war – on Wednesday, 29 July 1914 the price per sack was 1 shilling and by the following day it had risen to 1 shilling and 6 pence. The rich were encouraged to reduce their bread consumption because they could afford to buy more expensive foods. Meat, fish and eggs were financially procurable and therefore should be eaten instead of puddings, which contained bread and flour.[265]

By Royal Proclamation, the British people were asked to abstain from the consumption of bread by at least a quarter of what they would have normally consumed. This would ensure that those who could not afford to eat much other than bread, had enough in order to survive in times of 'grave stress and anxiety'.[266]

Baroness Reitzes, who sold her pearl necklace for £17,000 to buy bread for Vienna's poor. (*The War Illustrated*)

German prisoners waiting for bread pending distribution of their rations (Mrs C.S. Peel, *How We Lived Then 1914-1918*)

The need for bread was so desperate that Baroness Reitzes sold her pearl necklace for £17,000 to buy bread for Vienna's poor. Everyone – including Prisoners of War – would queue for hours or wait at fences in the hope of requisitioning some.

Flour was always weighed to ensure that an excessive amount was not used. To assist the health of the country, Government leaflets were circulated imploring the sensible use of bread. These were particularly aimed at the better off so that bread was available to fill the diet of the working class.

APPENDIX V

OFFICIAL INDEX-NUMBERS OF AVERAGE CHANGE OF RETAIL FOOD PRICES

| Beginning of | 1914. | 1915. | 1916. | 1917. | 1918. | 1919. | 1920. |
|---|---|---|---|---|---|---|---|
| January | — | 118 | 145 | 187 | 206 | 230 | 236 |
| February | — | 122 | 147 | 189 | 208 | 230 | 235 |
| March | — | 124 | 148 | 192 | 207 | 220 | 233 |
| April | — | 124 | 149 | 194 | 206 | 213 | 235 |
| May | — | 126 | 155 | 198 | 207 | 207 | 246 |
| June | — | 132 | 159 | 202 | 208 | 204 | 255 |
| July | 100 | $132\frac{1}{2}$ | 161 | 204 | 210 | 209 | 258 |
| August | — | 134 | 160 | 202 | 218 | 217 | 262 |
| September | 110 | 135 | 165 | 206 | 216 | 216 | 267 |
| October | 112 | 140 | 168 | 197 | 229 | 222 | 270 |
| November | 113 | 141 | 178 | 206 | 233 | 231 | 291 |
| December | 116 | 144 | 184 | 205 | 229 | 234 | 282 |

*Economic and Social History of the World War*, British Series. *Prices and Wages in the United Kingdom*, 1914–1920. Carnegie Endowment for International Peace.

Retail food price changes (Mrs C.S. Peel, *How We Lived Then 1914–1918*)

### *Using up the Pieces*

If you do not learn to be clever at using up the pieces you will never keep the household bills to a reasonable figure, unless indeed by feeding your family in a dull and scanty fashion. I do not write this book from the point of view of the food reformer (though I think the diet of both rich and poor needs reforming), neither do I write as a vegetarian (though I sympathise with many of their views); but I do write it hoping that I may therefore help those people who wish to do their duty to their country, to utilize every atom of food as intelligently as possible.

Mrs C.S. Peel, *My Own Cookery Book*

The importance of not wasting food continued after the war with the Great Strike of 1926 when its effects were still felt.

I give you Dorothy's exact words so that the message is not lost in translation:

Scraps of food left over from a meal would be utilised as follows:

Scraps of meat or vegetables would be added to a soup.
Fat from a joint would be clarified and used for cooking purposes.
Bones would be boiled to make stock or soup.
Odd stale pieces of bread (if any) would be added to soup, soaked and used for puddings, or dried and rolled and used for coating rissoles, etc.

This advice is put into action within the following imaginative recipe guidance:

Let us suppose you find in the larder:

(1) 2 to 3 oz. of cooked meat; 1 teacupful of brown sauce; a few cooked peas; a portion of a rice pudding, not enough to serve again; a few spoonfuls of mashed potato; 2 or 3 cold boiled potatoes; a small piece of cheese.

Make a thick soup by mixing together the sauce and mashed potato, thinning it with stock or water, seasoning to taste.

Mince the meat, mix it with the rice pudding and peas, season well and place in pipkins or shells. Slice the potatoes thinly and lay over the meat. Grate the cheese over the potatoes and make very hot in the oven. The seasoning and cheese flavouring will take away any sweetness in the rice pudding and you will have an excellent, fairly substantial savoury to serve instead of a sweet; if desired.

(2) A little cold porridge; remains of cooked cabbage; a few potatoes; 2 or 3 prunes; 1 rasher of bacon; a little potted meat; the remains of a dish of stewed fruit, more juice than fruit;

Use the porridge for thickening a white soup.

Put the potatoes and cabbage through a mincer, mix together and season well. Form into cakes and fry for breakfast.

Use the fruit juice instead of milk to make a cornflour pudding; or stiffen it with gelatine and use it for a jelly.

Mrs C.S. Peel, *My Own Cookery Book*

## RATIONING RECIPES

There follow recipes created by Dorothy – 'Granny Dot' – some of which have been adapted for twenty-first century tastes. The recipe remains largely unchanged where during straightened times, its essence is in the rationed ingredients used. If you would like to try them, I have adapted the weights and instructions, though Granny Dot herself may amply guide you through the process.

The chart in the Appendix provides imperial, metric and cup measurements and comparable oven temperatures are given in electric.

### RECHAUFFES
*In the average household where economy must be carefully studied, we cannot afford to feed our family on fillets of beef, chops, steaks, game and poultry, and joints, which make perhaps one reappearance cold and never appear upstairs again ... The haughty person who demands freshly cooked meat at each meal, and yet insists*

*that the bills shall be kept to anything between 10s and 12s a head a week must be brought to see reason.*

Mrs C.S. Peel, *Learning to Cook*

**Mock Venison**
This recipe is perfect for using thrift in your leftovers. Its grand title applies only when mutton and port are used. Otherwise it suits the more humble title of *Hash*.

In the words of Granny Dot:

*Take the joint of cold mutton (ham, chicken, pork, beef etc) and slice the meat as neatly as you can (use the bits for a mince), and remove all skin and gristle. Now please do not omit to do this, for a well-made hashed mutton should be made entirely of the eatable pieces of the joint. Having done this in ample time, put the meat on a plate. Mix one glass of port, one of mushroom ketchup, a tablespoonful of currant jelly (or any jam), the same of lemon juice, pepper, three cloves, and a finely shred onion, and some salt and pour it over the meat, and leave until one hour before the hash is required. If you cannot afford the port, use a little stock and less ketchup, and if you have not the ketchup you must do without it. While the meat soaks make some good brown sauce. Now strain the marinade (for that is what the liquid in which the meat has soaked is called) into the sauce, taste and season, and place it with the meat in an earthenware casserole. Cover, and cook very very gently for one hour. Serve very hot with mashed potato. If you like to add snippets of crisp fried bread do so, but on no account profane the hash with horrid little bits of leathery toast.'*

*If you cook and serve your hash thus, and especially if you call it Mock Venison, I doubt if it will not prove a popular dish. But if you cannot afford the port and ketchup, hashed mutton it must be, for it is those ingredients which give the venison taste to the mutton.*

*Please note that if you cook a hash fast it will be hard and tasteless, whereas reheated slowly and gently it is rich and tender.*

Mrs C.S. Peel, *Learning to Cook*

Ingredients
225g mutton or other cooked leftover meat, cut into bite size pieces
1tsp redcurrant jelly
100ml port (optional)
100ml gravy, mushroom ketchup or a mixture of both
Vegetable Oil or butter

½ onion, chopped
400g Leftover roast potatoes, boiled potatoes

Serves 2

1. Place the meat, redcurrant jelly, port, any leftover gravy, and some mushroom ketchup, into a bowl for an hour for the meat to moisten.
2. Put a knob of butter or some oil in a frying pan and when hot, fry the onion until glossy.
3. Add the meat with its sauce and heat through gently for up to an hour until tender.
4. You may like to add some vegetables such as peas, broccoli, chopped carrots, or chopped tomatoes.
5. Serve with fried or mashed potatoes and, if you like, some fried bread alongside.

### Rissole
*Now a rissole may be a most delicate preparation made with chicken and cream and truffle – a dish for a king; but of whatever material you make it, it must be creamy inside and crisp outside.'*

Mrs C.S. Peel, *Learning to Cook*

This is a truly memorable way to use up leftovers, something advocated by many. There is no end to the variety of ingredients you may use.

In the words of Granny Dot:

*If you wish to make a rissole, first prepare the mince. Then heat it in a good thick brown or white sauce, according to the colour of the meat you use, and be very careful about the seasoning, which may consist of pepper, salt, celery salt, cayenne, parsley, finely grated lemon peel, mushroom ketchup, and (if you are using chicken and game) a little ham or bacon.*

*Warm the well-flavoured mince in well-flavoured sauce, and see that the mixture is of the thickness of porridge. Then turn it on to a dish and let it become cold. When cold it will stiffen a little more, and with well-floured hands you can form it into the shape you prefer. Have ready a beaten egg yolk, and brush over, and roll in fine crumbs. Then fry, drain and serve very hot.*

Mrs C.S. Peel, *Savouries Simplified*

Ingredients
200g thick white sauce, p.133 with 40g each of butter and flour
100g cooked meat or fish
70g cooked vegetables
1 tbsp chopped herbs, spices and seasoning
1 free range or organic egg, beaten
Dried breadcrumbs
50g butter or vegetable oil

Makes 4 rissoles

1. Mix all of the ingredients together except the egg, breadcrumbs and oil. It is easiest to do this with your hands.
Herbs such as dill for fish, parsley or thyme for chicken, paprika for lamb and seasoning should be added.
2. Shape the mixture into rissoles (choose a shape you prefer).
3. Put the egg and breadcrumbs on separate plates. Coat the rissoles in the egg followed by the breadcrumbs and lay them on a baking tray. Set it in the fridge to firm up so that they will not fall apart when cooked.
4. Preheat the oven to 200°C/Gas Mark 6. Remove the rissoles from the fridge and use a pastry brush to paint them with oil or melted butter. Bake the rissoles for 20 minutes until lightly browned. Alternatively, heat the oil or butter in a pan and fry until golden.
Serve

## EGG DISHES

*Eggs are dear, but the dried eggs now placed on the market are excellent food value. They can be used in the same manner as fresh eggs, but care must be taken not to add too much water, otherwise they separate. The correct amount is generally three times as much water as egg by weight. If a dried egg is needed in a hurry, soak in warm water on the stove, and when the egg begins to rise beat it up well over heat.*
Mrs C.S. Peel, *The Victory Cookery Book*

### Custard Sauce
This tastes a little like Bird's Custard. It is a very good replacement in the absence of eggs. While colour could be used, as suggested by Granny Dot, it is not necessary.
    In her words:

*Materials. – 1oz. either corn flour, potato flour, arrowroot or a mixture of all, sufficient egg colour to give the desired colour (egg colouring is sold by most grocers), 1 pint boiling milk, 1 oz. sugar, flavour essence, a pinch of salt.*

*Method. – Mix the flour and egg colouring with a tablespoonful of milk until smooth. Boil the remainder of the milk with the sugar and pour over the flour mixture, stirring all the time. Add a pinch of salt and flavouring essence. Stir until well mixed and serve hot or cold.*

Mrs C.S. Peel, *The Victory Cookery Book*

Ingredients
500ml full fat milk
25g cornflour
25g sugar (use vanilla sugar if you have some)

Serves 4

1. Heat the milk.
2. In a bowl mix the cornflour and sugar together with a little milk, then add the remaining milk, stirring all the time.
3. Transfer the mixture to the pan and heat, stirring constantly until it thickens a little. Serve with a pudding.

### Mayonnaise Sauce without Oil

This liquid form of mayonnaise may have its place in dressing a salad, though this is not something I can imagine eating unless desperate. For interest's sake, do go ahead and make it, but not for culinary pleasure.

In the words of Granny Dot:

*Materials. – 2 yolks of eggs, 1 tin unsweetened condensed milk (fresh milk cannot be used in this recipe), vinegar as required, half-teaspoonful mustard, salt and cayenne pepper.*

*Method – Mix the yolks of eggs with salt and stir the milk into them as if it were oil, then add the vinegar, mustard, salt and pepper.*

Mrs C.S. Peel, *The Victory Cookery Book*

Ingredients
2 free range or organic egg yolks or 1 egg and 1 yolk
¼ tsp mustard powder
1 tsp vinegar
400ml of evaporated milk
Salt to taste

Serves 6

125

1. Whisk the yolks, mustard powder and vinegar. It is easier to do this in a blender or food processor, in which case use 1 whole egg and 1 yolk instead of 2 yolks.
2. Put the evaporated milk in a jug and pour it very slowly onto the egg mixture, whisking all the time. Season to taste.
Because this is more liquid than mayonnaise, use it as a salad dressing.

### *Egg Turnovers*

In the following recipe, wheat flour is replaced with rice flour and tapioca. It can also be replaced with semolina, potato flour, mashed potato and so on. The tapioca included in this recipe may be replaced by rice pudding.

This is not preferable to the pastry we are used to in pasties, but if I did not have the ingredients for a layered sumptuous pastry, this would certainly fill the gap.

In the words of Granny Dot:

*Method. – Prepare short paste, fill with scrambled eggs, and shape as turnovers. Bake in a hot oven. Other material may be added, such as cooked flaked fish, chopped nuts, cooked chopped potato, grated cheese, herbs, etc. Serve hot or cold.*

*Short Paste*
*Materials. – ½ oz. rice flour, ½ oz. tapioca, ½ oz. milk powder, 2 gills water, ¾ oz. fat, ½ lb rice flour, ¼ lb flour, ¼ oz baking powder, ¼ oz. salt.*

*Method. – Mix the first three ingredients cold in one gill of water, and boil until stiff, stirring all the time. Mix the rice flour, flour, baking powder, fat and salt together, add the boiled preparation and mix all together, adding sufficient water to make a fairly soft paste (about 1 gill). Roll and use. This is excellent for turnovers, pies and tarts.*

Mrs C.S. Peel, *The Victory Cookery Book*

Ingredients
for the Paste
15g rice flour
55g tinned or prepared tapioca
150ml full fat milk

for the Crust
25g fat
225g rice flour
110g plain flour
¼ tsp baking powder

¼ tsp salt
Extra milk, if needed

For the Filling
Use any filling you like. Scrambled egg is an example.

Makes 12-20, depending on the size you make

1. Preheat the oven to 200°C/Gas Mark 6.
2. Put the paste ingredients together in a pan and warm through.
3. Add them to the crust ingredients and mix well, adding a little more milk until a firm paste is formed which is not sticky.
4. On a lightly floured surface roll the pastry out and cut with a biscuit cutter or a knife.
5. Prepare some undercooked scrambled eggs, and place a spoonful in the centre of each pastry round.
6. Seal the pastry by crimping it together with your fingers or a fork, using water if necessary. Place the turnovers on a baking tray.
7. You could brush the prepared turnovers with milk or egg or leave plain.
8. Bake in the oven for five minutes or so until the crust has dried.
These are best served immediately.

## Omelette with Dried Eggs
Provided you mix the dried eggs and water together and set aside for an hour before use, you will produce an omelette which is very good. In order to hold its shape, the mixture needs to cook for longer than a fresh egg omelette.

In the words of Granny Dot:

*Materials and Method.- Omelettes are made as well with dried eggs as with fresh. The eggs should be beaten till thoroughly blended but not frothy. Season with salt and pepper and any addition desired, such as parsley, cheese, minced ham, potato, shrimps, chopped fish, vegetables, etc. Only ½ oz. fat should be used for 2 or 3 eggs – more fat spoils the omelette. Have the fat hot in the pan before adding the eggs. Be careful when using dried eggs not to add more water than three times the weight of egg, otherwise the mixture will separate in the cooking, and they must be thoroughly soaked for at least 12 hours and be quite smooth.*

Mrs C.S. Peel, *The Victory Cookery Book*

Ingredients
1 tbsp dried egg
130ml water

127

Fat for frying (butter, plain oil, lard or dripping)
Seasoning

Serves 1

1. Mix the dried egg in a bowl with the water and set aside for an hour. Season.
2. Heat the frying pan and melt some fat.
3. When it is sizzling, add the omelette mixture.
4. Cook the omelette until it is reasonably firm – this is necessary because it will easily fall apart.
Serve

### Scrambled Eggs with Bread Sauce
Like many rationing recipes, in the absence of an alternative, the bulk in the addition of the bread and milk produces an effective result.

In the words of Granny Dot:

*Materials. – 2 oz. bread, ½ pint cold milk, salt and pepper and nutmeg or mace, 2 dried eggs, e.g. 1 oz. dried egg and 3 oz. or 3 tablespoonfuls of water.*

*Method. – Break up the bread and pour the cold milk over it, season to taste. Boil very slowly. The bread will break up easier this way than when breadcrumbs are used. When soft, work well to make it creamy, or pass through a sieve. Add to this the dried eggs. (It takes almost 8 hours to soak for granulated eggs and 1 hour for powder.) Work well together, then scramble all together and season to taste. No fat is required.*

*This makes a creamy mass, and of course much larger quantity than when eggs alone are used.*

Mrs C.S. Peel, *The Victory Cookery Book*

Ingredients
10g dried eggs
90ml water
300ml full fat milk
60g bread
Seasoning
Serves 2

1. Mix the dried eggs with the water in a bowl and set aside.
2. Pour the milk over the bread in a pan.
3. Stir the mixture over a medium heat until the bread has broken up into a creamy mass.

4. Put the mixture through a sieve if it is not completely smooth.
5. In the pan, mix the eggs with the bread and milk mixture. Stir over a low heat until scrambled.
6. Season to taste.
Serve

### Polenta

This is included as an essential part of the two recipes which follow.
   In the words of Granny Dot:

*Materials. – 1 quart water, ½ pint maize semolina (yellow), ½ oz. salt, 1 oz. fat, a little cheese (if this is added, fat may be omitted).*

*Method. – Boil the water, add salt and fat and semolina or cornmeal (yellow). If white maize is used, double the amount of maize meal is required. Boil for 15-20 minutes, stirring all the time, or place in a porringer[1], and cook for an hour. Turn out to cool, cut into slices, and flour and fry in a frying-pan, with a little fat. Sprinkle with grated cheese or serve plain.*

Mrs C.S. Peel, *The Victory Cookery Book*

Ingredients
750ml water
1 tsp salt
250g polenta
25g butter
grated cheese (optional)
Serves 6

1. Bring the water and salt to the boil.
If using a non-fast action variety of polenta, preheat the oven to 180°C/Gas Mark 4 and prepare a buttered oven-proof dish before the next step, as you will need to bake the polenta before it can be used.
If you are making polenta cakes use a frying pan or board for 2 cm high cakes. If not, use a deeper dish. Have some buttered foil ready to cover the dish.
2. Gently pour the polenta through your fingers into the pan, whisking all the time with a balloon whisk to avoid lumps. Keep whisking until all of the water has been absorbed.
3. Mix in the butter and cheese.
4. Now is the time to pour the polenta into the appropriate container. For non-fast action polenta bake it in the oven for 40 minutes; for fast-action polents transfer to the appropriate container and cool.

### Maize Woodcock

To interpret this title, it is scrambled eggs on polenta with anchovy. Sliced polenta toasted on a griddle pan with lightly scrambled eggs topped with anchovy and a little parsley or chives is more substantial than using toast, and with limited bread, an effective alternative.

In the words of Granny Dot:

*Materials. – Scrambled eggs, a round of polenta, a few fillets of anchovy.*

*Method. – Lay a layer of scrambled eggs on a square or round of polenta. Place a few fillets of anchovy crosswise on the top, and heat in the oven.*

Mrs C.S. Peel, *The Victory Cookery Book*

Ingredients
Polenta set in a frying pan to a height of 2cm (see page 129)
2 knobs of butter
12 free range or organic eggs
12 anchovies
Chives, finely chopped

Serves 6

Maize Woodcock (*Author's own*)

130

1. Preheat the oven to 200°C/Gas Mark 6
2. Cut the polenta into 6cm x 9cm rounds.
3. Heat a griddle pan and melt a knob of butter in it.
4. When it sizzles, add the polenta, frying for about 3 minutes on each side until lightly browned.
5. In a separate pan, lightly scramble the eggs in a knob of butter, bearing in mind that they will be cooked further in the oven.
6. Lay the rounds of polenta on a baking tray and spoon some scrambled eggs on top of each.
7. Place 2 anchovy fillets on the eggs in a cross, and bake for 5 minutes.
8. Remove the tray from the oven and serve.

**Buck Rarebit**
This is a delicious alternative in the absence of bread.
Here is Granny Dot's recipe:

*Materials – A round or square of polenta, a tablespoonful of rarebit mixture, a poached egg.*
*Rarebit Method – Spread the cheese mixture on the polenta. Bake to a golden brown, place the poached egg, well drained on the top.*

Mrs C.S. Peel, *The Victory Cookery Book*

Ingredients
25g ground rice or plain flour
280ml full fat milk
50g grated cheese such as cheddar or Parmesan
½ tsp Dijon or English mustard
Salt and pepper
Pinch of cayenne
Polenta set in a frying pan to a height of 2cm
Knob of butter
6 free range or organic eggs

Serves 6

1. Preheat the oven to 200°C/Gas Mark 6.
2. To make the rarebit mixture, combine the flour with some milk into a paste.
3. Heat the remaining milk in a pan and add the paste, whisking until it thickens.
4. Add the cheese, mustard, cayenne and seasoning. Set aside, covered.
5. Cut the polenta into 6 rectangles.
6. Melt a knob of butter in a griddle pan and when it is sizzling, add the polenta

131

slices, frying for about 3 minutes on each side until lightly browned.
7. Place the polenta on a baking tray and spoon 1½ tbsp of rarebit mixture on top of each.
8. Bake in the oven for 10 minutes or until the rarebit mixture is bubbling and lightly browned.
9. In the mean time, poach the eggs.
10. Serve the polenta rarebits with a poached egg on top.


## SAUCES
*All thick sauces should be poured through a strainer, and into a very hot sauce boat. No matter how well made, a half-cold sauce can never prove attractive.*
                                                    Mrs C.S. Peel, *Learning to Cook*


### Curry Sauce
This is mild and comforting, a good way to introduce curry to children. Being spoiled by the plethora of wonderful spices and curries we have in the UK this may, in contrast, not be very exciting. If you like the curry sauce sold with fish and chips in England, however, you are bound to like this.
    In the words of Granny Dot:

*For a curry sauce peel and chop two onions and half an apple, and fry in fat until quite a deep yellow and soft. Pour 1 gill of boiling water over a tablespoonful of dessicated cocoa-nut, and add to it enough stock to make half a pint. Take two teaspoonfuls of curry powder, and mix it smooth in some of the stock. Stir all together, add some salt, and simmer; thicken with brown roux and sieve before serving. The sauce is greatly improved by being left to steep in its pan on a cool part of the stove for several hours. It should be thick and taste thoroughly cooked, and only just pleasantly hot. Some people add a few sultanas and a little lemon juice to the onion, as well as a pinch of turmeric.*
    *The usual fault of curry sauce is that it is insufficiently cooked and not sufficiently thick; it is, in fact, gravy flavoured with uncooked curry powder.*
                                                    Mrs C.S. Peel, *Learning to Cook*


Ingredients
150ml boiling water
1 tbsp desiccated coconut (this and the water may be replaced with 150ml coconut milk)
50g butter
1 onion diced

½ apple diced
2 tsp plain powder or 1 tsp curry paste
1 tbsp flour
300ml vegetable or chicken stock
Sultanas may be added and lemon juice for flavour, if liked

Serves 4

1. Pour the water over desiccated coconut in a bowl. Set aside.
2. Melt the butter in a pan and add the onion and apple, stirring until soft.
3. Add the curry powder and flour and cook for a minute or two, stirring occasionally.
4. Stir in the coconut with its water and the stock.
5. Simmer together for 5 minutes. Season to taste.
6. Blend.
Serve

### White Sauce

Six ears pricked up and one of my three dogs turned his head as if to say, 'What happened?' I had a Eureka moment. I can't believe that a recipe for white sauce written during the rationing period at the end of the First World War in 1918 made me shriek with joy! Its purpose was to eliminate the risk of lumps and therefore waste during constrained times. I was thanking Granny Dot aloud – you never know, maybe she is looking on and enjoying the fact that her great-great-granddaughter is finding her work enlightening a century later?

In her words:

*Materials. – ½ oz fat, 2/3 oz. flour, ½ pint milk, salt and pepper, grated nutmeg.*

*Method. – Mix the fat with the flour cold, add milk, salt, pepper, and a pinch of grated nutmeg, place on a small flame without stirring until it comes to the boil, whisk quickly to produce at once a smooth sauce. Made in this way the sauce does not require straining; there will be no lumps.*

Mrs C.S. Peel, *The Victory Cookery Book*

Ingredients
20g unsalted butter, cold
20g plain flour
300 ml full fat milk
pinch of salt
grind of pepper
sprinkling of nutmeg (optional)

1. If you have some disposable cooking gloves, they are useful for the following task. Take the butter and mush it up with the flour into a paste with your hands. You can use a fork, but it is easier and less messy with gloved hands.
2. Put the paste and the milk in a small pan over a medium heat.
3. When it is hot turn the heat up so that it boils and whisk thoroughly and lightly until you can feel it thicken – et voila – you have a smooth sauce.
4. Season to taste.

### Imitation Bread Sauce
For an imitation bread sauce, this is delicious. My now favourite spice, mace, is added here. Long slow cooking is important for a smooth texture.
   In the words of Granny Dot:

*Materials. – ½ gill semolina or white maize meal, 1 pint of milk, 1 small onion stuck with a clove, tiny piece of mace and pinch of salt, pepper.*

*Method. – Soak the semolina or maize meal in the milk, adding the onion, mace and salt. Bring to the boil, and place in a double cooker for 1 hour (having removed the clove from the onion), pass through a sieve. Finish with a little cayenne or pepper.*
                                        Mrs C.S. Peel, *The Victory Cookery Book*

<u>Ingredients</u>
1 small onion
1 clove
50g semolina or polenta
1 blade of mace
600ml full fat milk
Fat to grease an overproof dish, if using

Serves 8

1. This can be cooked in the oven or over the heat. If you choose the oven, preheat it to 170°C/Gas Mark 3.
2. Stick the clove into the onion and put it with the semolina or polenta and mace into a pan. Add the milk and stir over a medium heat until combined.
3. Either cook on a low heat, stirring now and then for an hour
or
Place in a greased oven proof dish, covered with a lid or foil. Put it in the oven for an hour.
Serve with roast chicken or turkey.

## CEREAL DISHES
*Those persons who cannot digest pulse foods often find that cereals suit them admirably.*
Mrs C.S. Peel, *Eat Less Meat Book*

### *Italian Paste* (pasta)
If someone had asked me to guess what First World War rationing recipes included, pasta would not have been on my list. The Italian food writer, Anna del Conte, who has allowed me to use her pasta instructions, says that the standard ratio should be 1 egg to 100g of flour (refined Italian flour).

Standard flour is used in Granny Dot's recipe so it is included here for authenticity, as well as water instead of an extra yolk. In making the rationing recipe for fresh pasta, using water in place of egg discolours it a little. The aim is to have a smooth dough which is not sticky.

In the words of Granny Dot:

*Materials. – ½ lb of household flour, half a teaspoonful of salt, one egg, and two to three tablespoonfuls of cold water.*

*Method. – Mix the flour and salt in a small basin and stir in the egg and water with a knife. After a preliminary kneading in the basin the paste is rolled on a table or marble slab under the palms of both hands until it resembles a long roll, then reversed and gradually kneaded into a short roll with the palm of the right hand just above the wrist, applying considerable pressure. The alternate movements are continued from twenty to thirty minutes, until the paste is elastic and quite smooth. The paste is more easily handled if halved and rolled into two sheets almost as thin as paper instead of one larger one. Just a little flour may be sprinkled on the table, but none on the rolling pin. Leave the sheets of paste spread out for about two hours. In this state the paste breaks easily, but cutting is speedily accomplished by means of a knife strong and sharp enough to go through many strips of paste placed one on top of the other. Though this paste may be cooked as soon as it is cut, it is better if kept overnight spread in single layers to harden before being used.*

Ingredients
225g plain flour
½ tsp salt
1 free range or organic egg
2-3 tbsp cold water

Serves 2

1. Put the flour on the work surface and make a well in the middle. Add the salt,

egg and water. Use a fork or your fingers, mix the eggs and water and draw in the flour gradually. Work quickly until it forms a mass. Scrape the work surface clean and wash your hands.

   Alternatively you can use a food processor. Put in the flour and salt, switch on the machine and drop in the eggs and water through the funnel. Process until a ball of dough is formed. Transfer the dough to a lightly floured work surface
2. Knead the dough for about 5-7 minutes, until smooth and elastic. Wrap in clingfilm and leave to rest for at least 30 minutes – or up to 3 or 4 hours.
3. Unwrap the dough and knead on a lightly floured surface for 2-3 minutes, then divide into 4 equal parts. Take one piece of dough and keep the remainder wrapped in clingfilm. Roll out the dough using a rolling pin, or by machine following the manufacturer's instructions.
4. Cut the pasta sheets into strips by hand or with a machine. Drape the strips over tea towels on the back of a chair to dry.
5. Boil the pasta for 2 to 3 minutes. Drain, reserving some of the pasta water. Toss in olive oil or butter to stop it sticking together. Add to a sauce. If necessary, add some of the reserved pasta water.
Serve .

### Nouilles au Gratin
*Nouilles* is french for noodle which suggests that Granny Dot's pasta recipe came from France, which she visited in 1917 in order to view feeding regimes.
   Granny Dot again:

*Materials.- 3 oz. nouilles, salt, boiling water, 1 oz. of margarine, half a pint of hot milk, one tablespoonful of grated cheese, breadcrumbs.*

*Method.- Boil 3 oz. of nouilles in salted water for fifteen minutes and drain. Melt one ounce of margarine and stir in as much flour as it will moisten. When it has cooked gently for five minutes add a half-pint of hot milk, salt, pepper, and a grain or two of cayenne. Stir and boil gently till smooth, then withdraw from the fire and add a tablespoonful of grated cheese. Place the nouilles in a buttered pie-dish in layers with the sauce spread between. Cover the final layer of nouilles lightly with mixed bread-crumbs and cheese, add several small pieces of butter, and bake in a fairly hot oven till nicely browned.*
Mrs C.S. Peel, *The Eat Less Meat Book*

Ingredients
100g pasta
50g butter plus extra for the dish
1 tbsp plain flour

300ml full fat milk
50g Grated cheese, adding more, dependent upon the strength of the cheese
seasoning
Dried breadcrumbs

You will need an ovenproof dish 20 x 15

Serves 2

1. Preheat the oven to 200°C/Gas Mark 6.
2. Make the white sauce on page 133 using the quantities given.
3. Add the cheese, enough to taste.
4. Boil the pasta until al dente and put it in a buttered dish.
5. Add the sauce and top with breadcrumbs.
6. Bake until the breadcrumbs are browned.
Serve

### *Ravioli Maigre*

I made this for Anna del Conte. It was a storm-ridden day so when I took them to her house they were almost blown off the tray as I transferred them from car to kitchen. We served them with sage and butter, but the choice is yours. Because of the higher water content of the pasta recipe, it may discolour a little. An alternative is to replace the water with egg.

In the words of Granny Dot:

*Materials. – ½ lb. Italian paste, 1 lb. spinach, one tablespoonful of grated cheese.*

*Method. – Prepare half a pound of Italian paste, roll it out as thin as possible, and dry it for one hour. Boil one pound of spinach in a little water, and after draining thoroughly chop it finely. In a little hot butter or margarine lightly brown a teaspoonful of very finely chopped onion, sprinkle in a heaped teaspoonful of flour, and when it has cooked for a few minutes stir in the spinach. Season to taste, and when cool stir in a small tablespoonful of cheese and put all through a sieve. Cut the paste into rounds one and half inch in diameter; wet the edges of one half with water, place in the centre a little of the spinach, and cover with the remaining rounds of paste. Seal the edges by pressing them together, and drop the raviolis into boiling salted water. Boil them gently for about half an hour and drain them well. Serve in a fireproof dish with a little white sauce mixed with cheese, or with tomato sauce poured over.*

*This home-made macaroni is delicious just tossed in butter, seasoned with pepper and salt, and served with poached eggs or as a centre to cutlets or fillets, or with boiled chicken or rabbit, or for that matter plain, and is infinitely superior to the hard, tasteless, stale macaroni so often bought in England.*

Mrs C.S. Peel, *The Eat Less Meat Book*

137

<u>Ingredients</u>
400g spinach
50g butter
½ onion, diced
1 tbsp plain flour
2 tbsp parmesan
seasoning
250g pasta sheets (see page 135)

Serves 6

1. Put the spinach in large pan, add a splash of water to it and stir until wilted. Remove from the heat, drain and set aside.
2. Fry the onion in the butter until it is lightly browned and add the flour. Mix it in and allow it to become pale brown. Set aside.
3. Finely chop the spinach.
4. Add 2 tbsp of Parmesan to the spinach and mix it in to the onion and flour. Season and set aside.
5. Lay the pasta sheets on a floured surface. Put a spoonful of spinach on top at approximately 5cm intervals.
6. Take some water and with your finger make a circle of water around each spinach spoonful.
7. Lay another sheet of pasta on top, carefully trying to avoid air pockets, sealing over the water circles.
8. Use a pastry cutter or a sharp knife to cut the ravioli.
9. Leave the ravioli on a lightly floured surface so that it does not stick. This is vital as it is so sad when it is ruined.
10. Boil some salted water.
11. Place the ravioli in the boiling water for 2 to 3 minutes and then drain.
Serve with melted butter with added sage and Parmesan.

### Risotto
I love it when I cook something with trepidation and it is a huge success – this is delicious, particularly when considering it formed part of rationing.
    In the words of Granny Dot:

*Materials. – Half a pint of milk, small teacupful of raw rice, four small onions, six good sized tomatoes, 1 oz. finely grated cheese, pepper and salt to taste.*

*Method. – Place onions, tomatoes, (these latter ingredients should be chopped finely), pepper and salt into a saucepan with the milk, boil all together until soft, stirring occasionally, and adding more milk if necessary, sieve them, then add the rice and cook until soft. Add a little more milk if necessary. Just before serving stir in the finely grated cheese.*

Mrs C.S. Peel, *The Eat Less Meat Book*

Ingredients
2 onions, roughly chopped
150g chopped fresh tomatoes
280ml full fat milk
Seasoning
100g risotto rice
Parmesan cheese, grated
Chives, finely chopped
Black pepper, ground

Serves 2

1. Put the chopped onions and tomatoes in a medium saucepan with the milk and some seasoning.
2. Bring to a simmer and cook until soft.
3. Puree in a blender and pass through a sieve back into the pan.
4. Add the rice and stir occasionally until it softens but is slightly al dente. Add more milk if necessary.
5. Stir in 2 tbsp of Parmesan and garnish with additional Parmesan, parsley or chives and freshly ground black pepper.

### Gnocci

The end result was so good that I would go as far as to say that I prefer it to the potato gnocchi I am more used to. I recommend this alongside a crisp green salad.

Here is Granny Dot's recipe:

*Materials. – one tablespoonful of margarine, 4 oz. of semolina, 1 oz. of grated cheese, one pint of water, salt.*

*Method. – Boil the water with the margarine and some salt. Drop in the semolina by ° and stir until the mixture thickens (this will take about a quarter of an hour), add the grated cheese and leave it until it becomes cold. Grease a fireproof dish with margarine, and sprinkle it with cheese, and put tablespoonfuls of the semolina mixture all over it. They should stand up roughly like rock cakes; add a few little bits of margarine and bake to a golden brown in a fairly hot oven, which will take about twenty minutes.*

Mrs C.S. Peel, *The Eat Less Meat Book*

<u>Ingredients</u>
600ml boiling water
1 tsp salt
70g butter
85g semolina
85g grated cheese - cheddar
Parmesan cheese, grated

Serves 2 hungry people or 4 as a starter

1. Put the water, salt and 50g of the butter in a pan and simmer.
2. Pour the semolina through your fingers slowly, whisking all the time. Traditionally, I believe a wooden spoon was used, but a whisk prevents lumps forming.
3. Add the cheese and stir in until it is like thick double cream in consistency. This should take about 5 minutes.
4. Pour it onto a plate and let it cool completely.
5. Preheat the oven to 180°C/Gas Mark 4.
6. Spoon little pieces of the cooled mixture as neatly as you can onto a buttered dish.
7. Generously grate Parmesan on top and dot the remaining butter in tiny pieces on top of this.
8. Bake the gnocci for about 15 minutes until it is hot.
Serve

**FISH**
*Do not despise salt herrings (Government pickled herrings), for they are very nourishing.*

Mrs C.S. Peel, *The Victory Cookery Book*

***Fish Mock Turtle Soup***
A First World War rationing recipe using a fish head just had to be tried. I have re-jigged it little by blending all of the ingredients other than the head itself, rather than strain the liquid as recommended.

Here is Granny Dot's recipe:

*Materials.– Cod's head, 4 oz. onions, 4 oz. carrot, 1 tablespoonful oil, 1 lemon, 1 teaspoonful basil, half-teaspoonful marjoram, 1 clove of garlic, 1 bay leaf and equal amount thyme, 1 dozen peppercorns, 6 allspice, 1 dozen corianders, 1 bunch parsley stalks, 3 pints water, 3 oz. baked flour.*

*Method. – Slice the onions and carrot and place in a saucepan with the garlic, oil, bay leaf, thyme, peppercorns, allspice, corianders and parsley stalks. Cut the cod's head into pieces – e.g. (1) Tongue, (2) top of the head, (3) and (4) cheeks, (5) and (6) shoulders if left on the head.*

*Place the trimmings on the bed of vegetables, and arrange the pieces of cod's head on the top; sprinkle with salt . Add the lemon juice, cover with a lid, and simmer until the fish is cooked in its own liquor. Carefully lift the pieces of cod out of the pan and keep warm with a little stock. Remove the liquid of the fish, which is reserved until later, now add the water to the remaining bones, etc. Boil then cook for 10 minutes. Strain the liquid, make it up to 1 quart, to which add the flour (baked dry in an oven until it is fawn coloured), and whisk the stock to separate the flour, which does not lump after baking. Boil for 10 minutes. Now add the basil and marjoram and the reserved fish liquid, season to taste, and add a pinch of cayenne pepper. Simmer for 5 minutes more, then strain. Serve with cut lemon.*

*The fish used for making of the soup can be served to follow the soup with a fish sauce and potatoes, or can be used for fish pies, patties, cakes, salads and many other dishes. The heads of other fish can be used equally well for the purpose, but cod's head has a large amount of gelatine, which of course is required to make this kind of soup.*

Mrs C.S. Peel, *The Eat Less Meat Book*

Ingredients
1 fish head – I used sea bass but most white fish would be fine.
2 tbsp of oil such as sunflower, vegetable or olive oil
110g chopped carrot
110g sliced onion
1 bay leaf
1 sprig thyme
Seasoning
2 strips of orange peel
500ml water or stock
Seasoning
1 tbsp lemon juice
Parsley to garnish

Serves 2-4

1. With a very sharp knife remove any fish meat you can from the head.
2. Put the oil in a pan and add the vegetables and herbs. Season.
3. Place the meat you have removed from the head on top of the vegetables so that it cooks through. This will take about two minutes.

4. Remove the meat and set aside.
5. Add the orange peel, water, and the fish head and simmer for ten minutes.
6. Remove the fish head and peel; blend the soup.
7. Season to taste with salt, pepper and lemon juice.
8. Serve with the cooked fish and sprinkle with parsley.

### How to Use a Tin of Salmon (12 oz)
*Open the tin at the side instead of the top so that the whole contents can slide out of the tin. Place it on a plate; carefully remove skin and bone by splitting the salmon; reserve the best pieces for a gratin, the next best for salad or scallops, the smaller pieces for cakes and the remainder for sandwiches. Cheese is an important part of these dishes, but must be omitted when it is scarce.*

Mrs C.S. Peel, *The Victory Cookery Book*

In the *Victory Cookery Book* one tin of salmon produces five dishes, two of which follow. If ramekins and scallop shells are used, these are suitable for a dinner party starter.

### Salmon Baked
This is comforting and delicious served with crusty bread and butter.
   Here is Granny Dot's original recipe:

*Materials. – Best pieces of salmon, white sauce, pepper, a few drops of lemon juice, a little grated cheese or crumbs.*

*Method. – Place the pieces of salmon in a fireproof dish, previously lined with white sauce. Add pepper to taste and lemon juice, cover with white sauce and sprinkle with grated cheese, and bake in a hot oven until brown.*
*The dish should be placed in another containing water white cooking.*

Mrs C.S. Peel, *The Victory Cookery Book*

Ingredients
Butter for the ramekins
110g tinned salmon
White sauce (see page 133)
2 tbsp lemon juice
½ tbsp chopped parsley
Seasoning
2 tbsp grated cheese
2 tbsp dried breadcrumbs (optional)

You will need 2 ramekins

Serves 2

1. Preheat the oven to $180^\circ$C/Gas Mark 4.
2. Butter the ramekins.
3. Mix the tinned salmon with the white sauce, lemon, parsley and seasoning.
4. Sprinkle cheese and breadcrumbs on top.
5. Bake in a hot oven for 20 minutes until lightly browned.
6. Remove from the oven and serve

### *Scalloped Salmon*
Quite a few years ago I saved some scallop shells, thinking that one day they would be useful; about ten years later they are! This is truly to be repeated.
  In the words of Granny Dot:

*Materials. – Salmon, mashed potatoes, a little oil, white sauce, cheese or breadcrumbs, salt to taste.*

*Method. – Make a border of mashed potatoes on a scallop shell by using a forcing bag and tube. Fill the centre with salmon and white sauce mixed, well season, sprinkle the fish with crumbs or cheese, baste with oil, then bake to a nice brown colour. The shells should be placed in such a position that the sauce cannot run over. The best method is to place the shell in a small heap of salt, which suffers nothing by being heated.*

Mrs C.S. Peel, *The Victory Cookery Book*

Scalloped Salmon (*Author's own*)

<u>Ingredients</u>
70g tinned salmon
200ml white sauce (see page 133)
1 teaspoon lemon juice, or so, to taste
Parsley
Seasoning
A little butter
Mashed potato made from one medium sized potato, milk and butter so that it is loose and creamy
Grated cheddar cheese and dried breadcrumbs

You need two scallop shells and a piping bag.
Serves 2

1. Preheat the oven to 200°C/Gas Mark 6.
2. Mix the salmon and white sauce together and stir in lemon juice, parsley and seasoning.
3. Butter the scallop shells and put half the mixture into each.
4. Pipe the mashed potato around the border.
5. Sprinkle cheese and breadcrumbs over the top of the salmon mixture.
6. Bake for 8 minutes or until lightly golden.
Serve

**MEAT**
*Large joints are now obtainable only by large families and in restaurants and institutions. As a rule, small pieces of meat have to be dealt with, and the housewife is never sure what part of an animal will be available. She must be content to take what she can get, and learn to cook her ration as economically as possible. Frying is an economical method of cooking, for any juices which escape are reclaimed when the gravy is made, and the process is saving of fuel ... Braising is not recommended as this is an expensive method of cooking and needs gelatinous stock, to produce for which much fuel is required.*
Mrs C.S. Peel, The Eat Less Meat Book

Due to the need to save fuel during wartime, it was recommended that meat was cut into portions so that large pieces were not used which demand greater fuel consumption to sufficiently cook.

*If, from lack of meat, a feeling of hunger is experienced, cheese or nuts are the items which should be added in small proportions to the diet. Meat is concentrated food, and it is therefore good for the general health of the country that it should be used as sparingly as possible; but as the desire for the quantity of meat to which most people have been accustomed must be satisfied, it should be served in such a manner as to supply the necessary bulk.[2]*

An example of the 'bulk' referred to is in a recipe for sausages in *The Victory Cookery Book*, 1918, the meat part of which would include fat and gristle, with the addition of an equal weight in breadcrumbs. Onion and vinegar are added to '*help to bring back the flavour which the meat has lost*'.[3]

### Mutton and Rice Stew

The point of this recipe is its simplicity dictated by necessity. So while you see below what the recipe is, I have altered it just a little.

In the words of Granny Dot:

*Materials.– 2 or 3 lb. scrag end of neck of mutton, 3 lb of onion, carrot, turnip, mixed seasoning, parsley, 2oz. rice.*

*Method.– Take the scrag end of neck of mutton and wash it. Then divide it and remove what fat you can. Place it in a pan with an onion, a carrot, and a turnip cut into dice, salt, parsley, also 2oz. of rice. Cover and simmer quite gently for four hours. Before serving remove the bones, leaving the meat in the broth. The proportions are about 2 lb. of scrag to 3lb of vegetables and two quarts of water. Taste the broth to see that it is well seasoned, and serve very hot.*

Mrs C.S. Peel, *The Victory Cookery Book*

Ingredients
50g fat (butter, plain oil, lard, dripping)
2 onions, chopped
1 small turnip, chopped into 1cm pieces
3 carrots, chopped into 2 cm pieces
1 tbsp tomato puree
450g scrag end of mutton, cut into bite-size pieces
Parsley
1 strip lemon peel
Bay leaf
200ml red wine
500ml chicken stock
30g rice
Finely chopped parsley and grated lemon zest for garnish

Serves 4-6

1. In a casserole, fry the vegetables in the fat until a little tender.
2. Add the tomato puree and stir.
3. Lift out the vegetables into a bowl with slotted spoon and set aside.
4. Fry the mutton in the casserole until lightly coloured.
5. Return the vegetables to the pan with the parsley, lemon peel and bay leaf. Add the wine and simmer for a couple of minutes.
6. Cover the contents of the casserole with the stock and simmer very gently for up to 4 hours until the meat is tender. Add the rice 20 minutes before removing the casserole from the heat.
7. Garnish with grated lemon zest and parsley.

### *War Galantine*

This is meatloaf boiled in a cloth. Baking it in a loaf tin lined with bacon, and topping it with dripping is a great improvement. Bulk is added with red lentils. Were you to have a rationing party and wanted to produce the genuine article, adding a few more herbs and a little lemon zest would not be cheating too badly. Serving it with Granny Dot's tomato sauce on page 197 is a suggestion. In Granny Dot's words:

*Materials.– 4 oz. of raw beef, 8 oz. cooked red lentils, 4 oz. sausage meat, 6 oz. fine dry bread-crumbs, one teaspoonful each of chopped parsley, grated onion, and mixed herbs. Salt and pepper to taste.*

*Method.– Mix all the ingredients with one raw egg beaten up with about one gill of stock. Form into a roll and tie in a well-floured clean cloth, leaving room for the roll to swell. The cloth must be wrung out in boiling water before flouring or the flour would not adhere. Place in boiling stock or water and simmer for two hours. Remove and strain and glaze with melted glaze. If preferred, add two ounces of chopped nuts to the galantine. The stock or water it was cooked in, if well skimmed, should be used as a foundation for a thick soup.*

Mrs C.S. Peel, *The Eat Less Meat Book*

Ingredients
12 streaky bacon rashers (you may need more)
110g raw beef, finely chopped (this can be replaced with sausage meat)
110g sausage meat
220g cooked red lentils
170g breadcrumbs
1 free range or organic egg

146

zest of 1 lemon
2 tbsp mixed herbs
1 tbsp parsley
Seasoning
Beef Dripping

You will need a loaf tin
Serves 6

1. Preheat the oven to 190°C/Gas Mark 5.
2. Line a loaf tin with bacon.
3. Combine the remaining ingredients other than the dripping. Mix well. I find this easiest with my hands.
4. Press the mixture into the prepared loaf tin. Place a few dots of dripping on top of the meat mixture and then fold the bacon over.
5. Bake for 45 minutes.
6. Remove from the oven and serve with tomato sauce or gravy.

### Cabbage Stew and Liver Dumplings

A dish which sounds so plain is made into something quite special by adding crisped liver dumplings which are mini rissoles, to the cabbage, well suited to limited produce.

In the words of Granny Dot:

*Materials.– 1 savoy or other large cabbage, 4 oz. raw chopped liver, a little salt, pepper, nutmeg and herbs, 2 oz. shredded onions, 2 oz. fat, 3 or 4 oz. breadcrumbs, 1 egg.*

*Method.– Clean the cabbage, cut into shreds and parboil; drain. Put 1 oz. fat into a saucepan, and when hot add the shredded onions, and sweat without allowing them to take colour. Add the cabbage, salt, pepper, a grate of nutmeg, and a little water, cover with the lid and bring to the boil, then simmer. Cream 1 oz fat with the egg, add the liver, season with salt, pepper, nutmeg, herbs, and add sufficient breadcrumbs to stiffen the mixture. Shape into balls, roll in flour or breadcrumbs, and place these with the cabbage, and cook for 30 minutes. Dish up the liver dumplings to form a border. Cook the cabbage so that there is just sufficient liquor left to form the gravy.*

Mrs C. S. Peel, *The Victory Cookery Book*

<u>Ingredients</u>
450g Savoy cabbage, finely sliced
100g fat (dripping, lard, butter or vegetable oil)
½ onion, finely chopped
Seasoning
Grated nutmeg
100g raw chopped beef, lamb, pork liver
1 free range or organic egg
200g dried breadcrumbs

Serves 4

1. Bring a pan of water to the boil and add the cabbage. Drain after a minute.
2. Melt 30g of the fat in a medium sized pan and add the onion. When it is glossy, add the drained cabbage and cook gently until soft, seasoning with salt, pepper and nutmeg. Add a little water if it catches on the bottom of the pan.
3. For the dumplings, in a bowl mix 30g of fat with the chopped liver, egg, 150g of breadcrumbs and seasoning.
4. Shape the dumpling mixture into 12 balls.
5. Put the remaining breadcrumbs on a plate and roll the balls in them.
6. Heat the remaining fat in a frying pan and fry the balls until crisp.
7. Once the cabbage and onion are cooked, season to taste and serve with the crisp liver balls on top.

### *Oatmeal Sausages*
In the absence of meat, these are a substantial replacement which would fill the hunger gap.
  In the words of Granny Dot:

*Materials.– ½ oz. fat. 2 oz. chopped onion, 1 or 2 oz. chopped suet, ½ pint of water, 1 gill vegetable gravy, 2 oz. medium oatmeal, 2oz. fine oatmeal, salt, pepper and spice.*

*Method.– Fry the onion and fat together, add the suet, water and vegetable gravy. Boil; then add the medium and fine oatmeal mixed. Stir over the fire for 15 minutes, season with salt, pepper and spice, and, when cooked and stiff, turn out to cool. Shape as required, coat and crumb, and fry or bake.*

Mrs C.S. Peel, The Victory Cookery Book

Ingredients
20g fat, but fat for frying (beef dripping, butter, lard or vegetable oil)
1 medium onion, finely chopped
25g shredded suet
140ml vegetable stock
300ml water
55g oatmeal
55g fine oatmeal
Seasoning
½ tsp mixed spice or ¼ tsp ground mace
50g plain flour
1 free range or organic egg
Dried breadcrumbs

Makes 6 sausages

1. Preheat the oven to 190°C/Gas Mark 5 if using the oven method in step 7.
2. Melt the fat in a pan and cook the onion over a medium/low heat until glossy.
3. Add the suet and liquids, followed by the oatmeals, seasoning and spice.
Simmer and stir until the mixture thickens considerably.
4. Leave the mixture to cool and then shape into sausages.
5. Put the flour, beaten egg and breadcrumbs on separate plates.
6. Roll each sausage in the flour, egg and then coat in the breadcrumbs.
7. Either fry in fat or brush with melted fat and bake in the oven for 10 minutes or until lightly browned.

### Savoury Oatmeal Pudding
This is a bulky dish, the aim of which was to fill the hunger gap when there was little else available.
    In the words of Granny Dot:

*Materials. – 5 oz. flour, 4 oz. medium oatmeal, 3 oz. suet (chopped) or shredded Atora, one tablespoonful chopped parsley, one dessertspoonful mixed herbs, salt, pepper, stock or vegetable stock or gravy to moisten it with, about one gill, one tablespoonful baking powder.*

*Method.- Mix the flour, oatmeal, suet, parsley, herbs, and seasoning in a basin, moisten with the stock and mix well, put into a well-greased basin, covered with a floured-scalded cloth, and boil two hours, or better still, cover with a greased paper and steam three hours. It can be eaten cut in slices and put round a stew, or can be eaten without meat served with a good brown sauce.*

Mrs C.S. Peel, *The Eat Less Meat Book*

<u>Ingredients</u>
Butter for the pudding basin
140g plain flour
1 tbsp baking powder
110g medium oatmeal
85g suet
1 tbsp chopped parsley, thyme, marjoram or mixed herbs
140ml of gravy or stock
Seasoning

You will need a 1 litre pudding basin
Serves 6-8

1. Butter the pudding basin.
2. Mix the ingredients together and place in the basin.
3. Place a layer of baking paper and a layer of foil (foil on top) on a worktop surface and fold a pleat into the centre to give room for the pudding to rise a little.
4. Place this on top of the basin and tie string around the edge tightly to secure it, folding a length of string across the centre and looping it under the opposite side to form a handle for lifting. Cut around the edges of the paper to form a circle and tuck the foil under the edges of the baking paper.
5. Now place the pudding in a pan of simmering water for 2 hours, ensuring the water is kept topped up to ¾ way up the basin.
6. Carefully remove the pudding basin from the water. Cut the string and remove the foil/paper. Loosen the sides of the pudding with a spatula. Put a serving plate on top of the basin and turn it over to unmould.
Serve

**Rabbit**
In the *Victory Cookery Book,* one rabbit produces five dishes, each dish for two people. These recipes are a lesson in economy with the bones being used for soup and any scraps of meat left on them added to rissoles. Culinary fashion at this time often involved white sauce where we may add a jus or gravy and some herbs.

***Fillets of Rabbit with White Sauce en Casserole***
Provided you cook the fillets for about 2 minutes on each side they should be tender.
    In the words of Granny Dot:

*Materials.– Fillets of rabbit (2), some white sauce, vegetables and potatoes, pepper and salt.*

150

*Method.– Cut the fillets from the back, flatten slightly, season with salt, a pinch of pepper, and brush over the fat. Place in a casserole, cover it, and cook the fillets on both sides without colouring, which will take about 5 minutes. Dish up, cover with sauce, and garnish with vegetables and potatoes.The above may be egged, crumbed and fried, or grilled and served with salad.*

Mrs C.S. Peel, *The Victory Cookery Book*

Ingredients
2 tbsp plain flour
1 free range or organic egg, beaten
4 tbsp dried breadcrumbs
2 back fillets of rabbit, flattened slightly by bashing lightly with a rolling pin
25g butter or lard
Seasoning

Serves 2

1. Put the flour, egg and breadcrumbs on separate plates. Take the fillets and coat them in the flour, followed by the egg, then coat them in breadcrumbs.
2. Melt the fat in a frying pan. Fry the breaded fillets for 1½ minutes on each side.
3. Remove from the heat when the crumbs have browned and the fillets have cooked through. This does not take long and it can be tough so make sure you do not overcook it.
Serve with white sauce (see page 133) flavoured with anchovy essence or well seasoned.

### Quenelles of Rabbit (One Leg)

Three out of the five rabbit recipes from one rabbit were created for Sunday lunch when my husband was away watching the Saracens vs Falcons rugby in London, so my children had to taste-test with me. Out of the mouths of babes: this, they said, tasted of nothing, so if you make it, the addition of herbs is essential. The tomato sauce on page 197 goes well with it.

Here is Granny Dot's recipe:

*Materials.–1 leg of rabbit, ½ oz. fat, 2 oz. bread panada, rice, salt, pepper and nutmeg, white sauce.*

*Method. – Bone the leg and remove all the sinews. Chop the meat finely together with the fat and bread, season with salt, pepper and nutmeg. If a mortar is available, pound the meat till thoroughly blended with the other ingredients, or put three times through a mincer to save time. Form into the shape of quenelles. Simmer 10 to 15*

151

*minutes in boiling stock or salted water. Drain well. Serve on a bed of rice and pour a creamy sauce over.*

Mrs C.S. Peel, *The Victory Cookery Book*

Ingredients
1 leg of rabbit, boned
55g bread soaked in water
1 tbsp dried thyme
Seasoning
Nutmeg
750ml chicken or vegetable stock
White sauce (see page 133)

Serves 2

1. Whizz all of the above except stock and white sauce in the blender.
2. Take two spoons and form the mixture into quenelles (neat oval shapes)
3. In a pan, simmer the stock and add the quenelles.
4. Simmer for 10 minutes.
5. Drain and serve on rice with seasoned white sauce.

### Cutlets of Rabbit (Second Leg)

The ingredients for this recipe are the same as the quenelle recipe but so different insofar as almost anything dipped in egg and fried in breadcrumbs is delicious. I added dried marjoram and would happily eat this again. My taste-testers (children aged 5 and 6) concluded that of the three rabbit dishes we were trying, this is 'definitely the best'.

Granny Dot's version:

*Materials.– Same ingredients as for quenelles, puree of peas as garnish, gravy or tomato sauce.*

*Method.– Prepare the same as for quenelles. Shape like cutlets; egg, crumb and fry;*

Mrs C.S. Peel, *The Victory Cookery Book*

Ingredients
1 leg of rabbit (boned)
55g bread soaked in water
Seasoning
Nutmeg
1 tbsp dried marjoram or thyme

1 free range or organic egg, beaten
120g dried breadcrumbs
50g fat (dripping, lard, butter or oil)
White sauce (see page 133)

Serves 2

1. Whizz the first 5 ingredients in a blender.
2. Form into cutlet shapes.
3. Beat some egg on a plate and put the breadcrumbs on another. Coat the cutlet shapes in beaten egg and then coat in breadcrumbs.
4. Leave in the fridge to firm up.
5. Heat the fat in a pan and fry the cutlet shapes until they are brown.
Serve with tomato sauce or gravy.

### Stewed Rabbit

This is similar to the *Mock Venison Hash* recipe on page 122. The necessity that fuel be saved for the war effort is seen in Granny Dot's comment below on the use of one casserole in this recipe and the consequent need for less hot water:

*Materials.– 2 shoulders of rabbit, 2 pieces of back (near the neck), 1 oz. of fat, a little corn flour, salt and pepper, a few potatoes, 1 small onion, stock.*

*Method.– Fry the pieces of rabbit lightly in the fat and season with salt and pepper. When browned, add a few potatoes cut into dice, and the onion. Fry all together carefully. If the rabbit is done before the vegetables, remove it and cook the vegetables longer. When done, dish up the rabbit and garnish it with vegetables. Rinse the pan out with stock, cook till all gravy is dissolved, thicken slightly with corn flour mixed smooth with a little water and brought to the boil. Add this to the boiling stock and stir together until clear. Pour over the rabbit. This dish may be, like so many others, cooked and served in the one casserole to save washing-up.*

Mrs C.S. Peel, *The Victory Cookery Book*

Ingredients
55g fat (dripping, lard, butter or oil)
1 small onion finely chopped
2 medium potatoes, diced
2 shoulders of rabbit, plus any leftover, cut into bite-size pieces
Gravy or another accompanying sauce

Serves 2

1. Bring the fat to a sizzle in a frying pan.
2. Add the onion and potato; cook for five minutes or so.
3. Add the rabbit and when cooked through, serve with a sauce.

### *Rabbit Soup*

So thorough was the use of every part during the First World War rationing period that scraps were taken from the bones used for the soup. When making this soup, I took 75g of meat from the bones of one rabbit after it had already been stripped of its meat for the first three rabbit recipes. This meat went into the Stewed Rabbit. This was impressive for meat which may otherwise have ended in the bin.

This soup did not taste of much. However, if you made it with less liquid added, perhaps it would be better, or with a wild rabbit which would have a stronger more gamey flavour.

Granny Dot's recipe:

*Materials.– Rabbit bones, 1 onion, 2 oz. raw rice, salt, 3 pints water, 1 teaspoonful curry powder, ¼ oz. cornflour.*

*Method.– To make the bones into stock, fry them with the onion and curry powder and cover with the water. Add rice and salt and cook until the rice is tender. To do this well takes one hour. Strain the liquid into a basin and remove all the bones with the meat. Crush the rice through a sieve or mincer, return to the soup, correct the seasoning, and thicken slightly with corn flour.*

Mrs C.S. Peel, *The Victory Cookery Book*

Ingredients
1 tbsp fat (dripping, lard, butter or oil)
1 onion finely chopped
1 tsp curry powder
50g rice
Bones of 1 rabbit
500ml of water, game, chicken or vegetable stock

Serves 2

1. In a pan fry the onion in the fat until glossy.
2. Stir in the curry powder for a minute before adding the rice and stirring again.
3. Add the bones and fry until pale brown.
4. Pour the liquid into the pan and simmer for an hour.
5. Remove the bones.
6. Blend the soup, season and serve.

## VEGETABLES

### *The Conservative Method of Cooking Vegetables*
*Vegetables contain minerals or salt which are necessary to health. For this purpose all vegetables should be cut into small portions and placed in a clean saucepan. Water may be added, but not more than will evaporate during the process of cooking, and a little fat of some kind is added – say half an ounce for every pound of vegetables. Vegetables can be blended with rice or other cereal by adding this to the vegetables, with as much liquid as the cereal will absorb. In this way many appetising dishes can be prepared in one saucepan; meat or fish may be added if required.*

Mrs C.S. Peel, *The Victory Cookery Book*

### *Potted Beans*
This is referred as an emergency food. It is very good provided hot water is used, and paprika. Without the butter it is like hummus, though I think better.

In the words of Granny Dot:

*Method. – Soak the beans from the previous day, then cook slowly til quite tender. Beat them through a sieve with the cheese and onion. Add the other ingredients. Stir vigorously over the fire for a few moments, then pound in a mortar or basin til perfectly smooth. Pot tightly and pour melted margarine over the top. As an emergency food potted haricots are invaluable and will keep ten days if stood in a cool place.*

Mrs C.S. Peel, *Eat Less Meat Book*

Ingredients
110g cooked haricot beans
25g grated cheese
15g chopped onion
25g fresh breadcrumbs
Seasoning to taste
Paprika (optional)
50g butter

Serves 2

1. Blend or mash the beans, cheese and onion together, with a little hot water to moisten.
2. Stir in the breadcrumbs and once blended, transfer to a saucepan and heat through, stirring constantly.
3. Add seasoning and the paprika.

4. Put the mixture into a ramekin.

5. Melt the butter, let it settle for a few moments and then pour the clarified butter which has risen to the surface on top of the bean pâté.

Serve with toast.

### *Jerusalem Artichoke Soup*

With some minor alternation, this is my favourite soup in the world, so far.

In the words of Granny Dot:

*Materials.– 2lb. Jerusalem artichokes, three pints of any white stock, one gill milk or cream, salt, pepper, 1oz. margarine.*

*Method.– Wash and peel the artichokes, put into a pan with the stock, bring to the boil, skim, and simmer till soft. Rub through a sieve, return to the saucepan, add the milk, and bring to the boil, stirring all the time, add the margarine bit by bit, stirring well, season, and serve. If rice or macaroni stocks are too thick a little water can be added to them before using.*

Mrs C.S. Peel, *The Eat Less Meat Book*

Ingredients
Half an onion, chopped
30g butter
30ml olive oil
600g Jerusalem Artichokes, peeled and sliced
600ml chicken stock (homemade if poss) or vegetable stock
80ml single cream (a little at a time, according to taste)
Salt
Chives, chopped

Serves 4

1. In a casserole fry the onion in the melted butter and olive oil until glossy.
2. Add the artichokes and coat in the oil.
3. Add the stock and simmer for about half an hour until completely mushily tender.
4. Whizz in the blender and pass through a sieve.
5. Add the cream and season to taste.
6. Garnish with chives and a little truffle oil if you have any.
This is really good with sourdough bread.

### *Mulligatawny Soup*

This soup is a lovely surprise, reminding me of the first curries I had in the mid 1980s, using curry powder as opposed to the more exotic mixes now widely available. My mother used to make prawn curry for Granny Dot's grandson, my grandfather, every time he came to stay because he loved to be reminded of his time with the Indian troops during World War Two. Though delicious, I am not sure it was comparable!

Here is Granny Dot's recipe:

*Materials.– 4 oz. shredded onion, 1 oz. fat, ½ oz. curry powder, 2 oz. rice, 1 oz. chopped chutney, ¼ oz. salt, 1 or 2 tomatoes, 1 small sour apple, bunch of aromatic herbs, half a lemon, 3 or 4 crushed cardamom seeds, 1 quart of water or stock, 1 teaspoonful of corn flour, 1 tablespoonful cooked rice for garnish.*

*Method. – Fry the onion with the fat, and as soon as the onion begins to cook add the curry powder and fry together. Cover with the water or stock, add the rice, chutney, tomatoes, the apple cut finely, cardamom seeds, herbs and salt. Cook for 30 to 40 minutes. Drain off the liquid, pass the drained material through a mincer, return to the liquid and thicken with the corn flour. Taste and correct the seasoning, and garnish with cooked rice.*

Mrs C.S. Peel, *The Eat Less Meat Book*

Ingredients
50g fat (butter, dripping, lard or oil)
2 chopped onions
1½ tbsp curry powder
60g rice
90g chutney (at least 25g of this being mango chutney)
2 medium tomatoes, diced
1 small Granny Smith apple
Juice of half a lemon
3 or 4 crushed cardamom seeds
½ tsp salt
8 curry leaves (optional)
1.2 litres water
¼ stick of cinnamon

Serves 4

1. Fry the onion in the fat until glossy.
2. Add the curry powder and cook, stirring now and then for 1 minute.

3. Stir the rice into the mixture before adding the remaining ingredients.
4. Simmer until the apple is very tender and the rice is soft.
5. Remove the cinnamon stick, blend and return to the pan.
6. Re-heat and season to taste with salt and additional chutney if necessary.
Serve as it is or with rice and a squeeze of lime.

### Stewed Cabbage and Rice

This is exactly what I imagined rationing cooking would involve. It tastes good and could be eaten as a meal or served as an accompaniment. At a rationing dinner hosted at Sutton Waldron Village Hall, Dot Swift, who cooked this, added a little curry powder. It was delicious.

Here is Granny Dot's recipe:

*Materials.– 1 oz. fat. 2 oz. shredded onion, 1 lb shredded cabbage, 1 gill water, 1 gill raw rice, pinch of salt and pepper.*

*Method.– Heat the fat, add the onion, and 'sweat' together until the onion is half cooked, then add the cabbage and water, also a pinch of salt. Cover the saucepan and place on a gentle heat, and simmer until the cabbage is nearly tender. Add the rice, stirring with a fork to mix the rice and cabbage well, and cover with sufficient water to be just level with the cabbage surface – about 1 gill. Correct the seasoning by tasting, adding sufficient salt and pepper. Cover the saucepan with a cloth and the lid. This is done to prevent any undue evaporation. Cook for 20 minutes, taking care that the heat is very gentle so that the contents cannot burn. After that time the whole will be cooked. Serve as a vegetable or in place of meat.*

Mrs C.S. Peel, *The Victory Cookery Book*

Ingredients
30g butter
½ onion, finely sliced onion
450g Savoy cabbage, finely sliced
140g rice
Seasoning

Serves 6 as an accompaniment

1. Melt the butter in a casserole, add the onion and cook, stirring now and then for five minutes.
2. Add the cabbage and some seasoning and stir occasionally. When it is tender, add the rice and enough water to just cover the ingredients.

158

3. Place a tea towel under the lid and let the mixture cook over a low-medium heat for about 20 minutes or until the rice is cooked
Set aside until you are ready to eat.


## BAKING USING SUBSTITUTES
*Almost all sweets and pastry require two of the most restricted articles of food – fat and sugar, and others which are scarce and dear.*
Mrs C.S. Peel, The Victory Cookery Book


Puddings were deemed a luxury, reserved for children. Alcohol was used in part substitute of fat, a little fat always being necessary. In place of flour, potato may be used whether in the form of potato flour or mashed potato. Vegetables such as beetroot, carrot and parsnip were also used in substitute, and honey in place of sugar.


### *Pastry*
*When using but little fat, rice flour and corn flour help to shorten the pastry. It will be seen, therefore, that it is yet possible to supply sweets and pastries by combining various substances such as are still available, especially in the preparing of nursery meals, where the protein and starchy foods are of primary importance.*
Mrs C.S. Peel, The Victory Cookery Book


Various pastry alternatives are given in *The Victory Cookery Book* containing substitutes of mashed potato, tapioca, rice flour, polenta, cooked rice and even haricot beans. When a sweet filling was available these would be used to create pastry where flour was scarce. Puddings were created during the war using ingredients which were available to help ease the burden on the housewife.


### Potatoes, Maize and Leftover Bread
*Fortunately we can often make use of potatoes in pastry, scones and buns, and then a little white of egg helps to give them the required body. Without this addition they are usually doughy, especially when a large amount of potato is used.*
Mrs C.S. Peel, The Victory Cookery Book


### *Potato Gateau*
This recipe is unaltered. There is not a huge amount I could think of doing other than replace the mashed potato completely, though grated potato may be an improvement! The texture is unlike any I have had in a sweet dish before. It is certainly different.

In the words of Granny Dot:

*Materials.- 4 oz. dry mashed potato, 1 oz. fat, 1 oz. sugar, 1 gill of milk, 1 beaten egg, flavouring to taste, 1 oz. corn flour or other starch, 1 tablespoonful of jam, some pie crust.*

*Method.- Line a greased sandwich tin with pie crust. Mix the potato, fat, sugar, milk, egg, flavouring and corn flour together. Line the crust with the jam and pour the potato mixture in the centre and spread out level. Bake in a moderate oven for 20 minutes.*

*The whole can be covered with paste or with strips of paste in trellis fashion, according to taste.*

Mrs C.S. Peel, *The Victory Cookery Book*

Ingredients
Pastry case, using egg turnover short paste on p.126
Half a pot of jam
450g mashed potato (I made mine using cream, and butter, enough to be of dropping consistency)
110g cornflour
4 free range or organic eggs
110g caster sugar
2 tsp vanilla essence

You will need a 24cm diameter tin.
Serves 10

1. Preheat the oven to 180°C/Gas Mark 4.
2. Line the tin with the pastry, reserving some for an optional lattice top.
3. Spread the jam into the pastry case.
4. Thoroughly mix the remaining ingredients and put them in the case on top of the jam. Do some lattice covering if you like.
5. Bake for 25–30 minutes.
Serve with cream or ice cream.

### Potato Pancakes with Bacon
It is suggested that the following recipe for potato and bacon pancakes may have syrup added to it for a sweet alternative. I have not found this recipe in Dorothy's books before the war and so think suggestions were made in order to allow one dish to satisfy both sweet and savoury appetites. This is similar to American pancakes with maple syrup.
Here is Granny Dot's recipe:

*Materials.- 1 lb. raw potatoes, 4 oz. bacon, 1 egg, juice of half a lemon, ½ lb. self-raising flour, salt, pepper and nutmeg.*

*Method.- Place the lemon juice in a basin, and grate the potatoes into it. Add the egg, salt, pepper and a little nutmeg, and when mixed, add the flour. First fry the bacon, then use the bacon fat to fry the pancakes. This quantity will make about 12 small pancakes. The potato pancake can also be served with sweet syrup, in which case leave out the pepper and nutmeg. With minced meat, cooked ham or cheese folded inside they make a good breakfast dish.*

Mrs C. S. Peel, *The Victory Cookery Book*

Ingredients
225g grated potato
1 tbsp lemon juice
a pinch of salt
Nutmeg (a few shavings)
1 free range or organic egg
110g self raising flour, sifted
12 rashers of Bacon
Butter for frying
Maple Syrup

Makes 6 pancakes – these are filling so one per person is probably enough.

1. Combine the first 5 ingredients together in a bowl.
2. Add the flour and mix.
3. Fry the bacon in a frying pan and when cooked remove on to a warm plate. Using a biscuit cutter, about 7cm in diameter, put some of the potato mixture into the hot pan, adding butter if necessary.
4. Remove the pastry cutter leaving the potato pancake in the pan while you fit however many more you have room for alongside.
5. Cook through over a medium high heat for about five minutes. Because the potato is raw, it does need cooking. It should be slightly crisp to bite in to.
Serve with the bacon and maple syrup.

### *Potato Scones*
This denser version of scones would be satisfying with some jam and butter or cream.

Here is Granny Dot's recipe:

*Materials.- ½ lb. dry mashed potatoes, 4 oz. rice flour, a pinch of sugar (not essential), 1 beaten white of egg, 4 oz. flour, ½ oz. baking powder.*

Potato Scones (*emmafarquharphotography*)

*Method.- Mix the potato, rice-flour, and sugar together, and allow to rest for a few hours, then add the beaten white of egg (or half a dry egg), flour and baking powder. Mix lightly into a soft dough, shape into balls the size required, place on a floured board and press flat with the lid of a cocoa tin to form a round. Let rest for 10 to 15 minutes, then place on a girdle or frying-pan, and bake on the hot-plate or in the oven.*

Mrs C.S. Peel, *The Victory Cookery Book*

Ingredients
225g mashed potatoes
110g rice flour
½ tsp sugar
1 free range or organic egg white
110g plain flour
1 tbsp baking powder
Full fat milk

Makes 10-12

1. Mix the potato and rice flour in a bowl. Cover and set aside for an hour or so.
2. Add the remaining ingredients to the bowl, adding a little milk if necessary for binding the mixture.
3. Form the mixture into scones 1.5 cm high.
4. Place on a hot griddle or frying pan and cook for a couple of minutes on each side.
Serve warm with butter or cream and jam.

### *Potato Shortbread*
These are significantly dense in comparison with traditional shortbread, but at the same time, would fill a hunger gap quite satisfyingly.

*Materials.- ½ lb. mashed potato, 6 oz. rice flour, 2 oz. fat, a pinch of salt, 2 oz. sugar, 2 oz. self-raising flour.*

*Method. – Work the mashed potato warm with the fat and sugar and salt, then add the rice flour, last of all the self-raising flour, or flour and baking powder. Roll out on a floured board, but to shapes desired, and bake to a very light fawn colour.*
Mrs C.S. Peel, *The Victory Cookery Book*

Ingredients
225g mashed potato
85g rice flour
55g self raising flour
55g caster sugar
55g fat
Pinch of salt
Full fat milk if necessary
Caster sugar for sprinkling

Makes 12 biscuits

1. Mix together all of the ingredients apart from the caster sugar for sprinkling, adding a little milk to moisten if necessary.
2. Form the mixture into a cylindrical shape and wrap in cling film. Place in the fridge for half an hour or so to firm up.
3. Preheat the oven to 180°C/Gas Mark 4.
4. Remove the cylinder from the fridge and slice into 1cm thick biscuits.
5. Place on a non stick baking tray and with a fork, prick holes in each biscuit.
6. Sprinkle with caster sugar.

7. Bake in the oven for 15 minutes or until cooked through.
8. Remove the baking tray from the oven and leave the biscuits for 5 minutes and then transfer them onto a cooling rack.
Serve with tea.

### Potato and Cheese Pudding

This is like a cheese scone with cheese sauce. While my children refused to eat it (I think they had had enough of a rationing frenzy!) their two friends asked for seconds.
   In the words of Granny Dot:

*Materials.- 8 oz. mashed potato, 2 oz. grated cheese, a little chopped onion, salt, pepper or cayenne and nutmeg, 1 beaten egg, 1 oz. fat, 8 oz. self-raising flour, white sauce.*

*Method.- Mix all the ingredients together, fill in a greased basin and steam for 2 hours. Serve the pudding with white sauce, to which add a little grated cheese.*

Mrs C.S. Peel, *The Victory Cookery Book*

Ingredients
30g butter, plus extra for the basin
225g mashed potato
225g self raising flour
2 tbsp finely chopped onion
1 free range or organic egg, beaten
White sauce with 80g cheddar cheese added (see page 133)

You will need a 600ml pudding basin
Serves 6

1. Butter the pudding basin.
2. Mix all of the ingredients together except the white sauce and transfer them into the basin.
3. Take a double layer of baking paper with a layer of foil on top of it. Fold the centre so that there is a pleat which will allow for expansion of the pudding. Place over the pudding basin.
4. Tie a string tightly around the edge of the basin with a tight knot, and then loop the string from one side of the basin to the other where you will loop it under the surrounding string to form a handle. Tuck the foil under the round of baking paper.
5. Place the pudding in simmering water ¾ way up the basin for 2 hours, topping the water up so that it does not dry out.

164

6. Carefully remove the pudding basin from the water. Cut the string and remove the foil/paper. Loosen the sides of the pudding with a spatula. Put a serving plate on top of the basin and turn it over to unmould.
Serve with cheesy white sauce.

### Potato Lemon Pudding

Having made an awful lot of mashed potato in testing other rationing recipes, using baked potatoes was somehow a relief! This pudding is very edible, the lemon zest adding a great deal of flavour. I served it with the rationing *Custard Sauce* on page 124.

In the words of Granny Dot:

*Materials.- 1 lb. baked potatoes, 2 oz. sugar or syrup, the grated rind of a lemon, 2 dried eggs, 4 oz. prepared flour, 1 gill of milk, custard sauce.*

*Method. – Take the pulp of the potatoes, mix with the other ingredients. Grease a pudding basin, fill in the mixture and steam for at least 2 hours. Serve with custard sauce.*

Mrs C.S. Peel, *The Victory Cookery Book*

Ingredients
Fat for greasing the basin
450g of baking potatoes
60g caster sugar or syrup
Grated zest of 1 unwaxed lemon
10g dried egg
110g plain flour
140ml full fat milk

You will need a 600ml pudding basin
Serves 6-8

1. Bake the potatoes and remove their insides.
2. Mix the potato insides with the remaining ingredients in a bowl.
3. Transfer the mixture into the pudding basin. Cover with a double layer of baking paper and foil, pleated, and secured with string tied tightly around the edge of the basin with a knot. Take the string from one side of the basin to the other and loop it with the surrounding string to form a handle. Tuck the foil under the baking paper.
4. Place in a heavy-based saucepan. Pour in boiling water ¾ way up the basin and simmer for 2 hours, keeping the water topped up.

5. Carefully remove the pudding basin from the water. Cut the string and remove the foil/paper. Loosen the sides of the pudding with a spatula. Put a serving plate on top of the basin and turn it over to unmould.
Serve with custard or cream.

### Ginger Nuts
This is an unusual recipe containing mashed potato and beetroot. Changing the recipe completely would defeat its purpose, so here it is unadulterated.

*Materials. – 8 oz. dry mashed potato, 1 oz. syrup, 4 oz rice flour, 4 oz. self-raising flour, 4 oz. chopped beetroot, 1 teaspoonful ginger (heaped), 1 gill of water or milk.*

*Method. – Mix all the ingredients together, dissolve the syrup in the moisture, add a pinch of salt. Roll on the pastry-board to form a roll, flatten slightly and cut into slices ½ inch thick. Bake on a greased baking-sheet for 15 to 20 minutes. When half baked, turn over and finish cooking.*

Mrs C.S. Peel, *The Victory Cookery Book*

Ginger Nuts (*emmafarquharphotography*)

Ingredients
225g mashed potato
1 tbsp golden syrup
110g rice flour
110g self raising flour
110g chopped beetroot
1 tsp ginger
140ml water

Makes 22

1. Preheat the oven to 180°C/Gas Mark 4.
2. Mix all of the ingredients together, adding the water slowly as you may need more or less, dependent upon the consistency of the mashed potato.
3. Flour a worktop and roll out the pastry. Cut it into biscuit sized rounds.
4. Place on a baking tray and bake for fifteen minutes or until firm.
5. Remove from the oven and place the biscuits on a cooling rack.
Serve with tea.

### *Potato and Jam Rings*

My children loved these. I then took them to dinner with friends who concluded that in the absence of choice these would satisfy the gap.

Here is Granny Dot's recipe:

*Materials.- 2 oz syrup, ½ lb. potato puree, ½ oz. fat, 1 teaspoonful baking powder, 1 dried egg, ¼ lb. rice flour, 1/ lb. standard flour, jam for filling.*

*Method. – Mix the syrup, potato puree, fat and egg together, beating as lightly as possible. Add the rice flour, standard flour and baking powder. Fill in a forcing-bag with star or rose tube and force out on to a baking-sheet, greased and dusted with flour, to form rings. Bake in a moderate oven. When baked, fill the centre with jam.*
Mrs C.S. Peel, *The Victory Cookery Book*

Ingredients
55g golden syrup
225g mashed potato
1 tbsp butter, lard or beef dripping
1tsp baking powder
1 free range or organic egg
110g rice flour

Potato and Jam Rings (*emmafarquharphotography*)

450g plain flour
120ml full fat milk
A jar of jam
Makes 25-30

1. Preheat the oven to 180°C/Gas Mark 4.
2. Mix all of the ingredients except the milk and jam, together in a mixing bowl.
3. Add milk gradually, so that when you hold a spoonful of the mixture above the bowl, it easily drops.
4. Either use a strong piping bag with a centimetre nozzle or your hands, wetted with water, to form 7cm lengths of the mixture.
5. Lay the lengths on a non-stick baking sheet and join the ends together into circles.
6. Bake in the oven for 15 to 20 minutes.
7. As soon as you remove the biscuits from the oven, add a teaspoonful of jam to the middle.
8. Leave them to cool for 5 minutes before carefully placing them on a cooling rack.
Serve with tea.

**Potato Buns**

The texture of these buns is slightly chewy; the benefit of this is that they do not fall apart, yet remain light.

*Materials.– ½ lb. mashed potato, 4 oz. rice flour, ½ lb ordinary yeast dough, ½ oz. sugar, a little spice, 1 oz. liquid fat, fruit or beetroot chips (a handful of raisins).*

*Method.– Mix the potato with the rice flour and let this rest for two hours or more. A natural ferment will change part of the starch into sugar, and the paste will be quite sweet after that time. To the bread dough add the prepared mixture, spice, sugar and liquid fat or oil, fruit or beetroot chips. Shape into buns, place on greased tins dusted with flour, cover and let fully prove, then bake in a hot oven for 15 to 20 minutes.*

Mrs C.S. Peel, *The Victory Cookery Book*

Ingredients
For the Dough
150g Strong white bread flour
¼ tsp salt
1tsp of yeast
100ml tepid water

For the Bun
110g rice flour
225g mashed potato
15g caster sugar
½ tsp mixed spice
30g melted lard or butter
225g yeast dough above
A handful of raisins or other dried fruit

Serves 8

1. Start by making the dough. Combine the dry ingredients together in a bowl and gradually add the water, mixing with a knife.
2. When enough water has been added so that the dough is not sticky, sprinkle a little flour on a clean dry surface and put the mixture onto that. Knead it for ten minutes, using the heel of your hand until the dough is smooth.
Alternatively knead with a machine using a dough hook for 5 minutes.
Leave the dough to rise in the bowl, covered with a tea towel for 1 hour.
3. For the bun, mix the rice flour with the mashed potato, sugar, spice and fat. Set aside while the dough rises.

4. Weigh 225g of the dough and mix it with the ingredients in the bowl.
5. Form into buns and set well spaced on a baking tray dusted with flour.
6. Leave the buns for half an hour to prove.
7. Preheat the oven to 200°C/Gas Mark 6.
8. Bake for 10 minutes or until when you tap the bottom of the buns they sound hollow.
9. Place the buns on a cooling rack.
Serve with butter or cream and jam.

### Potato Cheese
When hot, this is delicious; less so when cold. As part of a cheese toasty, this would be a satisfactory replacement.
    Granny Dot's recipe:

*Materials. – 1 lb. mashed potato, 2 oz. fat, 2 oz. rinds of cheese grated finely or chopped, 1 oz. salt, cayenne (as much as will lie on a sixpence), 1 gill of milk, 4 oz. potato flour, 1 oz. milk powder, 1 teaspoonful of mustard, colouring.*

*Method. – Work all the ingredients well together, place over the fire and stir until boiling hot. Place in a muslin in a basin with a saucer or small plate on top. When cold, take out of the basin and keep for one week before use. This will cut like cheddar cheese. Crushed with a fork and with a little white sauce added, it forms a creamy mixture which makes excellent rarebits when spread on polenta or toast and baked until just browned in a fairly hot oven or under the gas grill.*
Mrs C.S. Peel, The Victory Cookery Book

Ingredients
50g butter, lard or beef dripping
225g mashed potato
25g grated cheese rind (I used Parmesan)
1 tbsp salt
30ml full fat milk or more to loosen the mixture
½ tsp English mustard or mustard powder

You will need a 300ml pudding basin and a muslin or cheese cloth.

1. Melt the fat in a pan.
2. Add the remaining ingredients and mix into a paste over the heat. Milk can be added so that the mixture is not too stiff.
3. Line the pudding basin with muslin and push the mixture into it.

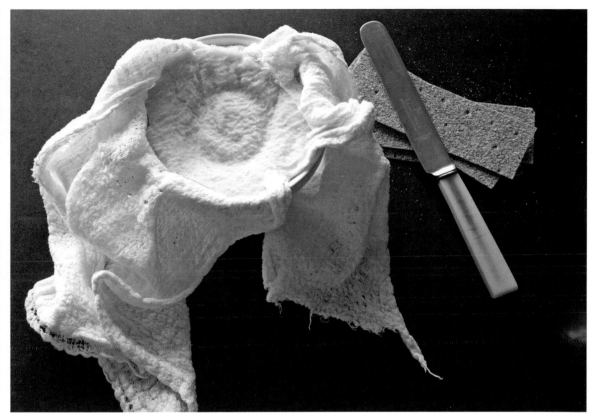

Potato Cheese (*emmafarquharphotography*)

4. Let it cool and keep in the fridge or larder for two or more days so that the flavour develops.

5. Slice the potato cheese and bake it as you would for a toasted cheese sandwich.

### *Maize and Potato Bread*
*A bread of which one cannot eat much*

I think the reason Granny Dot says this is that it is so filling. It tastes fine, and may not have received too many complaints without an alternative.

In the words of Granny Dot:

*Materials. – 1 lb. potatoes, ½ oz. salt, ½ lb. maize semolina, 1 ½ lb. flour, 1 oz. yeast, 4 oz. rice flour.*

*Method. – Boil the potatoes and ½ oz. of salt in water. When done, drain (reserve the water) and mash. Return the potato to the liquid, which should be 1 pint. Boil again, and add the maize, cooking until all moisture has been absorbed. Place in a*

171

Maize and Potato Bread (*emmafarquharphotography*)

*tin or double cooker and steam for 1 hour. Prepare a bread dough with the flour, yeast and ½ oz. salt. When the maize is cooked, turn out and allow to cool until just tepid, then mix with the bread dough. Shape into loaves, and place in greased bread tins using the rice flour in the shaping. This will give 4½ lb. of bread, which will keep well and is very satisfying.*

Mrs C.S. Peel, *The Victory Cookery Book*

Ingredients
225g cooked floury potatoes with water reserved
1 tsp salt
110g polenta
350g plain flour
7g sachet yeast
110g rice flour
300ml water

You will need a loaf tin.
Serves 10-12

1. Measure the reserved potato cooking liquid and add water until it measures 600ml.
2. Put the liquid in a pan with the salt and bring it to a simmer. Add the polenta, pouring it through your fingers and whisk the mixture until the liquid has been absorbed.
3. Spread the polenta on a board or dish to cool.
4. In a bowl mix the flour and yeast with the water. Turn it out on to a clean worktop and knead until it is smooth and elastic.
Alternatively knead the dough in machine with a dough hook for 5 minutes.
Leave the dough to rise in the bowl, covered with a tea towel for 1½ - 2 hours.
5. Knead the polenta with the potatoes dough and rice flour.
6. Put the mixture in an oiled bread tin and leave to rise for an hour.
7. Preheat the oven to 200°C/Gas Mark 6.
8. Bake the loaf for 30 minutes.
9. Turn out onto a cooling rack.
Serve

### *Maize Batter Pudding*

Maize/Polenta was associated with animal feed and so adding it to recipes was met with reluctance by some. If you use a good non-fast action type of polenta the pudding will have a greater texture which adds to the pleasure of eating it. In the words Granny Dot:

*Materials.– 2oz. maize meal, ½ pint water, 3 oz. rice flour, 2 oz. suet, half teaspoonful baking powder, 1 egg, 1 gill of milk, 1 oz. sugar, 1 oz coconut, flavouring.*

*Method.– Boil the water and suet, add the maize, and cook till the moisture is absorbed. Add sugar, milk, coco-nut and egg; work well. Mix the rice flour and baking powder together and add to the other ingredients. Grease a pudding basin, fill in the material and steam for 2 hours, or divided into four smaller shapes 1 hour would be enough. Serve with jam and custard.*

Mrs C.S. Peel, *The Victory Cookery Book*

Ingredients
Fat for greasing the basin
280ml boiling water
55g suet
55g polenta
85g rice flour
25g desiccated coconut

Maize Batter Pudding (*Author's own*)

pinch of salt
1 free range or organic egg, beaten
25g caster sugar
140ml full fat milk
½ tsp vanilla extract

You will need 600ml pudding basin
Serves 6

1. In a pan add the suet to the boiling water. Let the dry ingredients fall through your fingers into the water. Whisk vigorously so as to avoid lumps.
2. When the liquid has been absorbed, stir in the remaining ingredients.
3. Transfer the mixture to the greased pudding basin.
4. Take a sheet of baking paper and a sheet of foil (foil on top), folding a pleat in its centre which will allow the pudding to rise. Place it on top of the basin with the baking paper nearest the pudding. Secure it with string twice around the circumference of the basin and looped over the top to form a handle. Cut off the excess baking paper and tuck the foil under the baking paper. Place the basin in a pan of simmering water for 2 hours. Ensure that the water is ¾ way up the basin and is kept at that level throughout cooking.
5. Loosen the edges with a spatula, place a plate on top of the mould, turn it over; tap the top until the pudding falls.
Serve with jam.

### Bread and Jam Pudding

Before rationing was enforced in 1918, using up the scraps was already a necessity with the price of food having risen and submarine warfare reducing the amount of produce successfully arriving on our shores from primarily Canada and America.

So often many of us find stale bread in the bread bin and if we do not have chickens to throw it to, ducks on a pond nearby, or space in the freezer, it may end in the bin. Here we are reminded of what we can do by Granny Dot in the form of bread puddings:

> *Manage as carefully as one will it is difficult to prevent pieces of bread from accumulating in the bread-pan. These pieces, however, must be cherished, for they are the foundation of many excellent puddings...*
> *Bread and Jam Pudding. – Soak as before, flavour with grated lemon peel. Part fill a greased pie dish. Bake for a few minutes, cover with jam, and a layer of fine crumbs, and bake until brown and crisp.*
>
> Mrs C.S. Peel, *Learning to Cook*

175

<u>Ingredients</u>
Butter for the dish
85g white bread pieces, broken up
150ml full fat milk
Finely grated zest of a medium unwaxed lemon
1 tsp caster sugar
2 tbsp jam
3 tbsp dried breadcrumbs
Cream for serving

You will need a small ovenproof dish; I used a round 12cm diameter dish.

Serves 2

1. Preheat the oven to 200°C/Gas Mark 6.
2. Butter the dish.
3. Soak the bread in the milk and when the milk has been absorbed, mix in the lemon zest and sugar. This will satisfactorily break up the bread. You may need to add more milk depending upon the moisture content of the bread. Spoon the bread and milk mixture into the dish.
4. Dollop some jam on top of the mixture, spreading a little, but don't worry about this too much, just dot it around.
5. Sprinkle with the breadcrumbs (I keep a bag in the freezer and use them directly from it).
6. Bake the pudding for 12 minutes or until golden.
This is best eaten straight away and is even better with cream.

### *Lunch or Nursery Cake*

To complete the rationing recipes, I include my favourite. Every person who has tried it has said it is among the best cakes they have had. It is my father-in-law's favourite. Anna del Conte described this cake as 'perfection' – what better recommendation?

I admit to drastically altering the quantities of ingredients and adding Demerara sugar for a wonderful finish. The recipe comes from *Learning to Cook* which was published in 1915. 'Spiced Sultana Cake' is a better description than *Nursery* or *Lunch Cake.*

Here is Granny Dot's recipe:

*1 lb. of flour, one teaspoonful of baking powder, half a saltspoonful of salt, a quarter of a teaspoon of allspice or ground ginger, and 4 oz. of brown sugar.*

Lunch or Nursery Cake (*emmafarquharphotography*)

*Mix thoroughly, then rub in 4 oz. of brown sugar. Mix thoroughly, then rub in 4 oz. of clarified dripping or half margarine and half dripping, or all butter. Add 4 oz. of sultanas, and mix with half a pint of milk added gradually and mixed well. Bake in a greased tin in a moderate oven, increasing the heat a little after the first ten minutes. This recipe may be varied, adding currants and peel or using white sugar instead of brown, adding one or two beaten-up eggs, and substituting caraway seeds for fruit, but when eggs are used they should be stirred up with the milk and less milk used. In cake making use too little liquid rather than too much, for more may be added, whereas what is put in cannot be taken away. The dough should not be wet but fairly firm.*

Mrs C.S. Peel, *Learning to Cook*

Ingredients
150g unsalted butter, softened, plus extra for the tin
150g plain flour
120g caster sugar
1 tsp baking powder

1 tsp mixed spice
2 free range or organic eggs
100g sultanas
1 tbsp Demerara sugar

You will need a 20cm cake tin.
Serves 10

1. Preheat the oven to 190°C/Gas Mark 5.
2. Butter the cake tin and line with baking paper.
3. Mix all of the ingredients together except the Demerara sugar.
4. Put the mixture in the tin and sprinkle the Demerara sugar on top.
5. Bake for 25 minutes or until a skewer comes out clean.
6. Leave to cool in the tin for 5 minutes. Remove it and place on a wire rack to cool.
Serve when it is time for tea

CHAPTER 12

# Recipes Before and After the Great War

*When setting the table for a dinner party a tumbler is not required, but three or more wine glasses, according to the wines given – for example, one for sherry, one for hock, one for champagne, and one for claret.*

Mrs C.S. Peel, *How To Keep House*

Granny Dot's recipes amount to hundreds, if not thousands. Her writing was combined with an awareness of the need to ease the pressure of feeding a family on a limited budget. Rather than focusing on this, which could take up a separate book, the recipes which follow are among my favourites, both in interest and flavour and deserve to be brought back to life.

## RECIPES

*Very good food is expensive, just as very good clothes or motor-cars are expensive, and he who is not rich cannot have any of them. But if the cook knows her business, she can have simple and inexpensive dishes well cooked.*

Mrs C.S. Peel, *Learning to Cook*

## BREAKFAST

*Personally the British breakfast is a meal which I fail to appreciate. In a large and rich and leisured household it may be a pleasant repast, but in the average small home, where the cook-general reigns, it has few attractions. The Continental habit of partaking in coffee and rolls in the morning, of lunching well and early, and dining well and late, is cheaper and far more convenient in small houses, where all the hardest work must be done in the early morning. However, I am well aware that such ideas will not meet with general approval, so let us face our breakfast and make the best of it.*

Mrs C.S. Peel, *Learning to Cook*

179

***Sausage and Potato Rolls***
This is perfect for leftover mashed potato. Granny Dot puts this under the heading of Breakfast but it is equally good as a children's tea.

*Moderate oven or frying pan. Time, 20 minutes.*

*Materials.– Half a sausage for each person; potato pastry.*

*Method. – Skin the sausages, cut them in half, roll out some potato pastry, cut it into squares, lay a half sausage on each square, fold over. Press the edges together. Mark with the back of a knife, put on a greased baking sheet and bake in a moderate oven for 20 minutes, or until pale brown. If the oven is not in use the rolls can be cooked on a greased frying pan turning once. These can be prepared the day before, and baked or cooked in a frying pan in the morning.*

<u>*Potato Pastry*</u>
*Materials.- ½ lb mashed potatoes; 4 ozs. of flour, or flour and fine oatmeal; 1 ½ ozs. of dripping; 1 teaspoonful of baking powder; salt.*

*Method.– Mix the flour, salt and baking powder; rub in the dripping. Add the potatoes and mix well and lightly. Make a stiff paste with cold water. Four a board and roll out ¼ inch thick. It should be baked in a quick oven and can be used in place of ordinary pastry.*

Mrs C.S. Peel, *The Daily Mail Cookery Book*

<u>Ingredients</u>
225g mashed potato
110g plain flour or a mixture of flour and fine oatmeal
40g dripping
1 tsp of baking powder
a pinch of salt
Full fat milk, to be used if necessary
3 large cooked sausages, halved

Serves 6

1. Preheat the oven to 200°C/Gas Mark 6
2. Mix all of the ingredients except the sausages together. Knead the mixture until it is well combined, using milk to help bind if necessary.
3. Roll out the pastry to no more than 1cm thickness. Cut into 6 rectangles.
4. Shape the pastry around each half sausage and place on a baking tray.

5. Bake in the oven 15 to 20 minutes or until lightly browned.
Serve hot with tomato sauce or chutney.

### Wheatmeal and Oatmeal Bread

Years ago on holiday in Scotland when aged about nine, I remember asking for a bread recipe; the lady in question would not give it to me. This recipe reminds me of that so perhaps thirty years later I am tasting it again. It contains cooked porridge yet is light and delicious, good for breakfast toast, bread to have with pâté, and particularly good with anchovy butter (on page 190).

In the words of Granny Dot:

*Materials.- 1 ½ lbs of Standard flour; ¾ lb of cooked oatmeal; ½ pint of tepid water; ¼ oz. of yeast; ¼ teaspoonful of sugar; 1 teaspoonful salt.*

*Method. – Boil 2 ozs. of oatmeal until soft in the usual way. Drain well and beat it to a paste. Add it to the flour, while warm, together with the salt, mix well. Cream the yeast and sugar, add the tepid oatmeal water, and stir into the flour. Mix all well into a dough, adding a little more warm water if necessary. Set to rise in a warm place for two or three hours. Then take it up and knead well, adding a little more flour if necessary. Form into loaves, put them into greased tins and set to rise for half an hour, or until the dough rises to the top of the tin. Bake in a hot oven 30–40 minutes.'*

Mrs C.S. Peel, *The Daily Mail Cookery Book*

Ingredients
40g porridge oats (produces about 160g cooked porridge)
300ml water divided up into two separate 150ml amounts
350g wholemeal flour
7g sachet of yeast
¾ tsp salt
½ tsp brown sugar

You will need a loaf tin or a baking tray for a free-form loaf
Serves 10

1. Make the porridge by mixing 150ml water with the oats and stir in a small pan over a medium heat until the mixture is formed. Set aside on a plate to cool.
2. Weigh the remaining dry ingredients into a bowl and add the porridge when it is just warm. If you add it when it is too hot it will kill the yeast.
3. Warm the remaining water to a blood temperature and mix into the bowl until a dough is formed. You may need more water.

4. Knead the dough until it is no longer sticky. The kneading can be done in a machine using a dough hook for 5 minutes.
5. Put the dough into a bowl and put a tea towel on top of it. Allow it to rise for two hours.
6. Knock the dough back by punching it. Shape it into a loaf and place on a baking tray or in an oiled loaf tin.
7. Leave to prove for an hour.
8. Preheat the oven to 220°C/Gas Mark 7.
9. Bake the loaf for 20 minutes or until when you tap it on the bottom it sounds hollow.
10. Place on a cooling rack. (If you don't it will have a soggy bottom!).

### *Blackberry Jam*

The amount of liquid produced by blackberries differs and so it is important to measure the juice rather than rely on the weight of the blackberries.

Here is Granny Dot's wisdom:

*Wash the berries and pick off the stalks. Put into a preserving-pan, press with a wooden spoon, and let them simmer in their own juice until well heated and the juice is flowing freely. Rub through a hair sieve. Measure the pulp, and to each pint add ¾lb of sugar. Return the pulp to the pan with the sugar, stir well until it boils, then boil fast until it sets on being tested, about 25 minutes. Put into pots and cover.*

Mrs C.S. Peel, *The Daily Mail Fruit and Vegetable Book*

Ingredients for 1 large pot of jam
500ml blackberry juice
300g preserving sugar
Juice of half a lemon

1. Put the blackberries in a heavy-based pan over a low heat. When they are beginning to warm through, mash them with a potato masher to help the juice flow.
2. When the juice is freely flowing, put the blackberries into a sieve and press the juice through it into a bowl.
3. Measure the liquid in a jug and mix the appropriate amount of sugar to liquid.
4. If using a thermometer take the liquid to 100°C. I find that if taken to the jam setting point of 105°C, it may be too stiff.
5. Put a blob of the hot jam onto a cold plate. Leave it for a few seconds and then run your finger through it. If it crinkles it is ready.
6. Remove the jam from the heat and let it settle while you sterilise jars. I pour

boiling water into a jar and pour it out after a few seconds. It quickly dries out but if necessary, put it in a warm oven to do so.
7. Pour the jam into the jar and seal with wax paper.

### *Blackcurrant Jelly*
Two blackcurrant bushes produce so much fruit that our friends are guaranteed blackcurrant fool, coulis, sorbet and of course blackcurrant jelly. This recipe is adapted, but only a little.
Here is Granny Dot's version:

*Materials.- 4 quarts of black currant. To each pint of juice allow ¾ lb. of sugar.*

*Method.- Pick the fruit on a dry day; wash and free it from stalks. Put the fruit into a jar, cover, and stand it in a saucepan of cold water; bring to the boil, and simmer gently until the juice flows freely. Strain through a teacloth or jelly bag, but do not press it; boil the juice for a few minutes. Measure the juice, and allow 1 lb. of sugar to each pint; stir until the sugar is melted, then boil ten minutes longer, or until the jelly sets on being tested ... Put into small jars, and cover...*

*Note. – If sufficient sugar cannot be spared, 1 part of glucose to 2 parts of sugar may be used.*
Mrs C.S. Peel, *The Daily Mail Fruit and Vegetable Book*

Ingredients
1 kg blackcurrants
1 litre water
900g preserving sugar (450g per 570ml juice)

Makes 2 jars

1. Put the currants and the water in a large casserole or jam pan over a low to medium heat for about 20 minutes, or until the skins of most of the blackcurrants have split. Do not mash them, but let this happen naturally.
2. For a few hours or overnight, strain the contents of the pan though a muslin-lined sieve.
3. Measure the juice into the pan and add the appropriate amount of preserving sugar, making sure that the pan is large enough to hold the mixture when it boils.
4. Over a low heat, allow the sugar to dissolve. Turn the heat up and bring the mixture slowly to the boil where it should remain for a few minutes.
5. If using a thermometer take the liquid to 100°C. I find that if the temperature is taken to the jam setting point of 105°C, it may be too stiff.

7. Put a blob of the hot jam onto a cold plate. Leave it for a few seconds and then run your finger through it. If it crinkles it is ready.
8. Remove the jam from the heat and let it settle while you sterilise jars. To do this, pour boiling water into a jar and pour it out after a few seconds. It quickly dries out but if necessary, put it in a warm oven to do so.
9. Pour the jam into the jars and seal with wax paper.

### Rhubarb Jam

I asked my daughter what she would like to make with the little rhubarb we had and she categorically said, 'Jam!' It is a real treat and takes very little effort. In her *Daily Mail Fruit and Vegetable Book,* Granny Dot's rhubarb jams have added dates, figs or ginger. Because my favourite jam is rhubarb, I give it to you unadulterated, but first, from Granny Dot:

*Rhubarb and Date Jam*
*4 lbs of rhubarb; 2 lbs. of dates; 4 lbs. of sugar; 3 lemons.*
*Peel the rhubarb if old, cut it into small pieces, and place it in a dish; sprinkle 1 lb. of sugar over, and leave it for 24 hours. Wash and stone the dates, and put them into a pan with water to cover; add the rhubarb and lemons cut into quarters, bring to the boil, and simmer for 1 hour. Add the remainder of the sugar, stir until dissolved, then boil for 30 minutes, or until it sets on being tested. Remove the pieces of lemon, put into pots, and cover. The dates may be cut in halves or quarters, if liked.*
Mrs C.S. Peel, *Daily Mail Fruit and Vegetable Book*

Ingredients
550g rhubarb
550g preserving sugar
Juice of half a lemon

Makes 2 jars

1. Cut the rhubarb into small pieces and put it in a heavy-based pan with the sugar. Leave it for 24 hours.
2. Place the pan over a low heat until the sugar melts. This will take about half an hour.
3. Turn the heat up and let it simmer, stirring occasionally to break up the rhubarb and to ensure it does not burn.
4. If some scum comes to the surface, skim it off.
5. If using a thermometer take the temperature to 100°C. I find that if taken to the jam setting point of 105°C, may be too stiff.
6. Put a blob of the hot jam onto a cold plate. Leave it for a few seconds and then run your finger through it. If it crinkles it is ready.

7. Remove the jam from the heat and let it settle while you sterilise jars. I pour boiling water into a jar and pour it out after a few seconds. It quickly dries out but if necessary, put it in a warm oven to do so.
8. Spoon the jam into the jar and seal with wax paper.


## SAVOURIES SIMPLIFIED
*Savouries are always appreciated by men, and very often, nowadays, women prefer them to sweets; so that a small dinner, or even luncheon party, which does not end with a savoury of some kind, is short of much of its glory!*

Mrs C.S. Peel, Savouries Simplified

*Savouries Simplified* contains recipes designed to be eaten at the end of lunch or dinner. It is fun to serve a *Cheese Pufflet*, for example, at the end of a dinner, in place of a cheese board with perhaps some of Granny Dot's green grape jam.

### *Eggs au Gratin*
Comfort food which makes use of what you are likely to find in the fridge is a wonderful thing. I made two concoctions, one with added tomato, and one with creamed spinach. Once made, that's it, pop it in the fridge (it also freezes) until needed. Serve with crusty bread and butter for a real treat.
   Granny Dot's version


*Materials and Method.- Slice 4 hard-boiled eggs, not too thinly. Butter a piedish, and put a spoonful of any good, white sauce at the bottom of this, lay some of the sliced egg in, sprinkle with either grated cheese, or minced mushrooms, and pepper and salt; put in some more egg, and continue these layers till the dish is full, finishing off with some of the cheese, and a little chopped parsley; Dot some small pieces of butter over the top, put in the oven till nicely browned, and serve at once.*

Mrs C.S. Peel, Savouries Simplified

Ingredients
50g butter, plus extra for the dish
50g flour
600ml full fat milk
125g cheddar cheese, extra for sprinkling
3 large tomatoes, two handfuls of spinach, cooked
6 free range or organic boiled eggs (boiled for 7 minutes)
Dried breadcrumbs

Serves 4-6

1. Preheat the oven to 190°C/Gas Mark 5.
2. Melt the butter in a pan and add the flour. Cook, stirring for a couple of minutes over a gentle heat.
3. Remove the pan from the heat and slowly add half the milk while stirring until it forms a roux (or follow white sauce on p. 133 using quantities above.
4. Return the pan to the heat and add the remaining milk until the sauce is of double cream consistency.
5. Add the grated cheese. If you are using strong cheddar, you may need to add less.
6. Pour half the sauce into the bottom of a buttered dish.
7. Slice the eggs and lay them on top of the sauce.
8. Cover with a layer of sliced tomato or spinach
9. Pour the remaining sauce on top.
10. For the tomato version top with a little more finely sliced tomato before sprinkling some grated cheese and breadcrumbs on top.
11. Bake in the oven for 10 minutes and then serve.

### Cheese Pufflets

Sometimes you make something, having little idea of the outcome, and then when you taste it, it is so delicious that you almost squeal with delight that it has worked! Well, that is how I felt about this one, especially if served immediately as it really does puff up. Warning: it deflates like a soufflé and, dare I say, it is a close second.

Here is Granny Dot's recipe:

*Materials and Method.- Mix together 3 oz of grated cheese, 1 tablespoonful of flour, 1 egg, 1 teacupful of milk, and a pinch of salt. Have ready some ramekin cases, put the mixture into these, and bake for 10 minutes.*

Mrs C.S. Peel, *My Own Cookery Book*

Ingredients
85g of grated cheese
1 tbsp flour
1 free range or organic egg
100ml of full fat milk
Butter for the ramekins

You will need 2 ramekins
Serves 2

1. Preheat the oven to 180°C/Gas Mark 4
2. Mix the ingredients together.

3. Pour into buttered ramekins.
4. Bake for 10 minutes or until the cheese pufflets have risen.
Serve immediately before they deflate.

### Green Grape Jam

This is not a savoury recipe, but is the perfect accompaniment to a cheese board or a *Cheese Pufflet* and therefore sits well in this section. I saw a bowl of grapes which needed to be eaten that day and made this delicious accompaniment for cheese. I find myself longing for cheese more than I did before I made this; therein lies a friendly waistline warning.

In the words of Granny Dot:

*Materials and Method.- To each lb of grapes allow ¾ lb of sugar. Stalk and wash the fruit, and put it in a preserving-pan over a very gentle heat until the juice begins to flow; add the sugar, and stir until it melts. Then bring all to the boil, and boil fast until a little will jelly when tested. Put into clean, dry warm jars, and cover. This should be made of unripe grapes.*

Mrs C.S. Peel, *The Daily Mail Cookery Book*

Ingredients
450g of grapes
340g preserving sugar

You will need 1 jar

1. Stalk and wash the fruit and put it with the sugar in a heavy-based pan, over a very gentle heat until it melts.
2. '*Bring it to the boil and boil fast until a little will jelly when tested*' – do this by taking a small teaspoonful of the jam and putting it on a cold plate. Leave it for a few seconds and then run your finger through it. If it crinkles it is ready.
3. Sterilise a jar by pouring boiling water into it; pour it out after a few seconds. It quickly dries out but if necessary, put it in a warm oven to do so.
4. Pour the jam into the jar and seal with wax paper.
Serve with cheese and biscuits.

### Potato Soufflé

In *The Daily Mail Cookery Book* it is recommended that this is accompanied by white sauce. I am afraid that this does not appeal (sorry Granny Dot). I made a tomato sauce and it was so good that I repeated it for a dinner party. This soufflé is like mashed potato made in heaven.

Here's Granny Dot's version:

187

*Materials.- 1 1/2lbs cooked potatoes; 1 oz. margarine; salt; pepper; 2 tablespoonsful of milk; 2 eggs.*

*Method.- Rub the potatoes through a sieve. Melt the margarine in a pan, add the potatoes, seasoning, milk and margarine in a pan, add the potatoes, seasoning, milk and the yolks of the eggs. Mix well. Remove from the fire, whip up the white of the eggs to a stiff froth and stir in lightly to the mixture. Put into a greased soufflé mould with a band of buttered paper tied round it. Place in a saucepan with enough boiling water to come half-way up the tin. Place a greased paper on the top. Simmer from 40 minutes to an hour.*

*To Dish.- Loosen round the edge with knife, turn gently on to a hot dish. Pour white sauce over.*

*Garnishes.- Garnish with chopped parsley arranged in a pattern over the top, or with the yolk of a hard-boiled egg, rubbed through a sieve.*
   *This mixture can be put into a greased china soufflé dish and baked in a moderate oven 30 minutes, then send to table in the dish.*
                                        Mrs C.S. Peel, *The Daily Mail Cookery Book*

Ingredients
For the Tomato Sauce
3 tbsp olive oil
½ red onion finely diced
2 cloves garlic, whole
400g chopped tomatoes
50ml red wine

For the Potato Souffle
280g boiled potato, mashed.
30g butter, plus extra for the ramekins
1 tbsp full fat milk
salt
1 free range or organic egg, separated

You will need 2 ramekins and a roasting tin
Serves 2

1. First make the tomato sauce. In a pan, heat the oil.
2. Add the onion and when it is pale brown, add the garlic. Cook until the onion is deep brown and the garlic pale brown before adding the tomatoes and the wine.

Simmer for 15 minutes or until thick. Set aside.
3. For the soufflé, if using the oven instead of direct heat, preheat it to 180°C/Gas Mark 4. (see step 6.)
4. Mix the potato, butter and milk and season. Add the yolk (ensure that the potato is not so hot that it scrambles the yolk) and mix thoroughly.
5. In a separate bowl whisk the egg white until medium peak. Stir a tablespoonful of egg white into the potato mixture before folding in the rest.
6. Spoon the mixture into the buttered ramekins and place them in a roasting tin. Pour boiling water half way up the ramekins. Simmer for 40 minutes on direct heat or in the oven for 20 minutes covered lightly in a sheet of foil.
7. Spoon the sauce over the soufflé.
Serve immediately.

### Cheese Aigrettes

I make these either as a canapé, a starter or instead of cheese after dinner. You may like to serve chilli jam on the side for a twenty-first-century twist.

Here is Granny Dot's recipe:

*Materials and Method.- Put 1 oz of butter into a pan with 1 gill of water, and as soon as it boils fast, sift in 3oz of flour; stir this all well together till it forms a smooth, thick paste, then beat in 2 small eggs one at a time, and finally 2 oz of grated cheese, and season to taste with salt and pepper. Leave it to get cold, then fry in rough lumps for 10 minutes or a quarter of an hour. Serve very hot, dusted with grated cheese and coralline pepper.*

Mrs C.S. Peel, *Savouries Simplified*

Ingredients
150ml water
30g unsalted butter
90g flour
2 free range or organic eggs
50g grated cheese
seasoning
Oil for frying (sunflower, vegetable or other flavourless oil)
Cayenne pepper

Makes about 12

1. Put the water and butter in a pan over a high heat and as soon as it boils sift in the flour and stir vigorously.

2. Remove from the heat and let it cool a little by spreading out on a plate. Put it back in the pan with the eggs and cheese, being careful that the eggs do not scramble. Beat the mixture with a wooden spoon until the ingredients are incorporated.
3. Season to taste.
4. Heat the oil in a pan. Drop a little bit of the mixture into the oil. If it sizzles, the oil has reached the correct temperature.
5. Fry teaspoonfuls of the mixture until brown. Remove with a slotted spoon.
6. Drain on kitchen paper and serve hot dusted with grated cheese and cayenne pepper.

### Anchovy Butter
Granny Dot calls this *Green Butter*. Of course the parsley does make it greenish, but if I called it green anchovy butter, I think no one would make it! The dominant ingredient is anchovy so 'Anchovy Butter' it is. This has become something I have to stop myself from making on a regular basis as I could quite happily finish the lot.
    Granny Dot's recipe first:

*Materials and Method.- scald or blanch a small bunch of parsley, strip it from the stalk, rub it through a sieve; wash, bone, and pound 3 anchovies. Then pound together ½ lb butter, the parsley, and anchovies, when it is ready for use. Savoury butters are very useful for spreading on toast, for croutons, or even for some sandwiches.*

Mrs C.S. Peel, *Savouries Simplified*

Anchovy Butter with Wheatmeal and Oatmeal Bread recipe, p.181 (*emmafarquharphotography*)

Ingredients
110g unsalted butter
10g parsley
4–6 anchovy fillets, depending on their strength
A squeeze of lemon juice
Salt to taste

Serves 6-8

1. Soften the butter and chop the parsley and anchovies.
2. Mix it all together then add the lemon juice. Season if needed.
3. Put it in the fridge. You could wrap it in cling film to form into a cylinder and slice into rounds when needed.
Serve with toasted Wheatmeal and Oatmeal Bread (see page 181)

### Jellied Aspic

In *My Own Cookery Book*, we are told how to make aspic and savoury jellies. As a child on summer holidays with my great-grandparents in Murray Bay, Canada, I remember sitting in front of aspic moulded into clear oval shapes through which was a pretty picture of half a boiled egg surrounded by finely sliced vegetables. I am afraid that though it holds visually fond memories, they are not palatably fond. This version is made with fish stock and if you like oysters, you will love this. Traditionally, a calf's foot is used to make aspic, but I have simply followed Granny Dot's instructions (using fish stock) which do not involve feet of any kind.

*Materials.- 1½ pints of meat stock; ½ gill of tarragon vinegar and malt vinegar mixed; the strained juice of 1 lemon; 1 onion (sliced); ½ teaspoonful of salt; 2 oz. of gelatine; the white and shell of 1 egg; parsley; 8 peppercorns; 1 gill of water.*

*Method.- Place all the ingredients in a saucepan and whisk steadily over the fire until boiling. Simmer without stirring for 5 minutes. Just move away the froth so that the liquid can pour clear and strain through a jelly bag or clean cloth wrung out in boiling water. Strain a second or third time if needs be until the liquid runs clear. Leave to set.*

Mrs C.S Peel, *My Own Cookery Book*

Ingredients
1 litre fish stock
140ml vinegar (white wine, tarragon, sherry)
2 free range or organic egg whites and shells
½ tsp salt

191

sprig of parsley
1 onion, sliced
Juice of 1 lemon
A few peppercorns
6 sheets of gelatine (softened by soaking in cold water for 5 mins)
You will need a sieve lined with muslin and 8 moulds.

Serves 8

1. Put all of the ingredients in a pan and stir them gently with a balloon whisk until the mixture begins to boil. Remove the whisk.
2. Do NOT break the crust that has formed on top.
3. Remove the pan from the heat and let the bubbles subside.
4. Leave for 2 minutes and then bring it to the boil again. Remove it from the heat and leave it for 2 minutes.
5. Peek at the liquid under the crust and if it is not clear, repeat this. If it is still not clear, strain the mixture into a clean pan through a muslin and put it back on the heat with a fresh egg white and shell. Repeat the whole process until it is clear.
6. Strain the mixture through a muslin-lined sieve.
7. Now pour it into the moulds and let them set in the fridge.
8. If you would like to decorate it, then fill half the mould with liquid aspic and leave it to set for a couple of hours before gently adding brown shrimp, finely chopped tomato, chives, or whatever you like.
9. Pour more aspic on top so that the 'decorations' are covered. You may need to use a toothpick to push the 'decorations' back in place if they are displaced by the liquid.
10. Carefully put the moulds back in the fridge for about 3 hours until set.
11. To turn out, put each mould in boiling water for about 2 seconds to loosen the contents. Place a serving plate on top of each mould and tip it over so that the aspic unmoulds onto the plate.
Serve cold.

### Canapés à la Fribourg
These are hard to resist. To recreate exactly is a time-consuming process. We may have the luxury of a whizzing gadget and a fine sieve to speed things up a little. But first, here is Granny Dot's version:

*Materials and Method.- Steam a haddock, and work the flesh through a sieve, moistening it with a little milk, when necessary. Mix this pulp in a stewpan with a spoonful or two of cream, ½ oz of fresh butter, season with salt and a little cayenne.*

Canapes  a la Fribourg (*Author's own*)

*When quite hot, pile it up on fried croutons, smoothing it neatly, sprinkle with Parmesan cheese, and a few brown breadcrumbs, and serve very hot.*

Mrs C.S. Peel, *Savouries Simplified*

Ingredients
100g smoked or unsmoked haddock
50g butter, plus extra for frying
2 tbsp double cream
½ tbsp. lemon juice
Salt
3 slices stale bread
4 tbsp finely grated Parmesan
Parsley or chives to garnish

Makes approximately 20

1. Steam the haddock for 5 minutes or until it flakes.
2. Put the haddock, butter and cream into a blender and whizz until smooth. Mix in the lemon juice and some sea salt. Taste and add a little more if necessary.
3. With a 2½ cm pastry cutter, cut the bread into about 20 small discs. In a frying pan, heat a generous knob of butter until a breadcrumb sizzles when it is fried.

193

4. Fry the rounds of bread until lightly browned and then drain on kitchen paper.
5. Preheat the grill.
6. On a baking tray put teaspoonfuls of the paste onto the rounds of bread and pile a little grated Parmesan on top of these.
7. Grill until lightly browned.
8. Top with chives or parsley and serve immediately.

### *Devilled Bananas*

This has a real zing with an element of comfort, all in one mouthful. For me, this recipe is new and while hard to pinpoint exactly what it should accompany, I intend to have it for a Sunday evening supper that is neither sweet nor savoury, and alongside pork or lamb.

In the words of Granny Dot:

*Materials.- 8 bananas; 2 tablespoonfuls of sugar; a good pinch of red pepper; 1 teaspoonful of dry mustard; 2 tablespoonfuls of Worcester Sauce; 1 tablespoonful of vinegar; about 4 tablespoonfuls of olive oil.*

*Method.- Place the sugar, red pepper, mustard and Worcester in a jam basin and stand it in another of boiling water. Stir until the sugar has dissolved, add the vinegar and keep on stirring, add the oil. The sauce soon becomes thick and velvety looking, when it is ready for use. Peel the bananas and make them hot throughout, but do not fry them. Pour the sauce over them and serve very hot, accompanied by toast and butter.*

Mrs C.S. Peel, *My Own Cookery Book*

Ingredients
2 tbsp caster sugar
2 tbsp Worcestershire Sauce
1 tsp mustard powder
1 tbsp red wine vinegar
4 tbsp olive oil
3 bananas

Serves 6

1. Preheat the oven to 180°C/Gas Mark 4.
2. Place the sugar, Worcestershire sauce and mustard in a heatproof bowl over a pan of simmering water. Stir until the sugar has melted.
3. Add the vinegar and oil and keep stirring until a velvety sauce forms, the consistency of double cream. This will take about 5 minutes.

4. Put the whole bananas on an oven-proof dish in the oven and heat through for about 5 minutes.
5. Remove the dish from the oven and slice the bananas onto a serving plate. Pour the sauce on top.
Serve with toasted bread and butter.

### *Vienna Bread Rolls*

'Vienna' bread production is characterised by steam added to the oven, making the rolls slightly chewy with a good crust and worthy of serving with butter alone. They are still very good baked without steam, the essential part being to brush them with milk or beaten egg when straight out of the oven.

Here is Granny Dot's recipe:

*Materials and Method.- Warm a bowl, put in the flour and salt, rub in the butter. Put the yeast in a little basin with the sugar and two tablespoonsful of flour and work it smooth, add a gill of the milk and leave it to rise for a quarter of an hour. Whip the egg, add to it the remaining milk, pour it over the yeast and stir all into the bulk of the flour, kneading lightly. Leave the dough to rise an hour. Knead the dough again, divide it into 8 or 10 pieces, put them on a clean baking sheet and stand this over a pan of boiling water to allow the rolls to rise for a quarter of an hour. Put them in a quick oven, bake for about 10 minutes; as soon as they are done, brush them over at once with a little milk or egg.*

Mrs C.S. Peel, *Still Room Cookery*

Ingredients
450g strong white bread flour
30g butter, very soft
7g sachet dried yeast
1 tsp salt
1 free range or organic egg
300ml warm full fat milk plus extra for brushing on the rolls after baking

Makes 8–10

1. Put the ingredients except the milk in a mixing bowl.
2. Warm the milk to blood temperature and pour it into the mixing bowl gradually, stirring with a knife until the ingredients combine.
3. Knead on a worktop for 10 minutes until a smooth dough is formed.
Alternatively use a mixer with a dough hook for 5 minutes.
4. Leave to rise with a tea towel on top of the bowl two hours, or until doubled in size.

5. Remove the dough from the bowl and form it into buns. Place the buns on a baking tray.
6. Leave them to rise for an hour, less if they look well risen.
7. Preheat the oven to 200°C/Gas Mark 6. Place a roasting tin of simmering water in the bottom of the oven.
8. Bake the rolls on a shelf above the simmering water for ten minutes until golden, remove from the oven and brush immediately with milk. Set on a rack to cool.
Eat them within 24 hours as with all homemade bread, the sooner the better.

**SAUCES**
**Sauce Espagnole**
This is a very good accompaniment to fish and meat.
    Granny Dot's recipe:

*Materials and Method.- Slice an onion, half a turnip, and half a carrot; add 1 oz. of shredded celery, and some chopped parsley, six peppercorns, two cloves, and salt; moisten with 1 gill of the darkest stock you have, and cook gently until it turns a good reddish brown. Now add ½ pint of stock, bring to the boil, and simmer for ¾ hour. Strain, taste, add more salt and pepper, and a pinch of sugar as needed, thicken with brown roux, and melt it in, stirring all the time, 1 oz of glaze. This will produce a thick, smooth dark brown sauce, which can have tomato added, or be garnished with chopped gherkin or enriched with a little wine as required.*
                                        Mrs C.S. Peel, *My Own Cookery Book*

Ingredients
2 tbsp vegetable, sunflower or olive oil
1 carrot, roughly chopped
1 small onion, sliced
1 stick of celery, sliced
1 tbsp plain flour
½ tbsp tomato puree
300ml stock (any type)
Bouquet garni of 2 cloves, 6 peppercorns, 1 bay leaf, sprig of thyme, parsley stalk (cut a square of muslin, put the contents in and tie with string)
Seasoning

Serves 4

1. Heat the oil in a heavy-based pan over a medium heat and cook the vegetables until softened a little.

2. Add a level tablespoon of flour and stir for 1 minute to cook the flour.
3. Spoon in the tomato puree and stir for a few seconds.
4. Remove the pan from the heat and slowly pour in the stock, stirring.
5. When about half of the stock has been added, put the bouquet garni in the pan and return it to the heat. Gradually add the remaining stock. Turn the heat up and let it simmer for about half an hour until the vegetables are completely soft.
6. Remove the bouquet garni and put the mixture in a blender. Blend.
This will keep in the fridge for a few days until needed.

### Tomato Sauce
Simple to make and a valuable addition to many dishes in this book.

*Materials.- 4 tomatoes; 1/2 small onion; some bacon rinds; 1 oz cornflour; 3/4 pint stock from peelings or water in which cereals or vegetables have been boiled; 1 bunch of herbs, or a teaspoonful of dried, mixed herbs (tied in muslin); 10 peppercorns; salt; pepper.*

*Method. – Mince the onion, slice the tomatoes, and put the whole into a pan with the stock, bacon rinds, peppercorns and herbs. Simmer till soft. Rub through a sieve and return to the pan. Blend the cornflour with a little cold stock or water; add it to the puree and stir until it boils. Simmer 5 minutes. Season, and if necessary add a few drops of cochineal to improve its colour.*

Mrs C.S. Peel, *The Daily Mail Cookery Book*

Ingredients
4 rashers of bacon (optional)
1 tbsp olive, vegetable or sunflower oil
4 large tomatoes, peeled and roughly chopped
½ onion
350ml vegetable stock or water
Seasoning
1 tsp mixed herbs, thyme or marjoram

Serves 4

1. Fry the bacon in a hot saucepan, adding a little oil if necessary.
2. When the bacon is cooked, add all of the ingredients to the pan and simmer until the vegetables have softened, which will take about ten minutes.
3. Remove the bacon and whizz the mixture in a blender.
4. Sieve the sauce before serving for a completely smooth texture.

**Bread Sauce**

You need a really good loaf of stale white or brown bread for this. Long slow cooking produces a superior result.

In the words of Granny Dot:

*Materials.- 1 pint of milk; about 4 oz. of stale breadcrumbs; 1 onion; 2 cloves; 4 peppercorns; a pinch of mace; salt and pepper; 3 tablespoonfuls of cream of a walnut-sized knob of butter (optional)*

*Method.- Stick the cloves into the onion and lace in a pan together with the peppercorns, a saltspoonful of salt and the milk. Cook over a low fire until the milk becomes frothy, remove, let it cool a little and repeat the process. Gradually bring the sauce to the consistency of a puree. Taste, add a pinch of mace if the flavour is liked, add more salt and pepper if necessary, remove the onion, re-heat and finally stir in the cream or the knob of butter.*

Mrs C.S. Peel, *My Own Cookery Book*

<u>Ingredients</u>
1 onion
4 cloves
6 peppercorns
1 blade of mace
110g bread
300ml full fat milk
3 tbsp double cream
Seasoning

Serves 4-6

1. Halve the onion. Stick the cloves into it and add it to the dry ingredients in a heavy-based pan. Include the onion skin for a richer flavour.
2. Pour the milk on top of the ingredients.
3. Either leave the pan in a low oven 140°C/Gas Mark 1 for 2 hours, or stir the mixture over a gentle heat for half an hour. For a richer flavour use the slow oven.
4. Add the cream and season to taste.
Keep the sauce covered until use.

**SOUP**

**French Rice Soup**

Working my way through the recipes for this book has meant sampling them through the day and not stopping for lunch. My husband once turned up unexpectedly and I opened *The Daily Mail Cookery Book* in the hope that inspiration would pop out; French Rice Soup was the answer. There are variations using different stocks and toppings, such as fried garlic and onions. This is comfort food, perfect for a cold day or to warm you up. Granny Dot's recipe:

*Materials. – 2 ozs. rice; 1 onion; 2 cloves; 1 oz. fat; 1 1/2 pints of vegetable or cereal stock; 1 gill milk; 1 oz. cornflour; grate of nutmeg; salt; pepper.*

*Slow heat. Time, about 40 minutes.*

*Method. – Wash the rice in several waters. Drain. Melt the fat in a pan, and add the rice, stir in the fat, for 5 minutes, but do not brown; add the stock; bring to the boil; skim, add the peeled onion into which the cloves are stuck. Simmer gently till the rice is soft. Blend the cornflour with the milk and add. Boil 10 minutes, stirring well. Remove the onion and cloves, season, add the nutmeg, serve in a hot tureen.*

*Reasons for failure.– If the soup is not stirred the rice may sink to the bottom of the pan, and burn. If not stirred until boiling after adding the cornflour, it will become lumpy and may burn.*

Mrs C.S. Peel, *The Daily Mail Cookery Book*

Ingredients
25g butter
55g long grain rice
900ml vegetable stock
140ml full fat milk
25g cornflour
Nutmeg, grated

Serves 2

1. Melt the butter in a heavy based pan and add the rice, stirring over a medium low heat for 2 minutes, until the rice is palc brown.
2. Remove the pan from the heat and stir in the stock. Return the pan to the heat and simmer until the rice is soft, about 20 minutes.
3. In the meantime, whisk the cornflour and the milk together in a bowl or jug and when the rice is soft, stir it into the pan.
4. Simmer for about ten minutes stirring frequently so that the rice does not catch on the bottom of the pan.
5. Serve with nutmeg grated on top.

### Brown Haricot Soup

Sometimes the simplest ingredients produce the most hearty and satisfying soup. Here is Granny Dot's version:

*Materials and Method.- Wash the beans or peas and soak them in water for 12 hours Peel and slice the onions, carrots and turnip. Fry the peas and vegetables in the butter or margarine for 5 minutes. Add the liquid in which the beans were soaked and sufficient stock to make one quart in all, bring to the boil, add the celery seed, bacon rinds and seasoning and simmer for 2 hours or until the beans or peas are quite soft. Rub through a sieve and return to the pan. Add the milk and bring to the boil. Taste and add more seasoning if necessary. Sprinkle with finely chopped mint or with dried mint or with finely shredded crisped bacon.*

Mrs C.S. Peel, *My Own Cookery Book*

Ingredients
450g dry brown haricot beans
80g butter
2 large carrots, chopped
2 heads of celery, chopped
2 large onions, sliced
8 rashers of bacon
1 bay leaf
1 sprig of thyme (optional)
2 sprigs parsley, plus some chopped parsley for garnish
600ml vegetable bouillon
Salt and pepper to taste
Parsley or chives to garnish
Sherry (optional)

Serves 8

1. Put the beans in a bowl, cover them with water and soak overnight. Drain them and put in a heavy-based pan. Cover the beans with fresh water and simmer gently for 1 hour.
2. Heat another pan and add the bacon. Cook through, remove 4 rashers and finely chop. Set aside.
3. Melt the butter in the pan with the remaining bacon and add the vegetables, cooking until soft and lightly browned.
4. Pour the beans and their liquid over the vegetables and bacon. Add a bay leaf, thyme, parsley and bouillon. Simmer for another hour. Top the liquid up with water if necessary.

5. Remove the bacon, bay leaf and sprig of thyme before blending the soup.
6. Transfer the soup back into the pan and add more hot water if necessary.
7. Season to taste and sprinkle the reserved bacon and chopped parsley on top.
You may like to add a splash of dry sherry.


**FISH**
*In choosing fish, the housekeeper should always remember that when fresh it is firm and the eyes are bright, the gills red and the scales in good condition.*

Mrs C.S. Peel, *Fish and How to Cook it*


***Salmon, Cod or Hake and Tomatoes***
The sauce may be served over the fish or the fish can be broken up in pieces and added to the sauce. Flour was often added to sauces so that they were of a coating consistency. If you prefer to omit the flour, it will be just as good, perhaps better.
    In the words of Granny Dot:

*Moderate Heat. Time, 20 minutes.*

*Materials.– 2 cod or hake or salmon steaks; 1/2 lb. tomatoes; 1/2 small onion; 1/2 pint fish stock; 1 oz. fat; 1 oz. flour; blade of mace; half a lemon; salt; pepper.*

*Method.– Wash the steaks, wipe them dry with a clean cloth, sprinkle them first on one side then on the other with salt and pepper and rub them with lemon. Wrap them in buttered paper, place them on a greased baking sheet, and bake about 15 minutes in a moderate oven, or until the fish begins to leave the bone. While cooking make a sauce as follows: Peel and mince the onion, melt the fat in a pan, fry the onion without browning it for 5 minutes, add the flour (off the fire), mix smoothly, add the stock very gradually, the tomatoes cut in half, and mace. Return to the fire, stir until boiling, then simmer about 12 minutes. Season well and add.*

*How to dish.– Dish on a hot dish, strain the sauce over and serve. If the sauce is too thick add a little more stock. Tinned or bottled tomatoes can be used for this.*

*Reasons for failure.– If the fish is cooked too fast it becomes hard and dry. If the flour is not blended with the fat and stock off the fire it cooks before becoming blended and is lumpy.*

Mrs C.S. Peel, *The Daily Mail Cookery Book*


Ingredients
30g butter plus extra for the baking paper or foil

4 fillets of fish (1 per person)
Half a lemon
Seasoning
½ onion
½ tbsp flour
300ml fish stock
1 blade of mace
175g tomatoes, roughly chopped (and skinned if you prefer)

Serves 4

1. Preheat the oven to 180°C/Gas Mark 4.
2. Take a large sheet of baking paper or foil and butter it before laying on it the fish, skin side down. Season. Squeeze the lemon over the fish and place the remaining lemon on top.
3. Wrap it up, sealing and folding as best you can to prevent hot air escaping as it cooks. Bake the fish for 10 minutes or until cooked. Alternatively, steam the fish over simmering water until a knife easily parts the flesh.
4. While the fish is cooking put the butter in a casserole. Add the onion and cook until glossy. Add the flour and stir for two minutes and then add the stock gradually, followed by the mace and tomatoes.
5. Simmer for a few minutes.
6. When the fish is ready, either remove its skin and add to the casserole, or put it on a serving plate covered with the sauce.

### *Fillet of Fish with Beurre Noisette*
One of my favourites dishes is Skate with Beurre Noissette. This is Granny Dot's version:

*Materials.- 2oz of butter; 2 tablespoonfuls of lemon juice; parsley*

*Method.- Wash and dry the parsley and separate into tiny sprigs, free of stalk. Heat the butter in a pan, fry the parsley in it until crisp and brown and turn into a hot sauceboat. Heat the lemon juice and just before serving, pour it on to the parsley butter.*
Mrs C.S. Peel, *The Daily Mail Cookery Book*

Ingredients
500ml fish stock or water with a bay leaf, some pepper corns, and a slither of lemon peel
2 skate wings, trimmed and prepared
100g butter

2 tbsp chopped parsley
4 tbsp lemon juice
2 tbsp capers (optional)
Salt

Serves 2

1. Put the fish stock or water with the bay leaf, peppercorns and lemon peel in a wide saucepan which will accommodate the fish. Bring the stock to a gentle simmer and add the fish. When a knife easily slips through the flesh, drain the fish and set aside on a plate.
2. Pour out the liquid from the pan and melt the butter until brown, add the parsley and fry until crisp. Pour the lemon juice into the pan with capers if using. Season to taste.
3. Place the wings into the pan and coat with the sauce.
Serve

### *Fillet a la Maitre d'hotel*
When I made this, our local fishmonger who sells fish from his van arrived with the most beautiful smoked haddock. While smoked fish is not mentioned, it works very well.

In the words of Granny Dot:

*Materials and Method.- Make the required number of fillets and simmer them in stock made from their own trimmings, etc.; when cooked, place them on a hot dish and keep hot in the oven. Take ½ pint of good melted butter sauce, stir into it a tablespoonful of finely chopped parsley, beat up the yolk of an egg, add this and the juice of half a lemon, be careful not to let the sauce boil after these are added, pour over the fish and serve very hot.*

Mrs C.S. Peel, *Fish and How to Cook it*

Ingredients
300ml full fat milk with a slice of onion, a bay leaf and some peppercorns
2 fillets of smoked haddock
2 free range or organic egg yolks
1 tbsp lemon juice, plus extra if needed
100g unsalted butter, chopped into roughly 2cm cubes
Seasoning
½ tbsp chopped parsley

Serves 2

1. Put the milk, onion, bay leaf and peppercorns in a pan and bring to a simmer.
2. Add the fish and poach it for 4 or 5 minutes until a sharp knife inserts easily into the flesh. Set aside in a warm place while you make the sauce.
3. Put the yolks in a heatproof bowl over a saucepan of simmering water.
4. Whisk a tablespoon of lemon juice into the egg and add the butter, whisking in one cube at a time until a hollandaise sauce is formed.
5. Add lemon and salt to taste.
Garnish with chopped parsley and serve immediately.

### *Sole, Lemon Sole or Plaice au Gratin*
The addition of sauce is suggested, which I omitted as it is perfect as it is; thank you Granny Dot:

*Materials.- 1 Sole, 1 teaspoonful chopped parsley; 1 small onion or shallot; 3 button mushrooms; brown breadcrumbs; 1 oz margarine; half pint brown sauce; salt; pepper.*

*Method.– Wash and dry the fish, remove the skin, make an incision along the backbone at each side and slanting incisions on each side. Chop the mushrooms, shallot and parsley finely, and mix them together. Fill the incisions with the mixture, place the fish on a well-greased baking tin, cover with brown bread crumbs, put small pieces of the margarine at intervals over the top, and bake about 15 minutes in a moderate oven.*

*How to dish.– Serve on a hot dish and pour brown sauce round, in which the trimming of the mushroos have been simmered.*

Mrs C.S. Peel, *The Daily Mail Cookery Book*

Ingredients
4 prepared Plaice, Dover Sole or Lemon Sole
8 mushrooms
½ onion
1 tbsp parsley
Dried brown breadcrumbs
75g butter

Serves 4

1. Preheat the oven to 190°C/Gas Mark 5.
2. Finely chop the mushrooms, onion and parsley.
3. Make two incisions with a very sharp knife alongside the backbone of the fish so that you have pockets on either side.

4. Fill these pockets with the mushroom mixture. If the fillets are too thin, pile the mixture on top.
5. Sprinkle breadcrumbs on top of the fish and dot with butter.
6. Bake for 15 minutes until the breadcrumbs are crisp and the fish cooked through.
7. Serve, pouring any stray juices from the pan onto the serving dish.

## MEAT

### Mutton
*In the first place weigh the joint, and compare the weight given with that on the docket sent by the butcher, and if you find the joints weigh less than the amount charged let the butcher realise that in you he has a customer willing to pay promptly for what you order and not one who will endure dishonesty on his part.*

Mrs C.S. Peel, *The Single Handed Cook*

### *Cannelon of Mutton*
This has become a firm favourite. It does not take long to prepare and the result is very impressive.

Granny Dot's recipe:

*Materials.- 1lb of boned loin of mutton; 1lb of mixed vegetables; a bouquet of parsley, thyme, bay leaf, 2 slips of lemon peel, 1 blade of mace, 20 peppercorns, 2 cloves, tied together in muslin; 1 pint of well-flavoured stock; veal forcemeat; 1 oz of clarified fat; salt.*

*Method.- Wipe the meat, remove all skin and any superfluous fat, cut off the flat end and trim the remainder neatly. Beat the meat to flatten it, spread it with the stuffing and roll it up, the thin end inmost. Sew it into shape with a sharp packing-needle and washed string. Do not pull too hard or the meat may tear, but be sure that it is firm, and sewn so as to make a neat roll and to avoid any escape of the stuffing. Wrap the roll in greaseproof paper.*

*Melt the clarified fat in a stewpan, add the sliced vegetables and the herbs tied in muslin. Put the roll on top of the vegetables, cover the pan and put it in the oven (Regulo 4, 375 ° Elec.). The dish can be cooked on the hot-plate if more convenient but should properly be cooked in an enveloping heat. Cook gently until the vegetable juices start to run and the paper looks moist. Then add the stock, pouring it over the paper and putting some of the vegetables on top of the roll. Cover the pan and continue to cook gently, basting every 10 minutes for the first half hour and then*

205

*from time to time during the 1½ hours cooking. Take out the meat, drain it, remove the paper but not the string and put the joint away till cold. When cold, remove the string, trim the joint if necessary, brush it over with glaze and serve.*

*It may be served mounted on a bed of stiff chestnut puree or chestnut face or garnished with chopped aspic.*

*A loin of veal cooked in the same way is excellent.*

Mrs C.S. Peel, *My Own Cookery Book*

Ingredients
For the Mutton
450g of boned loin of mutton
50g butter
450g of carrots, sliced into sticks
600ml strong beef stock
Bouquet of parsley, thyme, bay leaf, 2 strips of lemon peel (no white pith), 1 blade of mace, 20 peppercorns, 2 cloves, tied together in a muslin

*For the Veal Forcemeat Stuffing*
1 beef, lamb or pork kidney, chopped (optional)
110g sausage meat
2 tbsp breadcrumbs
2 tbsp of chopped parsley
1 tbsp grated lemon peel
1 tbsp of chopped fat, suet or melted butter
Seasoning
1 free range or organic egg

Serves 4-6

1. Preheat the oven to 180°C/Gas Mark 4.
2. Lay the meat between two large pieces of cling film. Roll and bash the meat with a rolling pin until it is an even thickness. Remove the top layer of clingfilm.
3. Mix the stuffing ingredients together and spread over the mutton. This is easy with a palate knife.
4. Roll the meat into a sausage roll shape. Secure it with string.
5. Melt a knob of butter in a large casserole and place the mutton roll on top. Lightly brown.
6. Add the carrots to the pan and toss in the butter before adding the stock and the bouquet garni.
7. Cover the casserole with a lid and put it in the oven for an hour. Check that it is tender and if not, return to the oven for up to another half hour.

8. When it is ready, remove the casserole from the oven and place the meat on a board to rest. Remove the carrots with a slotted spoon to a serving dish and keep warm.
9. Taste the jus in the casserole and if not rich enough, place it over the heat and reduce by simmering until it has a richer consistency and flavour.
10. Remove the string and slice the mutton neatly.
Serve with the carrots and jus.

### Navarin of Mutton
Granny Dot's recipe is a perfect answer to leftover mutton and is also good when made using raw mutton following the same steps.

*Materials and Method.- Cut about 1 lb. of cold mutton (underdone if possible) into square pieces. Lay them on a dish and moisten them with a marinade made thus: two gills of mutton gravy (or stock), a tablespoonful of currant jelly dissolved in it, a spoonful of the vinegar from some walnut pickle, add a dust of salt and pepper. Let the meat lie in this, turning it occasionally for an hour or two. Then melt 2 oz. of butter and add a finely-shred onion, a sliced carrot and turnip, some celery and some chopped parsley; fry until the vegetable begins to brown, then add 1 oz. of flour and mix smooth. Add about a pint of stock, bring to the boil, and then simmer for half an hour. Rub this sauce through a sieve. Place the mutton and the marinade in the pan, pour the sauce over, and then heat very gently and slowly for one to two hours. Be sure that it does not boil, or it will be spoilt. The object is to cook the navarin very slowly and gently. If you use uncooked meat, fry it lightly before placing it in the marinade. Serve with sauté potatoes.*

Mrs C.S. Peel, *The Single-Handed Cook*

Ingredients
450g mutton, chopped into bite-size pieces
1 tbsp mushroom ketchup
1 tbsp redcurrant jelly
300ml gravy, mutton/lamb stock, or other meat stock
1 tbsp vinegar taken from walnut pickle, or white wine vinegar
1 wineglass of red wine
2 sprigs of rosemary
50g butter
1 onion finely sliced
1 large carrot, diced
25g plain flour
600ml mutton/lamb stock or water
1 bunch roughly chopped parsley

Serves 4

1. Put the meat in a bowl and marinate in the mushroom ketchup, redcurrant jelly, gravy, vinegar, red wine and rosemary. Leave it for at least 2 hours.
2. Melt the butter in a casserole and fry the vegetables for 5 minutes until tender. Add the flour and cook, stirring for a minute. Remove the casserole from the heat and stir in half the stock. Return the casserole to the heat and stir in the remaining stock.
3. Add the mutton and the marinade to the casserole and heat gently for $1\frac{1}{2}$ -2 hours until the mutton is very tender.
4. Garnish with parsley and serve with sautéed potatoes or wild rice and soured cream.

### *Ragout of Mutton*
I told two people I was making something with pearl barley and you'd think I had told them the pathways were lined with gold, so if you are not excited about mutton (which you will be if you try this), you may be about pearl barley!

In the words of Granny Dot:

*Materials.- ½lb of shoulder or neck of mutton; 2 onions; 2 carrots; 1 bay leaf; 1 oz. fat; 2 ozs pearl barley (soaked overnight); 1 1/2 pints stock, or water; 1/2 oz flour; salt; pepper.*

*Method.- Cut the mutton into neat pieces, removing any superfluous fat and bone. Peel and shred the onions, wash and scrape the carrots and cut into dice. Melt the fat in a casserole. Fry the mutton light brown both sides. Remove, fry the onions and carrots, and the flour and brown lightly, add the stock gradually, stirring well; bring to the boil, put in the meat, bay leaf, seasoning and barley, place the lid on the casserole and put in a moderate oven, or on the hot plate, and simmer the contents gently 1 hour, or until the barley is soft. Skim off the fat and serve in the casserole. If the barley absorbs the stock more must be added. If cooked over a gas ring it must be turned low and an asbestos mat should be placed under the casserole.*

*To Dish.– Serve in the casserole placed on a hot dish.'*

Mrs C.S. Peel, *The Daily Mail Cookery Book*

Ingredients
50g butter
2 onions finely sliced
1 large carrot, diced
1 bay leaf

1 sprig thyme or rosemary
450g mutton taken from the shoulder, leg or neck and chopped into bite size pieces
25g plain flour
1 tbsp tomato puree
120ml red wine
400ml water, lamb, chicken or vegetable stock
55g pearl barley
1 handful of chopped parsley and grated zest of 1 unwaxed lemon

Serves 4

1. Heat a casserole and melt the butter. Cook the vegetables until tender before adding the meat to brown.
2. Sprinkle flour onto the meat and vegetables and cook, stirring for a couple of minutes.
3. Stir in the tomato puree.
4. Gradually stir the wine and stock or water into the casserole. Add the barley and cover, simmering gently for an hour. Season.
Serve with vegetables and the parsley and lemon garnish.

**Meat Puddings and Pie**
*There are few dishes in cold weather more generally liked than a Beef-Steak Pudding, but on the principle of the 'large pigeon pie most skilfully made to consist almost wholly of beef,' partaken of by the Intelligent Family, a beef-steak pudding is little the worse for being made of shin of beef.*

Mrs C. S. Peel, *Learning to Cook*

**Beef-Steak Pudding**
*To a steak pie add a third of the weight of part-cooked quartered Spanish onion, and the sliced (raw) potato and plenty of stock. The whole secret of the success of a meat pudding lies in long and slow cooking, so allow four hours and cook with great gentleness.*

Mrs C.S Peel, *Learning to Cook*

Traditionally, the filling of a meat pudding is added to the pudding basin uncooked. My version uses a partly pre-cooked filling.

Ingredients
For the Beef filling
30g beef dripping

209

1 large onion, chopped
1 tsp mustard
2 carrots, peeled and diced
2 level tbsp plain flour
Seasoning
225g Silverside, shin, or stewing steak, cut into bite-size pieces
300ml ale
300ml beef stock
1 bay leaf

For the Suet Pastry
Butter for the pudding basin
110g suet or shredded Atora beef suet
450g plain flour
1 tsp salt
2tsp baking powder
Water – ice cold

You will need a 1.2 litre pudding basin.
Serves 6-8

Prepare the Filling
1. In a heavy based pan melt the dripping and fry the onion in it until glossy.
2. Stir in the mustard and the carrots and set aside.
3. In a mixing bowl, sprinkle the flour over the beef with some salt and pepper.
4. Add the beef to the pan and brown.
5. Stir in the ale and then the stock. Add the bay leaf and simmer for 5 minutes.

Prepare the pastry
1. In a mixing bowl, combine the shredded suet with the flour and baking powder.
2. Add cold water a little at a time and using your hands, mix until a firm but not wet paste is formed.
3. Butter the pudding basin and line with the paste to an even thickness of about 5mm.
4. With the leftover paste, roll a lid to fit snugly on top of the filled pudding.

Assembly
1. Spoon the beef filling into the lined basin and place the pastry lid on top, pressing the edges down so that no filling escapes.
2. Place a layer of baking paper and a layer of foil (foil on top) on a flat work

surface and fold a pleat into the centre to give room for the pudding to expand.
3. Place this on top of the basin and tie string around the edge tightly to secure it, folding a length of string across the centre and looping it under the opposite side to form a handle for lifting. Cut around the edges of the paper to form a circle and tuck the foil under the edges of the baking paper.
4. Now place the pudding in a pan of simmering water for 6 hours, ensuring the water is kept topped up to ¾ way up the basin.
5. Carefully lift the pudding basin from the water. Cut the string and remove the foil/paper. Loosen the sides of the pudding with a spatula, put a serving plate on top of the basin and turn it over to unmould.
Serve

### Bacon Pudding

In bringing the culinary past back to life, I tried this recipe having little idea of the end result: delicious. Suet puddings are new to me and I think this one will be what I choose the next time I have friends for dinner.

Here is Granny Dot's original recipe:

*Materials.- 4 ozs lean bacon; 4 potatoes (raw); 1 large onion; 1 tablespoonful of minced parsley; thyme, marjoram and sage; 1/4 lb suet paste or paste without fat; seasoning.*

*Method.- Roll out the pastry as for jam roll. Cut the bacon and peeled potatoes into dice. Mince the onion, spread all over the pastry and sprinkle the herbs and seasoning over. Roll up, tie in a scalded floured cloth and boil 2 hours.*

*To Dish - Turn out of the cloth on to a hot dish, and pour brown or tomato sauce round.*
Mrs C.S. Peel, *The Daily Mail Cookery Book*

Ingredients
For the Suet Paste
50g suet
pinch of salt
¼ tsp baking powder
110g plain flour
ice cold water

For the Bacon Pudding
110g suet paste
110g lean bacon
2 potatoes finely diced

211

½ onion finely chopped
1 tbsp Parsley, thyme, sage, marjoram finely chopped
Seasoning

Serves 4-6

1. Using your hands, mix the suet paste ingredients in a mixing bowl with a little cold water. Lightly flower a worktop. Roll the pastry out into a rectangle about 1.5cm thick. Lay bacon pudding ingredients on top of the suet paste and roll it up like a jam roly poly. Seal the edges by squeezing them together.
2. To steam, lay a pudding cloth or muslin on the worktop. Roll the pudding in the cloth and secure it by tying string so that it is in the shape of a Christmas cracker. Place the pudding in a casserole and pour boiling water on top so that it is completely covered. Allow to simmer over a medium heat for 2 hours, topping up with hot water when necessary.
or
Preheat the oven it to 180°C/Gas Mark 4.
Place a sheet of foil on a flat work surface with a sheet of baking paper on top of it. Butter the baking paper and place the pudding on top. Wrap the paper and foil loosely around the pudding, rolling and squeezing together so that hot air cannot escape and the pudding has some room to expand a little. Bake for 40 minutes until cooked.
3. Remove the pudding and when it is not too hot to handle, unwrap it.
4. Place the pudding on a serving dish and slice.
Serve with Granny Dot's tomato sauce (see page 197) or gravy.


## PIE PASTRY
*The crust of a pie is so important that if you cannot trouble to make it well it is better not to make it at all.*

Mrs C.S. Peel, *Learning to Cook*


### Rough Puff Pastry
This is crumbly, crisp and perfect for meat pies. Excess pastry may be frozen.
   Here is Granny Dot's original recipe:

*Materials and Method.-The following is the more usual pie pastry: 1lb. of dry and sifted flour (you sift the flour in order to avoid lumps). Put this in a basin and make a hollow in it (this is what cooks call making a well) and work into it 8 oz. of margarine or half margarine and half clarified beef dripping. Working in means*

212

*cutting the fat into pieces and then rubbing it lightly into the flour with delicately clean floured fingers. Add a teaspoonful of salt to the flour before you add the fat. When the flour looks like fine breadcrumbs add the yolk of one or two eggs (according to what you feel inclined to afford), and mix to a smooth dough with very cold water. Dredge the pastry board with flour and roll the paste out to the thickness of half an inch, fold in three, roll out again, fold in three again. Cover with a clean cloth and leave in a cool place. Repeat until you have given six rolls, then leave it for fifteen minutes. Roll out not quite half an inch thick. This sounds more tiresome than it is, but you can go on with other work in the intervals of pastry making, ...'*

Mrs C.S. Peel, *Learning to Cook*

Ingredients
450g plain flour
1 tsp salt
110g beef dripping or lard
110g unsalted butter
2 free range or organic egg yolks
Ice cold water

1. Combine the ingredients in a mixing bowl so that it resembles a very coarse crumble topping.
2. Add water and bring the pastry together with your hands. Ensure that it is not sticky; the less water you use, the more delicious.
3. On a lightly floured worktop roll it out into a long rectangle roughly 20cm x 40cm.
4. Fold it like a letter, folding the bottom third over the middle third, and the top third over the middle third. Turn it 90 degrees and roll again into the same long rectangle. Repeat the folds.
5. Wrap it in clingfilm and leave in the fridge for 20 minutes before repeating the process. Return it to the fridge and repeat the process again so that the pastry has had 6 roll and folds.
6. Refrigerate wrapped in clingfilm until needed.

### *Shortcrust Pastry*
Traditionally shortcrust pastry was made with added baking powder.
    In the words of Granny Dot:

*Hot oven. Time, according to the use to which the pastry is put.*

*Materials. – ½ lb. of flour; 3 oz. of fat (dripping, lard or clarified fat); ½ teaspoonful of baking powder; cold water to mix, pinch of salt.*

213

*Method.- Sieve the flour, salt and baking powder into a basin, rub in the fat and mix all to a stiff dough with the water. Flour a board and rolling pin. Roll out the pastry to the required thickness and use for meat pies, tarts, etc.*

*A richer pastry is made by using ¼ lb. of margarine or butter to ½ lb. flour, and mixing with sour milk, or milk and water.*

*Reasons for failure.– If mixed too wet the pastry will not roll properly; and becomes sodden and heavy. If put into too hot an oven it scorches before being cooked properly. If into too cold an oven, the pastry does not rise well and becomes hard.*
Mrs C.S. Peel, *The Daily Mail Cookery Book*

Ingredients
225g plain flour
½ tsp baking powder
A pinch of salt
55g beef dripping or lard, diced
55g unsalted butter, diced
Ice cold water

1. Mix the dry ingredients together in a mixing bowl and add the fat. Rub it in, lightly lifting the mixture as you crumble.
2. Stir in as small amount of cold water as possible so that the ingredients come together. Too much water equals tough chewy pastry.
3. Form the pastry into a disc shape and wrap it in cling film.
4. Put it in the fridge until needed.

### Italian Pie
This could not have been more welcoming on a winter's day after a cold mucking out session of a friend's horses in the rain.
Here is Granny Dot's recipe:

*Materials - 1/2 lb of any kind of cooked meat; 4 ozs. of macaroni; 1 teaspoonful of chopped parsley; 1/2 pint of white sauce (see page 000); salt; pepper; short-crust pastry.*

*Method.- Free the meat from skin and gristle, and cut it into dice. Boil the macaroni and mix it with the white sauce, meat, parsley, and seasoning. Grease and line a plain round cake tin with short-crust pastry, fill with the meat and macaroni mixture, cover with a round of pastry, seal the edges well. Bake in a moderate oven for 1 hour. Macaroni and cheese sauce baked thus in pastry is delicious.*

*To dish.- Turn out carefully on to a very hot dish.*

*Reasons for failure.– If cooked too fast the pastry will become too brown. If the oven is not hot enough when the pastry goes in it will become hard and not rise well.*
Mrs C.S. Peel, The Daily Mail Cookery Book

Ingredients
Rough Puff or Shortcrust pastry (see page 212 and 213)
300ml white sauce (see page 133)
55g strong cheddar, grated
225g diced ham
110g macaroni, boiled for ten minutes, drained and tossed in butter to prevent it sticking
Two handfuls of frozen peas
1 free range or organic egg, beaten

You will need a pie dish 20cm x 18cm
Serves 6-8

1. Preheat the oven to 200°C/Gas Mark 6.
2. Thinly roll out the pastry and line a pie dish (set aside enough for the lid).
3. In a pan warm the white sauce, add the cheese and stir until blended.
4. Mix in the ham, macaroni and peas before spooning it into the pie dish.
5. Carefully place the pastry lid on top and make a hole using a sharp knife in the centre for the air to escape. Use a fork to seal the edges.
6. Brush the top of the pie with egg.
7. Bake for 20 minutes or until golden brown on top. Remove the pie from the oven and serve at whichever temperature you prefer.
If you make this more than a day in advance and serve it warm, because the pie can become a little dry, you may like to make more of the cheese sauce to serve alongside.

**Additional Meat and Game Dishes**
***Jugged Rabbit***
In this recipe the addition of wine or port is essential for a rich flavour. In addition to the optional flour, you could also add celery and carrot with the onion for a more robust finish. If you cook this for longer than two hours, it will fall off the bone and become more of a ragout.
This is Granny Dot's original recipe:

Jugged Rabbit (*emmafarquharphotography*)

*Materials.- 1 rabbit; 2 onions; 12 peppercorns; 1 ½ pints of stock; 1 teaspoonful salt; ½ oz. flour; 2 ozs. Dripping.*

*Method. – Wash the rabbit well, and cut into neat joints. Soak the head in water for half an hour. Peel and slice the onions. Melt the fat in a frying pan, fry the pieces of rabbit brown on each side. Put into a jar or casserole, fry the onions and add to the rabbit with the stock; peppercorns and salt. Add some forcemeat balls, made of veal forcemeat, the last half hour. Cover the jar and bake in a moderate oven for 2 hours. Strain off the gravy into a pan. Blend the flour with a little cold water, add to the gravy with a teaspoonful of red currant jelly and stir over the fire until it thickens. Boil 3 minutes. A gill of claret added to the rabbit while cooking is a great improvement.*

*To Dish. – Send to table in the casserole or arrange the pieces of rabbit neatly on a hot dish, pour some of the gravy over. The remainder of the gravy should be sent to table in a sauce boat.*

*Garnishes usually served. – Forcemeat balls and red currant jelly.*
*Reasons for failure. – If the oven is too hot the rabbit cooks too quickly and becomes hard.*

Mrs C.S. Peel, *The Daily Mail Cookery Book*


Ingredients
For the Rabbit
1 rabbit, cut into joints, including the fillet from the back.
Seasoning
1 tbsp plain flour (optional)
55g beef dripping or lard
2 onions
1 carrot (optional)
1 celery stick (optional)
125ml of red wine such as claret, or port
850ml of chicken or rabbit stock
Salt and pepper
1 tsp redcurrant jelly

For the Veal Forcemeat Stuffing
55g fresh or dried breadcrumbs
25g suet
1 tbsp chopped parsley
1 tsp mixed herbs
Grated rind of 1 lemon
1 free range or organic egg
Seasoning

Serves 4

To make Forcemeat
1. Mix the forcemeat ingredients together in a mixing bowl. With wet hands form the mixture into 3cm balls.
2. Set aside on a plate ready to be added to the pot.

To make Jugged Rabbit
1. Preheat the oven to 150°C/Gas Mark 2.
2. Melt the fat in a casserole.
3. Season the rabbit joints and for a thicker sauce toss them in flour before adding to the casserole to brown.

4. Add the sliced onions (and optional carrot and celery) and stir occasionally until glossy.
5. Pour in the red wine or port and let the alcohol evaporate for a minute or so.
6. Stir the stock into the casserole, cover and place in the oven for 2 hours, or longer for the meat to fall from the bone.
7. Place the forcemeat balls in the casserole for the last 20 minutes of cooking.
8. Taste the sauce and add seasoning and redcurrant jelly according to taste.
This dish can be left in the fridge for a couple of days which if anything, improves its rich and delicious flavour.

### Chicken en Casserole
This is a dish I will cook again and again. The addition of mace is what makes it so special. In the words of Granny Dot:

*Materials.- A chicken, pheasant or rabbit; 4 rashers of bacon; parsley, lemon peel, 2 cloves, 8 peppercorns tied together in muslin; 1 onion; 1/2 pint water; a pinch of mace; salt and pepper; a dessertspoonful of glaze or a little browning.*

*Method.- The chicken may be cooked whole if the casserole is sufficiently large, but in that case it needs to be served on another dish, as it would be inconvenient to carve it in the high sided casserole. For that reason it is preferable to divide the bird. Cut it into neat joints. Cut the rashers of bacon into dice and place in the casserole. When the fat melts, put in the chicken, the finely minced onion, and cook till just coloured. Then add the water and bag of herbs. Cover the casserole and cook slowly in the oven for 1½ to 3 hours, according to the age of the bird. Remove the muslin of herbs. Stir into the gravy a spoonful of glaze or a few drops of browning. If liked, a little sherry may be added.*

Mrs C.S. Peel, *My Own Cookery Book*

Ingredients
250g bacon, chopped
50g butter
1 onion, sliced
1 free-range or organic chicken weighing approximately 1.8kg, portioned
Bouquet garni containing 2 cloves, ½ tsp powdered mace, 1 generous sprig of parsley, 3 peels of lemon (cut a square of muslin, put the contents in and tie with string)
300ml water

Serves 4-6

1. Preheat the oven to 170°C/Gas Mark 5.

2. Put the bacon in a casserole over a medium heat and fry until cooked, adding a little butter if necessary.
3. Add the onion to the casserole with some butter stirring occasionally until glossy. Remove from the pan into a bowl.
4. Season the chicken portions and fry them in the pan until golden, adding more butter if necessary.
5. Put the bouquet garni, onion, bacon and water in the casserole and bake with the lid on for 1½ hours. Remove from the oven.
Serve with perhaps mashed potato and sprouting broccoli.

### Poulet Marengo
Although the idea for this recipe came from Dorothy's autobiography, I did not find a recipe for it in her books. It was a favourite of Granny Dot's, produced by a cook she had in London.

*Then came to us Alice; an eighteen-year-old girl like a Persian kitten. We loved Alice and Alice loved us. She knew everything, more indeed than it was possible that she could know, and she made a delicious Poulet Marengo with a suspicion of garlic in it. This child became a family friend. ... At the flat Alice waited, beaming with joy; fires were burning, lights lit, spring flowers blooming. It was evident that the Poulet Marengo was cooking. When, after marrying a railway guard who retired and kept an inn, and bringing up a family, she died, we mourned our loss.*
Mrs C.S. Peel, *Life's Enchanted Cup: An Autobiography, 1872–1933*

Ingredients
1 free-range or organic chicken weighing approximately 1.8kg, portioned
3 tbsp plain flour
seasoning
100g butter
2 onions, sliced
2 cloves of garlic, finely chopped
1 pinch of cayenne
300ml of dry white wine
250g peeled chopped tomatoes
200ml chicken stock
400g mushrooms
1 tbsp parsley finely chopped
1 teaspoon lemon juice

Serves 4-6
1. Coat the chicken portions in seasoned flour.

2. Melt half the butter in a casserole or large frying pan and add the chicken. Fry until brown and set aside in a bowl.
3. Add the onions to the casserole and cook until glossy and then stir in the garlic and cayenne. Cook for a minute or two before adding the white wine.
4. Let the alcohol cook out for about 3 minutes before adding the tomatoes and the stock.
5. Return the chicken pieces to the pan and cover with a lid. Leave it to simmer for 30 minutes until the meat easily comes away from the bone.
6. While the chicken is cooking, fry the mushrooms in the remaining butter with some salt, and add to the casserole for the last ten minutes of cooking.
Serve with mashed potato or rice.

### Stewed Partridge with Cabbage (Old Birds)

I give you a succulent and mouth-watering recipe which, in Granny Dot's words may be applied to any old bird.

*Materials and Method.- Brown a brace of partridges in the stewpan, using clarified dripping, add a piece of pork or bacon cut in small pieces, a little chopped onion, two cloves, two chopped carrots, a bay leaf and some stock, and simmer for one and a half hours. Cut a Savoy cabbage into quarters, boil for twenty minutes, drain, and place in the stewpan with the rest about half an hour before it is done. Take out the cabbage, drain and press it, and place it in an entree dish. Arrange the birds in the centre. Strain the gravy, skim off the fat and pour it over the birds.*

Mrs C.S. Peel, *My Own Cookery Book*

Ingredients
25g fat – butter, goosefat, lard, beef dripping or oil
1 onion, finely chopped
1 carrot, finely chopped
1 stick celery, finely chopped
4 rashers bacon, chopped
50g butter plus a little more if needed
2 partridges
Seasoning
½ tbsp plain flour
1 tsp tomato puree
275ml chicken or game stock
½ Savoy Cabbage

Serves 2

1. Place the oil in a casserole over a medium heat and fry the vegetables until glossy.
2. Remove the vegetables from the casserole to a bowl and set aside.
3. Add the bacon to the casserole and when cooked but not crisp, remove and set aside.
4. Put the butter in the casserole over a high heat and season the partridges before browning them. Remove from the heat and set aside in a bowl.
5. Turn the heat down and return the vegetables to the casserole, adding more butter if necessary. Stir in the flour followed by the tomato puree.
6. Gradually pour the stock into the casserole, stirring as you do so.
7. Return the bacon and partridge to the casserole and cover with a lid. Place over a medium heat for an hour or until the meat feels tender and comes away from the bone. Twenty minutes before the cooking is finished put the cabbage, divided into segments in the casserole.
Serve.

### Salmi of Duck or Goose

The secret here is to add a Seville orange. If you use a standard orange, it will be good, but not special.

In the words of Granny Dot:

*Materials – 1 roast duck, or remains of roast goose; 3 shallots and 2 onions; pepper; cayenne; salt; 1 bitter orange.*

*Method.– Put the giblets of the duck or goose into some good stock with the finely shredded onions or shallots, cayenne, pepper and salt and stew gently for 25 minutes. Cut the bird into neat pieces, and add, simmer until hot.*

*To Dish.– Arrange the pieces of duck neatly on a hot dish, boil up the gravy, add the juice of the orange and strain over the duck. Serve very hot.*

Mrs C.S. Peel, *The Daily Mail Cookery Book*

Ingredients
25g fat – butter, goose fat, lard, beef dripping or oil
3 shallots, finely sliced
2 onions, finely sliced
1 duck, cooked and segmented
Cayenne pepper
Seasoning
Juice of 1 orange
1 Seville orange, peel (avoiding pith) and juice
60ml game or chicken stock

221

Salmi of Duck (*emmafarquharphotography*)

Serves 2

1. Melt the fat over a medium heat in a pan. Add the shallots and onions and cook until tender.
2. Sprinkle the duck pieces with a little cayenne pepper and some seasoning.
3. Add the duck to the pan with the stock juice and peel of the orange.
4. Heat through and serve.

## PUDDINGS

*'There are certain puddings which the woman who is obliged to cater economically must often order, and which may be very good and often are extremely nasty.*

*Suet Pudding is one of these. One meets it looking rather grey and greasy in the shape of a badly stuffed bolster, or sometimes it is made in a pudding basin. But the shape has little effect on its unpleasant consistency.*

*Now a suet pudding when well made is quite light and crumbly, and can appear plain to be eaten with brown sugar or treacle, or it may be enriched with sultanas, figs, marmalade, or jam. It is a very nourishing and wholesome pudding for children always supposing that it is properly made.*

*No matter what kind of suet pudding you make, be certain that the suet is untainted and free from every vestige of skin and fibre and shred it very finely. If you use Hugo's Atora suet use less than of ordinary suet. This suet may be bought shred fine and ready for use.'*

Mrs C.S. Peel, *Learning to Cook*

A friend said that if she had to choose a final dish, it would be a suet pudding. They conjure up memories of the good side of traditional school dinners, a Sunday lunch finale, or a modern day indulgence.

### *Burghwallis Sunday Plum Pudding*

Burghwallis Rectory in South Yorkshire belonged to the parents in law of Granny Dot. This recipe is seen in pre-war cookery books and wartime cookery books under the heading of *Plain Plum Pudding*. The most exciting thing about this is walking into the kitchen to be met by an amazing aroma of warm biscuits and sultanas.

In the words of Granny Dot:

*Materials and Method.- Sieve the flour and baking powder together, rub in the finely shredded suet, add the cleaned sultanas, stir in the well-beaten eggs and the syrup and add a little milk, sufficient to mix to a slightly runny consistency. Turn into a well-greased basin and steam for 4 hours. This pudding should be a deep golden brown in colour, light and crumbly in consistency.*

Mrs C.S. Peel, *My Own Cookery Book*

<u>Ingredients</u>
225g plain flour
1 tsp baking powder
1 pinch salt
170g suet
Zest of 1 unwaxed lemon
1 tsp mixed spice
225g sultanas or other dried fruit
2 tbsp golden syrup
2 free range or organic eggs, beaten
80ml full fat milk
butter for the basin

You will need a 1 litre pudding basin
Serves 8

1. Put the first 7 ingredients in a mixing bowl.
2. Warm the syrup and whisk it with the milk and eggs before mixing into the dry ingredients. For a light textured pudding do not over mix.
3. Butter the basin and lightly press the mixture into it.
4. Place a layer of baking paper and a layer of foil (foil on top) on a flat work surface and fold a pleat into the centre to give room for the pudding to rise a little.
5. Place this on top of the basin and tie string around the edge tightly to secure it, folding a length of string looping it under the opposite side to form a handle for lifting. Cut around the edges of the paper to form a circle and tuck the foil under the edges of the baking paper.
6. Now place the pudding in a pan of simmering water for 3 hours, ensuring the water is kept topped up to ¾ way up the basin.
7. Carefully remove the pudding basin from the water. Cut the string and remove the foil/paper. Loosen the sides of the pudding with a spatula. Put a serving plate on top of the basin and turn it over to unmould.
Serve with cream, custard or ice-cream.

### *Jam Roll*
Fillings of treacle, jam, mincemeat or a mixture of golden syrup, breadcrumbs and lemon juice are suggested. For a standard sized roly poly, use the quantity below. For a more delicate roly poly, make two smaller rolls. This petite pudding allows you to have three slices and to somehow feel a little less guilty!

Traditionally, suet puddings did not contain butter. Its addition does, however,

Jam Roll (*Author's own*)

benefits the flavour and gives it a pretty golden colour. Here is Granny Dot's original recipe:

*Method.- When the dough is mixed, roll it out on a floured board in a long strip. Spread with syrup, cover thickly with breadcrumbs, sprinkle with lemon-juice. Leave an edge all round the paste unspread. Roll up and seal the ends of the roll well together. Tie loosely in a cloth that has been wrung out in boiling water and well floured. Tie the ends with string. Place in a steamer or in a pan of boiling water and boil or steam steadily for 3 hours. Untie the cloth and serve the pudding on a hot dish.*

Mrs C.S. Peel, *My Own Cookery Book*

Ingredients
170g self raising flour
85g shredded suet or 55g suet and 30g unsalted butter
Pinch of salt
Zest of a lemon (optional)

225

60ml of full fat milk plus extra if needed
½ a jar of strawberry or raspberry jam

Serves 4-6

1. Mix the flour, suet, salt, lemon zest and milk together until combined. Do not over mix so that the pudding is kept light in texture.
2. Sprinkle a worktop with flour. Roll out the paste to 34cm x 28cm. You may prefer to make two smaller rolls measuring 14cm x 17cm each which will fit into a steamer more easily. If you make the larger version, it will not fit in the steamer and so you will need to bake it in the oven over a roasting tin of simmering water instead. In this case, preheat the oven to 180°C/Gas Mark 4.
3. Spread the jam over the top of the suet paste, leaving a 2cm edge around the circumference.
4. Roll the suet paste towards you lightly, so that it has room to expand, being careful not to lose the jam through the edges.
5. Put a sheet of foil on a flat work surface with a sheet of baking paper on top. Place the pudding in its centre.
6. Seal the foil and baking paper leaving a gap between it and the pudding so that it has room to expand.
7. Fold and scrunch up the edges of the paper and foil so that the roll is airtight.
8. Place the roll(s) in a steamer or in the oven for 1 hour.
If using a steamer, make sure the pan is topped up with water so it does not dry out while simmering. If using the oven, remember to place a roasting tin of simmering water below the pudding.
Serve sliced with ice-cream, custard or cream.

### *My Own Christmas Pudding*
This wins, hands down. We tested it against other puddings and it really is the best, I think largely because it is lighter texture due to the addition of suet.
   In the words of Granny Dot:

*The following quantities make about four 2-lb. puddings.*
*1lb. of raisins; 1 lb. of sultanas; 1 lb. of currants; ½ lb. of mixed candied peel; 2 oz. of almonds; 2 oz. of ground almonds; 1 teaspoonful of mixed spice; 1 nutmeg; 1 lb of suet or butter; 1/4lb of flour; 3/4 lb of fine breadcrumbs; 1 lb of brown sugar; ½ teaspoonful of salt; 9 eggs or 4 eggs, and quarter of a pint of beer; 1 lemon; 1 orange; ¼ pint of brandy.*
   *Pick over the fruit, stone the raisins, blanch the almonds by placing them in boiling water and removing the brown skins. Finely chop the almonds and candied*

Christmas Pudding (*Author's own*)

*peel. Grate the nutmeg and the rind of the orange and lemon. Dry the flour in the oven and sift it. In a large basin, mix together the breadcrumbs and finely shred suet, the fruit, the peel, the chopped and ground almonds, salt, nutmeg, spice, grated orange and lemon rind, and sugar. If butter is used, cream it and the sugar together and then add crumbs, etc. Add the sifted flour, and then mix in the beaten eggs. Add the strained juice of the orange and lemon, the milk or beer if used, and the brandy. Stir slowly. Cover the basin with a clean cloth and leave overnight. Stir well again and turn into greased pudding basins. Cover with pudding cloth, scalded in boiling water and well floured. Boil for 8 to 12 hours. Remove the cloth, allow the steam to escape from the pudding, cover them again with greaseproof paper and a clean cloth and keep in a cool, dry place until wanted. Boil for a further 6 to 8 hours when required for use.*

Mrs C S Peel, *My Own Cookery Book*

<u>Ingredients</u>
225g raisins
225g sultanas
225g currants
110g mixed candied peel (optional)

227

30g chopped almonds (optional)
30g ground almonds (60g if chopped almonds are not used)
½ tsp mixed spice
½ nutmeg, grated
225g suet or half suet, half unsalted butter
55g flour
170g breadcrumbs
225g brown sugar
2 free range or organic eggs, beaten
70ml beer
70ml brandy
Orange, rind and juice
Lemon, rind and juice
Butter for the basins

Makes 2 puddings in 1.2 litre basins
Serves 18-20

1. Mix all of the ingredients together in a mixing bowl. Cover with a tea towel and leave overnight in a cool place.
2. Turn the mixture into buttered pudding basins.
3. Place a layer of baking paper and a layer of foil (foil on top) on a flat work surface and fold a pleat into the centre to give room for the puddings to rise a little.
4. Put this on top of the basins and tie string around the edge tightly to secure it, folding a length of string across the centre and looping it under the opposite side to form a handle for lifting. Cut around the edges of the paper to form a circle and tuck the foil under the edges of the baking paper.
5. Place the basins in pans of simmering water for 6-8 hours, ensuring the water is kept topped up to ¾ way up the basin.
6. Carefully remove the pudding basins from the water.
7. Store in a cool place until use. The second pudding will keep until the following Christmas. Steam the pudding for a further 3 hours before serving.
8. Cut the string and remove the foil/paper. Loosen the sides of the pudding with a spatula.
9. Put a serving plate on top of the basin and turn it over to unmould.

Traditionally a sprig of holly is stuck into the top of the pudding. Half a cupful of brandy is then heated and poured over the pudding while being lit with a match. The pudding is presented in its flaming glory and served with brandy butter (delicious made with brown sugar).

### Banana Cake

This is more of a pudding than a cake insofar as it is quite dense, yet light, and when warm it suits being served as a pudding with cream, ice cream or custard.Granny Dot's recipe:

*Materials.- 4 bananas; glace cherries; 4oz. of brown sugar; 4 oz. of castor sugar; 2 eggs; 6 oz. of self-raising flour; 5 oz of butter or margarine; 1/4 pint of sour milk or milk.*

*Method.- Melt 2oz. of butter or margarine in the bottom of a cake-tin. Scatter in the brown sugar and arrange 2 sliced bananas and some glace cherries over it.*

*Cream the remainder of the butter, add the sugar and beat well until light and fluffy. Beat in the eggs. Stir in 2 mashed bananas and sift in the flour. Add the milk or sour milk and beat together. Pour into the tin on top of the sliced bananas and bake for 50 minutes in a moderate oven.*

Mrs C.S. Peel, *My Own Cookery Book*

Ingredients
250g butter
110g brown sugar
4 bananas, ripe
glace cherries, about 8 (optional)
110g castor sugar
2 free range or organic eggs
170g self raising flour
300ml full fat yoghurt, soured cream, full fat milk or a mixture

You will need a 20cm cake tin
Serves 10

1. Preheat the oven to 180°C/Gas Mark 4.
2. Put half of the butter in the cake tin and place the tin in the oven until the butter has melted.
3. Remove the tin from the oven and scatter the brown sugar over the butter. Neatly arrange 2 sliced bananas and some chopped-up glace cherries on top.
4. Cream the remaining butter with the caster sugar until light and fluffy.
5. Beat in the eggs and flour.
6. Mix in two mashed bananas
7. Add the milk or yoghurt and beat until fully mixed.

8. Spoon the mixture into the tin on top of the sliced bananas and bake for 45 minutes.
9. Remove from the oven and cool in the tin for ten minutes before removing the cake onto a cooling rack.
Serve warm.

### Canadian Lemon Pie
Granny Dot's recipe involves milk and cornflour which is much less time-consuming to make than many lemon meringue pie recipes. Part of the joy is in recreating the pastry which uses both lard and butter.

*Materials.- Short crust; 1½ tablespoonfuls of cornflour; ½ pint of milk; 5 oz. of sugar; 2 eggs; the grated rind and juice of 1 lemon.*

*Method.- Line a sandwich tin or flan case with short crust and make a neat dented edge. Prick the bottom, cover with greaseproof paper and fill with beans or crusts. Bake for 20 minutes (Regulo 7, 450 Elec.) and remove the paper and crusts.*

*Mix the cornflour smoothly with some of the milk, heat the remainder and pour on to the cornflour. Return to the pan and boil for 5 minutes, stirring well. Cool a little. Separate the yolks from the whites of the eggs. Beat the yolks and add them gradually to the cornflour, beating them well into the lemon rind, and strained lemon-juice, stirring all the time. Fill the pastry case with this mixture and bake for a few minutes in a moderate oven until set. Whisk the egg-whites very stiffly, sift the sugar, pile this meringue on top of the filling, dredge with castor sugar and dry gently in a cool oven for 20 minutes. Serve cold.*

Mrs C.S. Peel, *My Own Cookery Book*

Ingredients
Shortcrust pastry (see page 213)
3 tbsp cornflour
600ml full fat milk
280g caster sugar
Zest of and juice of 3 lemons
4 free range or organic eggs, separated

You will need a 23cm pastry tin, baking paper and baking beans.
Serves 10

1. Preheat the oven to 190°C/Gas mark 5.

Canadian Lemon Pie (*Author's own*)

2. Place the pastry on cling film or baking paper. Put another piece on top and roll out.
3. Remove the top layer of cling film or baking paper and turn the pastry dough over onto the tin and line it with the pastry.
4. Now scrumple up a piece of baking paper, then unscrumple and fit it snuggly on top of the lined pastry tin. Fill with baking beans.
5. Bake the pastry for 10 minutes.
6. Remove the pastry from the oven. Spoon the baking beans out of the case and remove the baking paper (be careful, I had hot beans flying around the kitchen with my poor dogs trying to eat them).
7. Return the pastry to the oven for another ten minutes and then remove. Set aside while you make the filling.
8. Heat the milk and mix a spoonful or two of it into a bowl with the cornflour. Mix it into a paste before adding the remaining milk. Return it to the pan and stir for a few minutes until it thickens.
9. Add 25g of sugar to pan and mix in. Allow to cool a little before mixing in the yolks, lemon zest and juice.
10. Pour the filling into the pastry case and bake for 20 minutes until the filling only wobbles a little.
11. Remove the tart from the oven and turn the temperature down to 140°C/Gas Mark 1.
12. In a large bowl whisk the egg whites and add the remaining sugar gradually. Keep whisking until you have a very stiff and glossy meringue.
13. Carefully spoon the meringue on top the lemon tart, creating peaks with a fork. Bake the tart for about 40 minutes. The pastry should be crisp and crumbly with a browned meringue top.
Serve warm or cold.

### *Apple Snow*
With its enticing name and apple meringue content, this is perhaps best suited for children.

In the words of Granny Dot:

*Materials.- 2lb. of cooking apples; 4 oz. of sugar; the thinly cut rind of a lemon; the whites of 2 eggs; 1 ½ oz. of ground almonds (optional); glace cherries; cream.*

*Method.- Peel, core and slice the apples. Stew them until tender with a very little water, the rind of the lemon and the sugar. Rub through a sieve. When cold, mix in the stiffly whipped egg-whites. Whip in the ground almonds and add more sugar if necessary. Serve in individual glasses decorated with cherries and whipped cream.*
Mrs C.S. Peel, *My Own Cookery Book*

Ingredients
2 free range or organic egg whites
80g caster sugar
300g apple puree (peel and core apples, roughly chop and place in a pan over a low heat with a little water until they soften)
Demerera sugar for sprinkling (optional)

You will need 4 glasses for serving.
Serves 4

1. Whip the whites to medium/stiff peak and whisk in the sugar.
2. Put the puree in a bowl and stir a spoonful of the whites into it.
3. Now fold the remaining egg white mixture into the puree and spoon into the glasses.
4. Sprinkle a little Demerara sugar on top of each filled glass and serve.

### *Almond Custard*

Adding jam to this pudding reminds me of a Bakewell tart without the pastry and with added coconut. If you would like to add orange flower water as in the original recipe, please do, though I would use teaspoons instead of the tablespoons in Granny Dot's recipe. Granny Dot advises to eat it cold. As a compromise, I think warm is perfect, with a dollop of cream.

In her words:

*Method.- 1/2 lb. sweet almonds, ½ lb. castor sugar, 3 tablespoonsful orange-flower water, 3 whole eggs, 4 oz. desiccated cocoanut, ¼ oz. bicarbonate of soda, and 3 gills milk.*

*Blanch the almonds, and pound them to a smooth paste in a mortar; add to this the sugar, orange-flower water and eggs, etc, mixing them well together and then adding the bicarbonate of soda; finally mixing it all thoroughly with the milk. Have ready a buttered piedish, put the mixture into this, and bake for 40 minutes. Leave the custard to cool, and serve cold in a glass dish, covered with whipped cream flavoured with castor sugar and vanilla essence.*

Mrs C.S. Peel, *Puddings and Sweets*

Ingredients
Butter for the dish
225g ground almonds
175g caster sugar

Almond Custard (emmafarquharphotography)

110g desiccated coconut
3 free range or organic eggs
140ml full fat milk
½ a jar of strawberry or raspberry jam

You need an ovenproof dish approximately 15cm x 20cm
Serves 6-8

1. Preheat the oven to 170°C/Gas Mark 3.
2. Butter a dish.
3. Put the almonds, sugar and coconut in a bowl. Beat the eggs with the milk in a jug and mix into the bowl. Add more milk if necessary so that the mixture easily drops from the spoon.
4. Spoon about half a jar of jam into the buttered dish and spread it over the base.
5. Pour the mixture on top of the jam and bake for 20-25 minutes.
Serve with cream at whichever temperature you prefer.

### Strawberry, Raspberry or Peach Shortcake
This is airy, light and pretty, though good luck in slicing it.
   In the words of Granny Dot:

*Materials.-4 oz. of butter; 8 oz. of flour; a pinch of salt; ¼ teaspoonful of baking powder; ½ oz. of ground almonds; 2 oz. of sugar; 1 egg; 1 lb. of strawberries, raspberries or peaches; ¼ pint cream.*

*Method.- Sieve together the flour, salt and baking powder. Cream the butter till light and frothy, add the sugar and cream again. Mix in the ground almonds and the beaten egg. Add the dried and sifted flour and mix to a stiff paste, adding a little milk if necessary.*
   *Have ready three buttered sandwich tins. Divide the paste into three portions and press with the hand into rounds to fit into the tins. Press into the tins and prick over with a fork. Bake for 30 to 40 minutes in a slow oven.*
   *Hull the strawberries and slightly whip the cream. Reserve about a dozen fine fruits for decoration: slice the rest and sprinkle with sugar. Shortly before serving, spread one of the rounds with strawberries, cover with a second cake spread in the same way and top with the third cake. Arrange the whole strawberries on top and pour on the slightly shipped cream.*
   *Raspberries will not require slicing; tinned peaches should be neatly cut up.*
                                        Mrs C.S. Peel, *My Own Cookery Book*

Ingredients
110g unsalted butter
50g caster sugar
1 tbsp ground almonds
225g plain flour
Pinch of salt
¼ tsp baking powder
140ml double cream
Icing sugar for sweetening (optional), and for sprinkling
A punnet of seasonal berries

You will need 3 x 20cm cake tins
Serves 10

1. Preheat the oven to 180°C/Gas Mark 4
2. In a mixing bowl cream the butter and sugar until light and fluffy and then add the almonds, flour, salt and baking powder.

3. Divide the mixture into 3 and press each into a cake tin.
4. Bake in the oven for 15–20 minutes until dry.
5. Remove from the oven and leave the shortbread to cool in the tin for 5 minutes before placing onto a cooling rack.
6. Shortly before serving, lightly whip the cream which you may like to sweeten a little with icing sugar.
7. Put one of the shortbreads on a serving dish followed by cream and fruit. Repeat the process with the other two layers until you have a pretty pudding.
8. Sprinkle with icing sugar and serve

### *Zabaglione*

This gloriously egg yellow and creamy zabaglione is to die for, eaten on its own or alongside poached pears or berries and plums in a cinnamon syrup, or any way you like.

In the words of Granny Dot:

*Materials.- The yolks of 6 eggs; 1 teacupful of castor sugar; 1 teacupful of Marsala, Madiera or sherry.*

*Method.- Place the egg-yolks in a basin, stir them well, gradually stir in the sugar and then the wine. Stand the basin over a pan of boiling water and whip over gentle heat until the mixture thickens and froths. Be very careful not to overheat the mixture or the eggs will curdle. Have ready some warmed Melba glasses. Turn the frothing mixture into these and serve immediately. Hand crisp sponge fingers or Cat's Tongue fingers with the Zabaglione.*

Mrs C.S. Peel, *My Own Cookery Book*

Ingredients
4 free range or organic egg yolks
50g caster sugar
1 tbsp or more according to taste of dark rum, brandy, Madeira, Poire William, peach schnapps, fruit liqueur, etc.

Serves 2-4

1. Put all of the above in a heatproof bowl set over, not in, a pan of simmering water.
2. Whisk for about 5 minutes until you have a thick and creamy zabaglione.
3. Serve warm or cover it with clingfilm and put it in the fridge until needed.

**Milk Puddings**
*The house keeper who is found down to a certain cash limit is apt to grumble that but little choice in the matter of puddings and sweets is possible to her. All good sweets, she complains, need eggs and cream. This is true of many recipes, but still there are a number of nice sweets which are quite inexpensive and in no way beyond the powers of the average single-handed cook. Cream, of course, is a luxury, but fortunately a little may be made to go a long way, for 1 gill is sufficient to add to a small soufflé or mousse or to the milk used in a bavarois. Machine-made cream or undiluted condensed milk can often be used and greatly lessen the expense.*

*The single-handed cook, if a sensible person, may often save herself much time and trouble by a little forethought.*

Mrs C.S. Peel, *The Single Handed Cook*

*Milk Pudding*
A Marmite recipe which is not everyone's cup of tea but most definitely mine.
In the words of Granny Dot:

<u>To Make Milk Puddings</u>
*Cool Oven. Time, 3 hours.*

*Materials.- 2 ozs. of any farinaceous food, such as rice, sago, tapioca; 1 pint of milk, or milk and water; 1 tablespoonful of sugar; pinch of salt.*

*Method.– Put the rice or any other cereal used at the bottom of a greased pie dish, add the salt, sugar and milk. Stir well, place in a cool oven, and cook slowly about 3 hours, until set. Stir occasionally the first hour. If liked nutmeg can be grated over the pudding, or any flavouring essence added to it. A little fat or suet can be added also if liked.*

*To Dish.– Place the pie dish in an entree dish, or on another dish.*

*Reasons for failure.– If the oven is too hot the pudding may boil over into it and waste. The moisture evaporates and leaves the cereal quite dry before it has cooked soft. Slow gentle cookery is required.*

Mrs C.S. Peel, *The Daily Mail Cookery Book*

<u>Ingredients</u>
Butter the dish
60g pudding rice, sago, or tapioca
1 tbsp caster sugar (I used vanilla sugar which is just caster sugar in which I put

237

vanilla pods, left forever really, until you need it.)
600ml full fat milk
Grated nutmeg
100ml double cream

You need a pudding basin or ovenproof dish with an 800ml capacity.
Serves 2

1. Preheat the oven to 140°C/Gas Mark 1.
2. Put the rice/tapioca/sago in the buttered dish with the sugar. Pour the milk on top.
3. Stir every now and then with a fork during the first hour. This helps to create a creamy pudding.
4. After an hour or so remove the dish from the oven and add some grated nutmeg (about ½ a nut) if you like. Return to the oven and then leave it for 2 hours until it is ready.
5. Taste it and if it would benefit from its addition, fold the skin over and carefully stir in some double cream.
I don't imagine that if you are eating rice pudding you are watching your waistline, but if you are, it is almost as good without cream, but not quite am afraid.
Serve with strawberry jam.

### Ground Rice Custard Pudding
Granny Dot's addition of a bay leaf is what makes this pudding perfect. A friend said it reminds her of her childhood.
   Granny Dot's recipe:

*Materials..- 1 pint of milk or milk and water; 1 bay leaf, or any flavouring essence liked; 2 ozs. of ground rice; 1 oz. of sugar; 1 egg*

*Method.- Put the milk and bay leaf into a pan, bring to the boil, remove the bay leaf, sprinkle in the ground rice, stir and simmer 6 minutes; remove from the fire and cool a little, beat up the egg with the sugar, add to the pudding, pour into a greased pie dish, and bake until set, in a cool oven.*

*Two dried eggs prepared according to directions may be used in place of an egg.*

*To Dish.- place the pie dish in an entree dish or on another dish and serve.*
*Reasons for failure. - If cooked too fast in the oven or too long the egg may curdle.*
                    Mrs C.S. Peel, *The Daily Mail Cookery Book*

Ingredients
Butter for the dish
600ml full fat milk
1 bay leaf
55g ground rice or semolina
25g sugar
1 free range or organic egg (optional)

You will need a small ovenproof dish. I used a round one 12cm in diameter.
Serves 2

1. Preheat the oven to 140°C/Gas Mark 1.
2. In a pan bring the milk to simmer with a bay leaf and add the ground rice through your fingers, whisking so it does not become lumpy.
3. Add the sugar and allow the mixture to simmer gently, stirring now and then until it is smooth.
4. Remove the pan from the heat so that the mixture can cool a little before adding the egg.
5. Whisk the egg and mix it in thoroughly.
6. Pour the mixture into the prepared dish and remove the bay leaf (you could leave it in if you would like to infuse the pudding further).
7. Bake for 30–40 minutes until it is reasonably firm.
Serve with jam

### *My Own Rice Mould*

Our neighbour Jane enjoyed this pudding so much she was unable to speak! It is creamy and really is a treat, especially the chocolate version. I think the past really is coming back to life in this pudding and I encourage you to try it.

In the words of Granny Dot:

*Materials.- 4 oz. of Carolina rice; 1 ½ to 2 pints of milk; 2 tablespoonfuls of castor sugar; 1 sheet of gelatine or ½ teaspoonful of powdered gelatine; the white of 1 egg; 2 or 3 tablepoonfuls of cream or undiluted condensed milk.*

*Method.- Wash the rice. Place it and the milk in a pan, bring to the boil and cook gently for 1 hour. Add the sugar and cook for a further 15 minutes. When the rice is perfectly soft through, turn into a basin and add the gelatine which has been dissolved in a little hot milk. Stir well and leave till nearly cold. Add the whipped cream or condensed milk and stiffly beaten white of an egg. Pour into a quart mould which has been rinsed out in cold water and left unwiped. Leave to set and turn out.*

239

*This Recipe results in a delicious, rich, creamy rice shape and may be used as the foundation for other cold sweets.*

Mrs C.S. Peel, *My Own Cookery Book*

Ingredients
55g pudding rice
700ml full fat milk
2 tbsp caster sugar
1 sheet of gelatine
110g chocolate buttons, broken up chocolate, or grated chocolate (optional)
1 large free range or organic egg white
2 tbsp cream
Vanilla pod (optional)

You will need 5 timbales or ramekins
Serves 5

1. Preheat the oven to 140°C/Gas Mark 1.
2. Place the rice and milk in a pan and simmer gently for 45 minutes, stirring now and then so that it does not catch on the base of the pan. You may like to add a vanilla pod, split in two lengthways.
3. Add the sugar and cook until the rice is softening. This will take about 8 minutes.
4. Soak the gelatine sheet in cold water until softened (a few minutes) and then add it to the rice.
5. If using, add the chocolate to the rice while it is still warm enough to melt.
6. Stir in the cream and set the mixture aside.
7. Whip the egg white until it reaches medium peak. Stir a spoonful into the mixture before folding in the remainder.
8. Take the moulds and rinse them in cold water.
9. Pour the mixture into the moulds and put them in the fridge for at least a couple of hours before turning out.
If you are not serving the puddings the day you make them, cover with cling film so that they do not dry out.
10. To serve, loosen the edges with a spatula, place a small plate on top of each mould, turn it over and tap the top until the pudding unmoulds.
   Bananas work really well with the chocolate version: put chopped banana in a pan over a medium heat and sprinkle 1 tbsp of Demerara sugar on top. When warm, serve with the chocolate rice mould.
   Berries are a good accompaniment with the vanilla version: put 3 tbsp of caster or granulated sugar in a pan over a low heat with about 1½ tbsp water until

melted. Pour this on top of a cupful of berries so as to bring out their full flavour, before serving.

Alternatively, just have good old strawberry or raspberry jam alongside.

### Honeycombe Cream

'That custard pudding was delicious, so light and yummy!' – the reaction of my taste tester. Here is Granny Dot's recipe:

*Materials.- 3 teacupsful of milk, 1 teacupful of castor sugar, 1 teaspoonful vanilla essence, 1/2 oz. best leaf gelatine, 3 eggs, some jam.*

*Method.- Put the milk, sugar, vanilla and gelatine into a pan and dissolve. Stir in the yolks very slowly and stir continuously, till it all thickens, but does not boil. Whip the whites to a stiff froth, stir them in, and turn it all into a mould, in which any jam to taste has been put. leave in a cool place to set.*

Mrs C.S. Peel, *My Own Cookery Book*

Ingredients
500ml full fat milk
125g caster sugar
4 sheets of leaf gelatine
1 tsp vanilla extract
3 free range or organic eggs, separated
4 tbsp of jam or fruit coulis
You will need 4 timbales or ramekins

Serves 4

1. Heat the milk and sugar in a pan until the sugar has melted. Stir in the gelatine and vanilla.
2. Cool the mixture for a few minutes before adding yolks. Stir over a low heat until the mixture thickens.
3. Whisk the whites to a medium peak and stir a third of them into the mixture. Fold in the remaining whites.
4. Rinse the moulds with water to aid the removal of the honeycombe cream when it has set.
5. Place some jam or coulis into the base of the moulds and spoon the mixture on top. Cover with clingfilm.
6. Leave to set in the fridge for about 3 hours or so.
7. To serve, loosen the edges with a spatula, place a small plate on top of each mould, turn it over and tap the top until the pudding falls.
You could smarten it up with some berries or eat as it is.

## TEA TIME TREATS

### *Feather Tart*

This is the first of the recipes I took from Granny Dot's books. It is perfect as it is, like a fancy jam tart. Everyone who has tried it has asked for the recipe.

In the words of Granny Dot:

*Materials.- 1lb of self raising flour; 2 oz of sugar; 4 oz. of butter, margarine, or margarine and lard mixed; 1 egg; 1 small teaspoonful of almond essence of rum; jam.*

*Method.- Sift the flour, rub in the fat, add the sugar, mix in the beaten egg and the almond essence or rum. Knead all together. Divide the paste into two portions. Roll out one portion on a well-floured board and use it to line a well-greased sandwich tin. Spread thickly with apricot jam. Cover all over with little pieces of the second portion of the paste, each piece being about as much as can be picked up between finger and thumb. Bake for 1 hour in a moderate oven.*

*If preferred, the second portion of paste can be rolled out, small circles stamped out and used to cover the jam, overlapping slightly.*

Mrs C.S. Peel, *My Own Cookery Book*

Feather Tart (*Author's own*)

<u>Ingredients</u>
225g self-raising flour
55g sugar
110g unsalted butter
1 free range or organic egg
1tsp of rum or almond essence if you like
A pot of jam

You will need a 20cm cake tin.
Serves 8-10

1. Preheat the oven to 190°C/Gas Mark 5.
2. Mix all of the ingredients apart from the jam, together. Do so with a light hand as it is, after all, a 'feather' tart.
3. Roll out half of the mixture on a lightly floured worktop. Press it into the cake tin.
4. Spread jam thickly over the top of the mixture in the tin.
5. Break off little pieces of the remaining mixture and put them on top of the jam. This creates a light 'feathery' effect.
6. Bake in the oven for 30–40 minutes until lightly browned.
7. Allow to cool in the tin for 5 minutes before turning out onto a cooling rack. Serve.

### *Hazel Cake*
The layers of this cake make it seem decadent, with its light and creamy texture and the added crunch of hazelnuts.
    In the words of Granny Dot:

*Materials.- 4 oz. of flour; 4 oz. of butter; 4 oz. of sugar; 1 teaspoonful of baking powder; 2 eggs; 2 oz. of hazel nuts; 1 teaspoonful of coffee essence; a little milk; butter icing for filling; white, chocolate or coffee glace icing or milk frosting.*

*Method.- Chop the nuts and roast them under the grill until well browned, taking care to toss and turn them about so that they do not burn. Reserve a few whole nuts for decoration. Warm a cake-tin, rub the inside with butter or margarine, flour it well and shake out any flour that does not adhere to the sides of the tin. Separate the yolks from the whites of the eggs. Cream the butter, add the sugar and cream again. Sieve together the flour and the baking powder. Beat in the egg-yolks one at a time. Gradually and lightly sift in the flour alternately with a few spoonfuls of milk. Add the chopped nuts and the coffee essence. Add the stiffly whipped egg-whites.*

*Bake in a moderate oven (Regulo 5, 425 Elec.) for about 45 minutes. Leave in the tin to cool a little before turning out. Slice into layers, spread with coffee butter icing and build back into position. Ice with glace icing or milk frosting and garnish with whole hazel nuts.*

Mrs C.S. Peel, *My Own Cookery Book*

Often Granny Dot's cakes are half the size of a standard cake. This is a single sponge divided into three layers which heightens it. It is topped with a glace icing which makes it very sweet, so perhaps to just add some florets of the coffee icing with some hazelnuts is preferable.

Ingredients
For the Cake
55g of hazelnuts plus a few for decoration
110g of butter, plus extra for the cake tin
110g of caster sugar
2 free range or organic eggs, separated
1 tbsp coffee essence, camp coffee or expresso
110g flour, plus extra for the cake tin
1 tsp baking powder
a little full fat milk (optional)

For the Icing
170g butter
280g icing sugar
1 tbsp espresso or coffee essence

You will need a 20cm cake tin.
Serves 10

1. Preheat the oven to 190°C/Gas Mark 5. When it has reached temperature, roast the chopped hazelnuts on a baking tray for a few minutes until browned. Set aside.
2. Prepare a cake tin by buttering it and then tapping flour over the butter. Tap out the excess.
3. In a mixing bowl beat the butter and sugar together until light and fluffy.
4. Mix in the egg yolks and coffee essence.
5. Sift the flour and baking powder into the mixture followed by the chopped hazelnuts. Loosen the mixture with some milk if necessary.
6. Spoon the mixture into the cake tin and put it in the oven for 20 minutes.
7. Remove from the oven and cool in the tin before removing the cake. With a very sharp and long knife, slice the cake into 3 horizontally.

8. To make the icing, in a bowl whip the butter with the icing sugar until light and fluffy and add the coffee.

9. Put the bottom layer of the cake on a serving plate. Spread the icing over the first two layers of the cake. Top it with the third layer. Put the remaining icing in a piping bag and pipe some florets on top of the cake. Top these with hazelnuts.

This cake was eaten quickly by a man building a gate; a lady helping with the garden; a man plugging the enormous cracks in the floor of our foundationless house which had flooded; our neighbour and her boyfriend; me; my Romanian friend; my two children and my husband – so it feeds ten!

### Streusel Kuchen
This is one of my favourite Granny Dot recipes, perfect for a weekend breakfast or coffee with friends.

In the words of Granny Dot:

*Materials.- For the Kuchen: 12 oz. of flour; 1 saltspoonful of salt; 3 oz. of sugar; 1 oz. of yeast; 1 egg; 3 oz. of butter; milk to mix.*

*For the Streusel: 3 oz. of flour; 3 oz. of butter; 4 oz. of sugar.*

*Method.- Start by making the Kuchen. Cream the yeast in a warm basin with a teaspoonful of sugar and add a few spoonfuls of warm milk. Cover and leave for 15 minutes to rise, putting the basin in a warm place out of draughts. Sieve together the flour and salt. Cream the butter and sugar together. Beat in the egg and lightly stir in the sifted flour. Add the yeast and sufficient warm milk to form a soft dough that will drop from the spoon. Cover with a clean cloth and leave in a warm place for 1 to 2 hours.*

*Make the Streusel by rubbing together the butter, sugar and flour until of the consistency of coarse crumbs. Butter a Yorkshire-pudding tin, turn the Kuchen mixture into it, pat it down, and strew the Streusel over it. Cover again and leave for half an hour and then put into a hot oven (Regulo 8, 465 Elec.) for 10 minutes. Reduce the heat to Regulo 5, 425 Elec, and bake for a further 20 minutes.'*

Mrs C.S. Peel *My Own Cookery Book*

Ingredients
For the Kuchen
80g butter
80g sugar

Streusel Kuchen (*Author's own*)

1 free range or organic egg
350g flour
1 teaspoonful salt
1 x 7g sachet yeast
80ml full fat milk

For the Streusel topping
85g butter
85g flour
110g caster sugar
A punnet of fruit (optional)
Muesli or oats (optional)

Serves 10

1. In a mixing bowl cream the butter and sugar until light and fluffy.
2. Beat the egg into the mixture.
3. Stir in the flour, salt and yeast.

4. Warm the milk so that it is blood temperature and mix with the ingredients so they form a dough which is not sticky.

5. Leave the mixture in a bowl at room temperature with a tea towel over it for two hours of rising.

or

Roll the mixture straight onto a non-stick baking tray and cover in a tea towel, leaving in a cool place over night, ready to bake in the morning. If you do this, skip instruction 7.

6. Prepare the streusel topping by lightly mixing the butter, flour and sugar together, so that it is a crumble topping resembling course breadcrumbs.

7. Roll the dough out onto a baking tray so that it is about 1.5 cm high. Leave it for another hour.

8. Preheat the oven to 200°C/ Gas Mark 6.

9. Lightly combine the Streusel topping with fruit, if using. Sprinkle the topping on the dough.

Any crumble topping is fine – for breakfast you may like to add muesli or oats as well.

10. Bake for ten minutes. Turn the oven down to 180°C/Gas Mark 4. Bake for another ten minutes.

Serve at any temperature. To reheat the Streusel Kuchen, do so at a high temperature so that the topping remains crisp.


### *Guglhupf*

Traditionally this was eaten by the Austrians for breakfast. When I made it I had not read the recipe through and so ended up taking it out for lunch with me so that I could transfer it from bowl to tin to prove after two hours of rising! It is very good, and yet another calorific carbohydrate wobble impacting recipe. So off I went with my Rhodesian Ridgeback for our third run in as many days!

In the words of Granny Dot:

*Materials.- 6 oz. of butter; 4 oz. of sugar; 1/2 teaspoonful of salt; 3/4 lb of finely sifted flour; 2 eggs; 4 oz. sultanas; 4 oz. blanched and chopped almonds; 1 oz. of yeast; 1 gill of tepid milk.*

*Method.- Blanch and finely chop the almonds. Cream the yeast with 1 teaspoonful of sugar until runny and add the tepid milk. Cover, set in a warm place, and leave for 15 minutes. Cream the butter, add the sugar and beat till fluffy. Beat in the eggs one at a time. Stir in the sifted flour and salt. Add the yeast and mix all together. Beat well. The dough should be moist and should slip easily from the spoon. Cover with a clean cloth and leave to rise for 2 hours in a warm place. Well butter a fluted ring mould or plain cake-tin. Warm the tin, turn the dough into it and leave for another 30 minutes in a warm place. Bake for about ¾ hour (Regulo 5, 425 Elec.). Turn out and sprinkle with sifted icing sugar when cool.*

Mrs C.S. Peel, *My Own Cookery Book*

Ingredients
170g butter, plus extra for the tin
110g sugar
2 free range or organic eggs
340g flour
1 x 7g sachet yeast
½ tsp salt
110g sultanas
110g almonds, roughly chopped
140ml full fat milk
Icing sugar

You will need a Guglhupf tin.
Serves 10

1. Cream the butter and sugar until light and fluffy.
2. Beat the eggs into the mixture.
3. Stir in the flour, yeast and salt, sultanas and almonds.
4. Gently warm the milk to blood temperature and pour onto the mixture, stirring with a knife. Cover with a tea towel and leave to rise for 2 hours.
5. Butter the tin and turn the dough into it.
6. Leave to prove for an hour.
7. Preheat the oven to 200°C/Gas Mark 6.
8. Bake for 30 minutes. Turn it out and sprinkle generously with icing sugar.
Serve warm with jam

### Nusskippferl

... or Nut Crescents. These are German biscuits, described by Jane as, 'like a sexy shortbread.' Can you think of a better description?

In the words of Granny Dot:

*Materials.- 3 oz. of butter; 5 oz. of flour; 1 oz. of sugar; 2 oz. of ground almonds.*

*Method.- Cream the butter and sugar together, add the ground almonds and the sifted flour and knead with the hand. Make into a long finger-thick rolls, cut these into 4-inch lengths and bend into small crescents. Bake in a moderate oven for 10 to 15 minutes, until slightly brown. Roll in icing sugar while still warm.*

Mrs C.S. Peel, *My Own Cookery Book*

Nusskipferl (*emmafarquharphotography*)

<u>Ingredients</u>
85g unsalted butter
30g sugar
140g flour
55g ground almonds
Icing sugar

Makes 12

1. Preheat the oven to 180°C/Gas Mark 4.
2. In a mixing bowl cream the butter and sugar until light and fluffy. Add the dry ingredients and mix into a dough.
3. In the palm of your hand roll pieces of dough into the size of a small golf ball. Flatten them into a wide finger shape and bend this into a crescent.
4. Place each crescent onto a baking tray, pressing them down slightly so that one side is flat.
5. Put the baking tray into the oven for 10 minutes.
6. Remove from the oven and dredge in icing sugar.
7. After 5 minutes, transfer the biscuits onto a cooling rack.
Serve

### *Madeleines*

While visiting my son's godmother who lives in Paris, I came home with a Madeleine tray. You can of course buy them in many cook shops, but this one feels special because it was bought in their country of origin. They were first made as early as the eighteenth century and named after their maker.

The first time I made these I followed the recipe exactly. The second time, I increased the butter content because it was just a little bit dry. They are more delicious shortly after they are made, so if you are not going to eat them straight away put them in a sealed container. Granny Dot suggests brushing them with jam or sprinkling with nuts or desiccated coconut. I sprinkled sugar on half of them and added jam to the other half; both very good, the former reminiscent of Savoyardi Lady's Fingers.

In the words of Granny Dot:

*Materials.- 2 eggs, 3 ozs. of flour; 1 oz. of margarine; 1/2 teaspoonful of baking powder; 2 ozs of sugar; grated rind of half a lemon; flavouring essence.*

*Method - Break the eggs into a basin, whisk a little, add the sugar and whisk until thick and creamy. Sieve the flour, baking powder and a pinch of salt, and stir lightly*

Madeleines (*Author's own*)

*to the eggs alternatively with the melted margarine, add the lemon rind and flavouring and put into small greased tins. Bake in a quick oven about 12 minutes. Turn out on to a sieve, and when cold brush over with a little jam rubbed through a hair sieve, or with a little dissolved red currant or crab apple jelly. Sprinkle with desiccated cocoanut, or chopped almonds or walnuts.*

Mrs C.S. Peel, *The Daily Mail Cookery Book*

Ingredients
2 free range or organic eggs
55g sugar
85g flour
¾ tsp baking powder
grated zest of 1 lemon
80 melted butter plus extra for buttering the tray
Icing Sugar

You will need a Madeleine tray, Yorkshire pudding tray, or a cupcake tray.
Makes 10

251

1. Preheat the oven to 200°C/Gas Mark 6 and butter the Madeleine tray. (You will be in trouble if you do not butter the tray, unless it is non-stick but for confidence I would still butter it.)
2. In a mixing bowl whisk the eggs and sugar until light and fluffy.
3. Add the flour, baking powder and lemon zest to the egg and sugar mixture and combine.
4. Stir in the butter.
5. Spoon the mixture into the tray and sprinkle sugar or nuts on now, if using. For jam or honey, paint on when baked.
6. Bake for 10 minutes.
7. Remove the Madeleines from the tray immediately and let them cool on a cooling rack. Seal very well if they are not being eaten straight away; they will not be good for long.

### *Daily Mail Shortbread*
I have made shortbread so many times using many different combinations. This is among the best and so you need look no further.
Granny Dot's recipe:

*Materials.- 6 oz. flour; 1 oz. of castor sugar; 4 oz. of margarine; pinch of salt. 2 oz. of ground rice and 4 oz. flour may be used in place of 6 oz. flour. Before baking place a piece of candied peel on each.*

*Method.- Cream the margarine and sugar, work in the flour gradually, knead well. Divide into 4 pieces, make each into a round cake with the hands, pinch the side into scallops with the thumb and first finger, prick the top with a fork, place on a greased baking sheet and bake in a moderate oven about ½ hour. See the bottom does not burn.*

Mrs C.S. Peel, *The Daily Mail Cookery Book*

Ingredients
110g butter at room temperature
25g caster sugar, plus extra for sprinkling on top
170g plain flour
Pinch of salt

Make 4 large biscuits

1. Preheat the oven to 180°C/Gas Mark 4.
2. Cream the butter and sugar until light and fluffy.

3. Add the flour gradually, beating in after each addition so that it does not fly all over the place. Do not over-mix.
4. Squeeze the mixture together and divide in 4.
5. Shape the biscuits on a baking sheet into circles. Scallop the edges with your thumb and index finger, using a little flour to help if necessary. You may need to put the mixture into the fridge before shaping if it is too soft.
6. Put the baking tray in the fridge for 20 minutes to firm up.
7. Bake for 20 minutes and then turn the oven off, leaving the door ajar. Let them cool in the oven to help them dry out.

### My Own Chocolate Cake

This cake is for adults for two reasons. Firstly, it is a little torte-like in texture and therefore rich and indulgent, and secondly adding whisky or rum to the icing reserves it for adults.

In the words of Granny Dot:

*Materials.- 3oz of chocolate or of sweetened chocolate powder or cocoa; 3 oz of butter or margarine; 3 oz. of sugar (4 oz. if cocoa is used); 1 egg; 4 oz. of flour; 1 teaspoonful of coffee essence, a scant ½ pint of milk; 2 teaspoonfuls of baking powder; a teaspoonful of bicarbonate of soda.*

*Method.- Place the chocolate, 1 oz. of butter and the milk in a pan and heat until the chocolate has dissolved. Stir occasionally. Cool. Cream together the butter and sugar, beat in the egg, add the cooled chocolate mixture and sift in the flour and then the baking powder and bicarbonate of soda. Stir and half fill a well-greased cake-tin. Bake in a moderate oven for 50 minutes.*

*Allow to cool in the tin and then turn out. If liked, this cake may be iced or split in half and sandwiched with butter icing.*

Mrs C.S. Peel, *My Own Cookery Book*

Ingredients
For the Cake
300ml full fat milk
85g dark chocolate, broken into small pieces. Better still, use chocolate chips
85g unsalted butter, plus extra to butter the cake tin
85g sugar
1 free range or organic egg
100g plain flour
1 tbsp cocoa powder
1 tsp coffee essence

2 tsp baking powder
1 tsp bicarbonate of soda

For the Icing
110g unsalted butter softened
225g sifted icing sugar
1–2tbsp whisky, rum or 1 tsp vanilla extract

You will need a 20cm cake tin.
Serves 8-10

1. Preheat the oven to 180°C/Gas Mark 4.
2. Butter the cake tin and line it with baking paper.
3. In a small pan, warm the milk. Mix in the chocolate and melt. Remove from the heat and cool.
4. In a mixing bowl cream together butter and sugar. Beat in the egg and coffee essence followed by the cooled chocolate milk. Sift the flour, cocoa powder, baking powder and bicarbonate of soda into the mixture and mix well.
5. Pour the batter into the cake-tin.
6. Bake for 30 minutes or until a cake skewer comes out clean.
7. Allow to cool in the tin and then turn out onto a serving plate.
8. To make the icing, in a clean bowl whip together the butter with the icing sugar and flavour. The longer you whip it together, the lighter and fluffier the icing will be.
9. Ice the cake with a palate knife and enjoy.
Because the cake is moist, it lasts longer than your average chocolate cake.

### *Almond Sponge Cake with Lemon Meringue Icing*
Granny Dot calls this Ring cake; I do not know why other than perhaps referring to the tin she used. This recipe is thrilling because of the added almonds and the subsequent texture of the cake. I am excited about the icing and while I realise that such icing is not a new to us, I did not expect to find it in a 1905 cookery book. So thank you Granny Dot.

*Materials.- 3 oz. of sugar; 5 oz. of butter or margarine; 2 or 3 eggs; 4 oz. of self-raising flour; 2 oz. of ground almonds; 3 oz. of sultanas; almonds for decoration; icing.*

*Method.- Beat the butter and sugar to a light, fluffy cream. Add the eggs, one at a time, beating each well in before adding the next. Lightly stir in the sifted flour, the ground almonds, and sultanas. Turn into a greased fluted tin. Bake in a moderate oven (Regulo 4. 375 ° Elec.) for 1 hour. Ice with frosting.*

*Frosting for Ring Cake*
*½ lb of sugar; ½ gill of water; the white of 1 egg; the juice of half a lemon.*
*Dissolve the sugar in the water and boil for 5 minutes. Stiffly whip the egg-white*
*and slowly pour on the syrup, whisking all the time. Add the lemon-juice, and when*
*thick, pour over the cake. Decorate with almonds that have been blanched, split and*
*browned in the oven.*

Mrs C.S. Peel, *My Own Cookery Book*

Ingredients
For the Cake
110g unsalted butter, plus extra for the tin
85g caster sugar
3 free range or organic eggs
110g self-raising flour, sifted
55g ground almonds
85g sultanas (optional)

For the Lemon meringue icing for cake
80ml water
225g caster sugar
White of one free range or organic egg
Juice of half a lemon

You will need a 20cm cake tin.
Serves 8-10

1. Preheat the oven to 180°C/Gas Mark 4. Butter the cake tin and line it with
baking paper.
2. Beat the butter and sugar until light and fluffy.
3. Add the eggs one at a time, mixing each in before adding the next.
4. Lightly stir in the flour, ground almonds and sultanas.
5. Spoon the cake mix into the tin.
6. Bake for 20 minutes or until a cake skewer comes out clean.
7. Remove the cake from the tin onto a cooling rack.
8. To make the icing, in a pan dissolve the sugar in the water over a low heat.
Bring the syrup to the boil for 5 minutes.
9. In a bowl stiffly whip the egg white and slowly pour the syrup into it, whisking
all the time.
10. When a thick icing is formed, stir in the lemon juice.
11. Pour the icing over the cake and spread it with a palate knife. Dip the palate
knife in hot water to assist in smoothing the icing over the cake.

Serve

**Welsh Cakes**
A cold and crisp day is perfect for light and crumbly Welsh cakes. They are also something children can easily help you make.

In the words of Granny Dot:

*Materials and Method.- 1lb. of flour, 6oz of butter, 6 oz. of castor sugar, 2 oz. of currants, half a pint of raw cream. Mix the butter and sugar well into the flour, then add currants and cream. Roll out until half an inch in thickness, cut the cakes with the cover of the flour dredger and bake both sides in a Dutch oven before a clear fire.*
Mrs C.S. Peel, The Single Handed Cook

Ingredients
250g plain flour
½ tsp baking powder
80g caster sugar
60g unsalted butter, chopped into cubes
60g lard chopped into small cubes, plus extra for cooking
70g currants
1 free range or organic egg white
30ml full fat milk

Makes about 12

1. Sift the flour and baking powder into a mixing bowl. Add the caster sugar, butter and lard.
2. With your fingers, as if you are making crumble, combine the ingredients.
3. When you have achieved this, add the currants and then mix in the milk.
4. In a separate bowl whip the egg white and fold it into the mixture.
5. Sprinkle flour on a worktop and roll out the mixture to about 1.5cm thick. Cut with a 6cm pastry cutter.
6. Heat a griddle pan and melt enough lard to moisten the surface.
7. Fry the cakes for 2–3 minutes on each side until they are golden brown. If they are a little black they are still delicious, some say more so.
8. While they are still hot cover them with caster sugar.
Now all you have to do is to go for a walk in crisp cold weather, put the kettle on when home, sit back with a cup of tea and a Welsh cake and relax.

## TO FINISH

### *Pear Sweets*

Pear sweets! I was given two large bags full of pears. I thanked my neighbour very much. Not knowing what I would do with them all, this recipe answered my question. If you are like me, and you need just a little something sweet after dinner and that little something may turn into a regretful helping, these are the answer. They are so sweet that one is enough!

In the words of Granny Dot:

*To Candy Greengages, Apricots, Plums, Cherries, and Pears.*
*Materials.-1lb. of loaf sugar; 1/2 pint cold water; 1 lb. of fruit.*

*Method.- Lay them (the fruit) in the prepared syrup, bring to the boil, and simmer gently until the fruit becomes clear. Skim well. Lift out the fruits one by one with a skimmer or fish slice; lay on the flat dishes in a dry place. Cover for 24 hours. Boil the syrup to the pearl degree. Lay the fruit in, and simmer gently until tender. Put on a flat dish again, cover, and leave another 24 hours. Reheat the syrup, put in the fruit again, and boil for a few minutes. Take out with the skimmer, and have ready some castor sugar; sift it over the fruit on both sides until quite white; then lay on wire trays in a moderate oven until dry. Turn occasionally.*

Mrs C.S. Peel, *The Daily Mail Fruit and Vegetable Book*

Ingredients
450g of granulated sugar
300ml cold water
Juice of half a lemon
10 pears, peeled, cored and halved
300g caster sugar (vanilla sugar if you have any)

Makes 20

1. Put the sugar and water in a heavy-based pan over a low heat. When it has melted, add the lemon juice and bring the syrup to the boil.
2. When the syrup has reached 100°C, add the fruit and let it simmer until it becomes clear.
3. Skim off any scum that rises to the surface.
4. Carefully lift the fruits out with a slotted spoon and lay them on a baking tray. Store in a cool place for 24 hours.
5. Set aside the pan with the syrup in it to re-use the next day.

Candied Pears (*Author's own*)

6. Reheat the syrup slowly to the 112°C. Add the fruit again, a few at a time, leaving in the syrup for about 5-7 minutes. You just want them to be candied a bit more. Remove them as you did in step 4 and set aside in the same way for 24 hours.
7. The next day reheat the syrup to 112°C and put the fruit back in. After about 3 minutes remove the fruit into a bowl of caster sugar.
8. Lay the fruit on a wire rack set over a baking tray to catch the sugar, and put it in the oven at 170°C for about 10 minutes and then turn the oven off. Leave the fruit in there to dry out a bit with the door ajar.
Store them on clean baking paper in an airtight container.

### *Caraway Comfit*
Caraway comfit has emerged via Granny Dot's autobiography:

*Aunt Charlotte was tiny and fair, with smoothly-parted hair, a bonnet, exquisite little kid boots, which she bought from a celebrated London bookmaker, and in winter a sealskin coat, in summer a silk jacket trimmed with lace and jet. And always she carried a sweet-smelling green Russian leather bag containing, amongst other things, a boxful of pink and white caraway comfit.*

*And always she wore a rakish-looking eye glass firmly fixed in one of her pretty blue eyes.*

Mrs C.S. Peel, *Life's Enchanted Cup, An Autobiography: 1872–1933*

I have not added food colouring to make some of these pink, and I am sure Aunt Charlotte would sniff at my attempt which I realise is not a great one, but the idea is there. Here it is:

Ingredients
300g granulated sugar
100ml water
1 jar caraway seeds

1. Put the sugar and water in a pan over a low heat to make a sugar syrup. Wait until the sugar has dissolved and do not stir as this will not help. When a syrup has formed, remove from the heat.
2. Heat a frying pan over a medium heat and add the caraways and two spoonfuls of the syrup.
3. Shake the pan gently to allow the syrup to coat the seeds and to dry up on them.
4. Add more syrup and keep repeating this process until the syrup is used up and the seeds become coated in white. If you manage to coat them better than I did, I envy you! They will last for ages, and if you like them, try adding some colour for fun.

### *Elderflower Cordial*
Once a year I make this and freeze several plastic bottles of it which I decant into a pretty one which stays in the fridge until it is time to be replenished. It is sweet, lemony and delicious, adapted using my Swedish grandmother-in-law's recipe. Granny Dot's version:

*Materials and Method.- Pick the berries from the stalks when quite ripe. Place in a broad deep earthenware jar, adding ½ pint of water to each quart of berries; cover and place in the oven until the juice flows freely. Strain through a cloth, and to each pint of juice allow ¾ lb of sugar, and to each 2 quarts of juice allow 1 oz. of root ginger, 1 dozen cloves, and a stick of cinnamon, all bruised. Boil ½ an hour. Strain, and when cold bottle.*

Mrs C.S Peel, *The Daily Mail Fruit and Vegetable Book*

<u>Ingredients</u>
80 large elderflower florets
4 lemons, juiced, peel removed
160g citric acid
3kg caster sugar
4 litres of boiling water

Makes 5 bottles

1. In a very large pan pour the boiling water on the sugar. Stir over heat until the sugar melts.
2. Add the lemon juice, lemon peel, elderflowers and citric acid to the pan.
3. Cover the pan with tea towels and leave for 4 days.
4. Remove the flowers with your hands, squeezing out the cordial. This makes sieving the cordial into bottles easier.
Keep one bottle in the fridge and use plastic bottles to store the rest in the freezer.

### *Mint Julip*
This refreshing cocktail feels like an excuse to drink at lunchtime!
   Granny Dot's original recipe:

*Materials.- The juice and half the rind of 1 orange; 1 sprig of mint; 1 teaspoonful of sugar; 1 wineglassful of gin or brandy; ice.*

*Method.- Peel the orange very thinly and squeeze out the juice. Strain it into a tumbler, wash the mint, dry a little, and add with the sugar and orange peel; add the gin or brandy. Fill up with crushed ice.*
                    Mrs C.S Peel, *The Daily Mail Fruit and Vegetable Book*

<u>Ingredients</u>
Juice of 2 oranges
80ml gin or brandy
1 tsp caster sugar (or more depending on your taste)
4 pieces of orange peel, carefully avoiding the pith which will add a bitter taste
A handful of fresh mint leaves
2 glasses worth of crushed ice

Serves 2

1. Put all of the ingredients in a cocktail shaker including crushed ice and shake away, then add to the glasses.

2. Be careful not to leave the mint or peel in the shaker as these are a pretty and tasty addition.

### Rum Punch

I served this on bonfire night. Beyond the initial tasting, I didn't have any as it was finished by friends very quickly!

This is Granny Dot's version:

*Materials.- 2 Seville oranges; 2 lemons; a small piece of stick vanilla; 4 cloves; 1 inch of stick cinnamon; 1 ½ lbs of sugar; 1 pint of water; 1 gill of brandy; 1 gill of rum.*

*Method.- Put the sugar and water into a pan, stir until the former is melted, then boil to a syrup. It should drop heavily from a spoon. Peel the fruit very thinly, and put it into a bowl with the flavouring and spices. Pour the hot syrup over, and infuse for 5 or 6 hours. Mix in the orange and lemon juice, add the brandy and rum, and strain through a fine cloth. Keep on ice until required.*

Mrs C. S. Peel, *The Daily Mail Fruit and Vegetable Book*

Ingredients
170g granulated sugar
120ml water
Peel or 2 oranges
Peel of 2 lemons
Vanilla pod
4 cloves
1 stick of cinnamon
150ml brandy
150ml dark rum
300ml orange juice
300ml lemon juice
Crushed Ice

Serves 8-10 people

1. Put the sugar and water in a heavy-based pan over a low heat until melted. You can jostle the pan, but do not stir.
2. When the sugar has melted, turn up the heat so that it almost boils and then add the peel of the fruit and the other spices.
3. Leave it to infuse for at least an hour, or for as long as you can before needed.
4. Add the brandy, rum and juice of the fruit to taste.
5. Serve on crushed ice.

### Noyeau

I have some relations who like to serve flavoured alcohol after lunch. This would certainly meet with their approval. For the almonds to make a difference, they need to be organic with their skins on. I like to serve this on ice.

Here's Granny Dot's version:

*To 1 gallon of whiskey, 3 lb. loaf sugar, the thin rind and juice of 3 large lemons, 1 lb. bitter almonds, blanched and bruised in a mortar. Let all these ingredients stand in a well-covered jar for 6 weeks, stirring daily; then filter through blotting paper and bottle.*

<u>Ingredients</u>
100g organic almonds
1 litre whisky
270g granulated sugar
Juice and rind of a lemon

1. Bruise the almonds in a pestle and mortar or bash them with a rolling pin.
2. Mix all the ingredients together in a bottle. After a week it will start to taste delicious. You could remove the almonds after six weeks.

# Conversion Tables

| Gas Mark | Fahrenheit | Celcius |
|---|---|---|
| 1 | 275 | 140 |
| 2 | 300 | 150 |
| 3 | 325 | 170 |
| 4 | 350 | 180 |
| 5 | 375 | 190 |
| 6 | 400 | 200 |
| 7 | 425 | 230 |
| 8 | 475 | 240 |

| Weights | | | |
|---|---|---|---|
| Imperial | | Metric | |
| ½oz | 6oz | 10g | 175g |
| ¾oz | 7oz | 20g | 200g |
| 1oz | 8oz | 25g | 225g |
| 1 ½oz | 9oz | 40g | 250g |
| 2oz | 10oz | 50g | 275g |
| 2 ½oz | 12oz | 60g | 350g |
| 3oz | 1lb | 75g | 450g |
| 4oz | 1 ½ lb | 110g | 700g |
| 4 ½oz | 2 lb | 125g | 900g |
| 5oz | 3 lb | 150g | 1.35kg |

| Imperial | Metric | American |
|---|---|---|
| ½ fl oz | 15ml | 1 tbsp |
| 1 fl oz | 30 ml | 1/8 cup |
| 2 fl oz | 60 ml | ¼ cup |
| 4 fl oz | 120 ml | ½ cup |
| 8 fl oz | 240 ml | 1 cup |
| 16 fl oz | 480 ml | 1 pint |
| 1 gill | 140 ml | 2/3 cup |
| 1 quart | 1.14 litres | 4 ¾ cup |

| American Weight Conversion | | |
|---|---|---|
| 1 cup flour/caster or granulated sugar | 5oz | 150g |
| 1 cup brown sugar | 8oz | 175g |
| 1 cup butter/margarine/lard | 6oz | 175g |
| 1 cup sultanas/raisins | 8oz | 225g |
| 1 cup raisins | 7oz | 200g |
| 1 cup currants | 5oz | 150g |
| 1 cup ground almonds | 4oz | 110g |
| 1 cup golden syrup | 12oz | 350g |
| 1 cup uncooked rice | 7oz | 200g |
| 1 cup grated cheese | 4oz | 110g |
| 1 stick butter | 4oz | 110g |

| American Liquid Conversion | |
|---|---|
| (1/4 pt) | 150mls |
| ½ pt | 275 |
| 1 | 570 |
| 1¼ | 725 |
| 1¾ | 1 litre |
| 2 | 1.2 |
| 2½ | 1.5 |
| 4 | 2.25 |

# Notes

**Part One**

1   Mrs C.S. Peel, *The Hat Shop* (1933)
2   Mrs C.S. Peel, *Life's Enchanted Cup: An Autobiography 1872-1933* (1933), p. 135
3   Mrs G.M. Young, *Early Victorian England* (1933)
4   Mrs C.S. Peel, *The Stream of Time* (1931)
5   Peel, *Life's Enchanted Cup*, p. 116
6   *Ibid.*, p. 136
7   *Ibid.*, p. 255
8   *Ibid.*, p. 97
9   *Ibid.*, p. 270
10  *Ibid.*, p. 40
11  *Ibid.*, p. 24
12  *Ibid.*, p. 16
13  *Ibid.*, p. 28
14  *Ibid.*, p. 29
15  *Ibid.*, p. 32
16  A Brougham is a closed carriage, most often with four wheels. It was an everyday vehicle used in the latter part of the nineteenth century.
17  Peel, *Life's Enchanted Cup*, p. 23
18  A Phaeton is a light four-wheeled open-sided carriage drawn by one or two horses.
19  Peel, *Life's Enchanted Cup*, p. 33
20  *Ibid.*, p. 49
21  *Ibid.*, p. 38
22  *Ibid.*, p. 34
23  *Ibid.*, p. 25
24  *Ibid.*, p. 56
25  *Ibid.*, p. 26
26  *Ibid.*, p. 50
27  www.oldbailyonline.org
28  Peel, *Life's Enchanted Cup*, 62
29  *Ibid.*, p. 85
30  *Ibid.*, p. 229
31  *Ibid.*, p. 60
32  *Ibid.*, p. 61
33  *Ibid.*, p. 77
34  *Ibid.*
35  *Ibid.*, p. 99
36  *Ibid.*, p. 118
37  *Ibid.*, p. 74
38  *Ibid.*, p. 127
39  *Ibid.*, p. 262
40  www.thehistorybox.com
41  Peel, *Life's Enchanted Cup*, p. 107

42  *Ibid.*, p. 110
43  *Ibid.*, p. 109
44  *Ibid.*, p. 127
45  *Ibid.*, p. 100
46  *Ibid.*, p. 149
47  *Ibid.*, p. 150
48  *Ibid.*, p. 36
49  *Ibid.*, p. 29
50  *Ibid.*, p. 20
51  *Ibid.*, p. 31
52  *Ibid.*, p. 17
53  *Ibid.*, p. 192
54  *Ibid.*, p. 142
55  www.bbc.co.uk/news/magazine-19544309
56  Peel, *Life's Enchanted Cup*, p. 28
57  *Ibid.*, p. 19
58  *Ibid.*, p. 37
59  Mrs C.S. Peel, *A Year in Public Life* (1919), p. 217
60  Peel, *Life's Enchanted Cup*, p. 8
61  *Ibid.*, p. 77
62  *Ibid.*, p. 126
63  *Ibid.*, p. 112
64  *Ibid.*, p. 87
65  Mrs C.S. Peel, *My Own Cookery Book* (1923), p. v
66  Mrs C.S. Peel, *How To Keep House* (1906), p. 70
67  Mrs C.S. Peel, *Learning To Cook* (1915), p. 28
68  Peel, *How To Keep House*, p. 197
69  *Ibid.*, p. 203
70  Peel, *Life's Enchanted Cup*, p. 117
71  *Ibid.*, p. 113
72  *Ibid.*, p. 261
73  *Ibid.*, p. 168
74  Peel, *How To Keep House*, p. 188
75  Peel, *Life's Enchanted Cup*, p. 43
76  *Ibid.*, p. 44
77  *Ibid.*, p. 49
78  *Ibid.*, p. 67
79  A Fly was a horse-drawn public coach or delivery wagon especially one let out for hire. In Britain, the term also referred to a light covered vehicle, such as a single-horse pleasure carriage or a hansom cab.
80  Peel, *Life's Enchanted Cup*, pp. 48, 57
81  *Ibid.*, p. 62
82  *Ibid.*, p. 64
83  *Ibid.*, p. 65
84  *Ibid.*, p. 67
85  *Ibid.*, p. 68
86  *Ibid.*, p. 69
87  http://shm.orxfordjournals.org

88  Peel, Life's Enchanted Cup, p. 69
89  *Ibid.*, p. 70
90  *Ibid.*, p. 88
91  *Ibid.*, p. 262
92  *Ibid.*, p. 270
93  *Ibid.*, p. 269
94  *Ibid.*, p. 121
95  *Ibid.*, p. 17
96  *Ibid.*, p. 62
97  *Ibid.*, p. 29
98  *Ibid.*, p. 97
99  *Ibid.*
100 *Ibid.*, p. 95
101 *Ibid.*, p. 97
102 *Ibid.*, p. 96
103 *Ibid.*, p. 262
104 Mrs C.S. Peel, *How We Lived Then 1914-1918* (1929), p. 8
105 Peel, *Life's Enchanted Cup*, p. 37
106 *Ibid.*, p. 72
107 *Ibid.*, p. 93
108 *Ibid.*, p. 76
109 *Ibid.*, p. 266
110 *Ibid.*, p. 68
111 Mrs C.S. Peel, The Eat Less Meat Book (1917), p. 16
112 Peel, *How We Lived Then*, p. 84
113 Peel, *Life's Enchanted Cup*, p. 21
114 *Ibid.*, p. 38
115 *Ibid.*, p. 148
116 *Ibid.*, p. 135
117 *Ibid.*, p. 264
118 Peel, *A Year in Public Life*, p. 27
119 Peel, *Life's Enchanted Cup*, p. 144
120 *Ibid.*, p. 145
121 Peel, *A Year in Public Life*, p. 27
122 Peel, *Life's Enchanted Cup*, p. 102
123 *Ibid.*,
124 *Ibid.*, p. 111
125 *Ibid.*, p. 35
126 *Ibid.*, p. 17
127 *Ibid.*, p. 30
128 *Ibid.*, p. 36
129 *Ibid.*, p. 18
130 *Ibid.*, p. 34
131 *Ibid.*, p. 46
132 www.fashion-era.com/rational_dress.html
133 Peel, *Life's Enchanted Cup*, p. 26
134 *Ibid.*, p. 98
135 *Ibid.*, p. 94

136 *Ibid.*, p. 86
137 *Ibid.*, p. 129
138 *Ibid.*, p. 117
139 *Ibid.*, p. 130
140 *Ibid.*, p. 131
141 *Ibid.*, p. 133
142 *Ibid.*, p. 268
143 *Ibid.*, p. 177
144 Peel, *How We Lived Then*, p. 53
145 *Ibid.*, p. 51
146 *Ibid.*, p. 108
147 Ian J. Cawood and David McKinnon-Bell, *The First World War* (2002)
148 Peel, *How We Lived Then*, p. 109
149 *Ibid.*, p. 113
150 *Ibid.*, p. 70
151 *Ibid.*, p. 67
152 *Ibid.*
153 Peel, *Life's Enchanted Cup*, p. 31
154 Peel, *How We Lived Then*, p. 11
155 Peel, *Life's Enchanted Cup*, p. 32
156 *Ibid.*, p. 265
157 *Ibid.*, p. 101
158 *Ibid.*, p. 153
159 Millicent Garrett Fawcett, 'The War Effect on Women's Work', *The War Illustrated*, 6 January, 1917 and www.thisismoney.co.uk
160 Peel, *Life's Enchanted Cup*, p. 128
161 www.bbc.co.uk/news/magazine/-19544309
162 Peel, *How We Lived Then*, p. 112
163 www.theguardian.com/world//2008/nov/11/first-world-war-wmone-home-front
164 Peel, *How We Lived Then*, p. 110
165 Peel, *Life's Enchanted Cup*, p. 266
166 *Ibid.*, p. 165
167 *Ibid.*, p. 167
168 Peel, *How We Lived Then*, p. 106
169 Peel, *Life's Enchanted Cup*, p. 167
170 *Ibid.*, p. 173
171 *Ibid.*, p. 169
172 *Ibid.*, p. 171
173 www.thehistorybox.com
174 http://ezitis.myzen.co.uk/russian.html
175 Peel, *Life's Enchanted Cup*, p. 175
176 *Ibid.*, p. 168
177 Peel, *How We Lived Then*, p. 129
178 Peel, *Life's Enchanted Cup*, p. 200
179 Peel, *How We Lived Then*, p. 179
180 Peel, *Life's Enchanted Cup*, p. 173
181 *Ibid.*, p. 40
182 *Ibid.*, p. 171

183 Peel, *How We Lived Then*, p. 55
184 *Ibid.*, p. 139
185 *Ibid.*, p. 40
186 *Ibid.*, p. 143
187 *Ibid.*, p. 161
188 *Ibid.*, p. 199
189 *Ibid.*, p. 145
190 Peel, *Life's Enchanted Cup*, p. 195
191 *Ibid.*, p. 196
192 *Ibid.*, p. 197
193 Peel, *How We Lived Then*, p. 163
194 Peel, *Life's Enchanted Cup*, p. 244
195 Peel, *How We Lived Then*, p. 163
196 *Ibid.*, p. 157
197 *Ibid.*, p. 152
198 Peel, *Life's Enchanted Cup*, p. 176
199 Peel, *How We Lived Then*, p. 61
200 Peel, *Life's Enchanted Cup*, p. 181
201 *Ibid.*, p. 263
202 Peel, *A Year in Public Life*, p. 84
203 Peel, *Life's Enchanted Cup*, p. 178
204 Peel, *How We Lived Then*, p. 52
205 *Ibid.*, p. 14
206 www.historylearningsite.co.uk/rationing_and_world_war_one.html
207 Peel, *How We Lived Then*, p. 103
208 Peel, *Life's Enchanted Cup*, p. 165
209 Peel, *A Year in Public Life*, p. 22
210 Peel, *How We Lived Then*, p. 88
211 *Ibid.*, p. 134
212 Mrs C.S. Peel, *The Victory Cookbook* (1918), p. 8. The quote is from the Right Honourable J.R. Clynes MP, Food Controller.
213 Peel, *A Year in Public Life*, p. 173
214 Peel, *Life's Enchanted Cup*, p. 221
215 Peel, *A Year in Public Life*, p. 16
216 *Ibid.*, p. 18
217 *Ibid.*, p. 149
218 *Ibid.*, p. 119
219 *Ibid.*, p. 120
220 *Ibid.*
221 Peel, *Life's Enchanted Cup*, p. 202
222 Peel, *How We Lived Then*, p. 82
223 *Ibid.*, p. 94
224 *Ibid.*, p. 95
225 *Ibid.*, p. 2
226 Cawood and McKinnon-Bell, *The First World War*, p. 53
227 Peel, *Life's Enchanted Cup*, p. 187
228 Peel, *How We Lived Then*, p. 84
229 Peel, *A Year in Public Life*, p. 24

230 Peel, *Life's Enchanted Cup*, p. 193
231 Peel, *A Year in Public Life*, p. 92
232 Peel, *Life's Enchanted Cup*, p. 194
233 Peel, *A Year in Public Life*, p. 49
234 Peel, *Life's Enchanted Cup*, p. 176
235 Peel, *A Year in Public Life*, p. 91
236 Peel, *Life's Enchanted Cup*, p. 202
237 Peel, *A Year in Public Life*, p. 168
238 Peel, *How We Lived Then*, p. 164
239 *Ibid.*, p. 95
240 *Ibid.*, p. 69
241 *Ibid.*, p. 57
242 Peel, *The Victory Cook Book*, p. 13
243 *Ibid.*, p. 239
244 Peel, *Life's Enchanted Cup*, p. 180
245 Peel, *How We Lived Then*, p. 57
246 Peel, *Life's Enchanted Cup*, p. 237
247 www.historylearningsite.co.uk/ration_and_world_war_one.html
248 Peel, *A Year in Public Life*, p. 136
249 *Ibid.*, p. 139
250 Peel, *Life's Enchanted Cup*, p. 217
251 *Ibid.*, p. 224
252 Peel, *How We Lived Then*, p. 179
253 *Ibid.*, p. 180
254 Peel, *The Eat Less Meat Book*, p. 15
255 Peel, *How We Lived Then*, p. 101
256 Peel, *The Eat Less Meat*, p. 40
257 Peel, *A Year in Public Life*, p. 114
258 Peel, *How We Lived Then*, p. 82
259 *Ibid.*, p. 93
260 *Ibid.*, p. 92
261 Peel, *The Victory Cook Book*, p. 233
262 *Ibid.*, p. 96
263 *Ibid.*, p. 45
264 Peel, *A Year in Public Life*, p. 84
265 Peel, *How We Lived Then*, p. 223
266 *Ibid.*, p. 220

**Part Two**

1    A smart bowl, typically with a handle, used for soup, stew or similar dishes.
2    Peel, *The Victory Cook Book*, p. 90
3    *Ibid.*, p. 91

# Index

Locators with '*p*' refers to pictures/photographs. Mrs C.S. Peel's books listed under the sections where they are mentioned, for example, under 'meat dishes'.

273